D0914274

NEW RULES FOR A NEW ECONOMY

Stephen A. Herzenberg, John A. Alic, & Howard Wial

NEW RULES *for a* NEW economy

Employment and Opportunity in Postindustrial America

A Twentieth Century Fund Book

ILR PRESS

AN IMPRINT OF

CORNELL UNIVERSITY PRESS

Ithaca and London

The Twentieth Century Fund sponsors and supervises timely analyses of economic policy, foreign affairs, and domestic political issues. Not-for-profit and nonpartisan, the Fund was founded in 1919 and endowed by Edward A. Filene.

First published 1998 by Cornell University Press

Printed in the United States of America

Cornell University Press strives to use environmentally responsible suppliers and materials to the fullest extent possible in the publishing of its books. Such materials include vegetable-based, low-VOC inks and acid-free papers that are recycled, totally chlorine-free, or partly composed of nonwood fibers.

Cloth printing   10 9 8 7 6 5 4 3 2 1

Library of Congress Cataloging-in-Publication Data
Herzenberg, Stephen.
    New rules for a new economy : employment and opportunity in
postindustrial America / Stephen A. Herzenberg, John A. Alic, Howard
Wial.
        p.   cm.
    "A Twentieth Century Fund book."
    Includes bibliographical references and index.
    ISBN 0-8014-3524-2 (alk. paper)
    1. Employment forecasting—United States. 2. Labor market—United
States. 3. Service industries workers—Supply and demand—United
States—Forecasting. 4. Manufacturing industries—Employees—Supply
and demand—United States—Forecasting. I. Alic, John A.
II. Wial, Howard. III. Title
HD5724.H43   1998
331.12'0973—dc21   98-18220

Contents

Foreword

From 1940 to the middle of this decade, the proportion of American workers employed in the service sector increased steadily from about half to three-quarters. The corresponding decline in the share of manufacturing employment has evoked great consternation throughout most of this period. Many feared that replacing the tangible, durable output of factories with the talk and paper that services spew forth would be akin to replacing Fort Knox with a house of cards. Indeed, the growth of services has been widely blamed for the declining productivity growth, stagnant wages, and rising economic inequality plaguing the United States since 1973.

But the derogatory stereotypes often assigned to service-sector work—"hamburger flipping" foremost among them—are ill-founded and misleading. Those who attribute the post-1973 economic blues to the expansion of services usually fail to note that this sector grew just as inexorably during the preceding decades of prosperity. It may be true that in some service industries productivity gains are difficult if not impossible to achieve. As the economist William Baumol has noted, a string quartet performance will always require four musicians to toil the same number of minutes. But services such as bank transactions, toll collections, and cashiering have become much more efficient with the advent of ATMs and electronic scanning devices.

Analyzing the impact of this sector's growth is extremely difficult because the service sector defies generalization: it really is not a sector at all. Rather, it is the remainder of the economy after subtracting manufacturing, most government activity, and agriculture. The limited commonality among lawyers, nurses, pilots, teachers, cooks, waiters, and jan-

itors may be that they all work in a service industry. Caution is therefore
advised for those who seek to draw connections between the increase in
service employment and such economic trends as the decline in unionization, the persistence of the U.S. trade deficit, the increasing presence
of women in the workforce, or the growth of "contingent" work.

The authors of this book, economist Stephen Herzenberg, engineer
John Alic, and lawyer-economist Howard Wial, do an admirable job of
mapping out a meaningful picture of the various components of the
service sector. Their reminder of the variety in the nature of service
work should be of great help in future attempts to make economic sense
of the broader economic developments related to the changing nature
of work. Investment bankers may have difficulty relating what they do to
the tasks performed by low- and average-wage employees, but the janitors, child-care workers, hospital orderlies, and others who toil in labor-
intensive, low-productivity service jobs have significant things in
common. The much larger share of service workers engaged in complex employment that requires substantial training (sales, administration, low-level management) also faces a set of circumstances that can
be similar in important respects.

In developing their subcategories of service employment, Herzenberg, Alic, and Wial strive to clarify the interactions between each group
and the economy as a whole. The authors draw boundaries around clusters of service jobs in ways that may convey a great deal of information
about the forces that have exacerbated income and wealth inequality
while hindering wage growth for middle-income Americans.

The Twentieth Century Fund / Century Foundation has energetically sought to document, understand the causes of, and develop ideas
for alleviating economic inequality. We have supported Edward Wolff's
seminal report, *Top Heavy,* demonstrating that wealth inequality in the
United States has worsened to a level last seen during the Great Depression. We also sponsored Robert Kuttner's *Everything for Sale: The Virtues
and Limits of Markets,* which devoted considerable attention to the connections between inequality and markets. Our roster of forthcoming
books includes the economists Barry Bluestone and Bennett Harrison's
analysis of the relationship between economic growth and inequality,
economics writer Jeffrey Madrick's exploration of slow productivity improvements, Cornell political scientist Jonas Pontusson's investigation
into why inequality is so much worse in the United States than in other
developed countries, journalist Simon Head's reporting on the role of

technology in inequality, Harvard's Theda Skocpol's bold proposals for federal action to alleviate inequality, and Wolff's examination of the extent to which schooling may or may not help eliminate inequality. Professor James K. Galbraith's forthcoming work on the effects of unemployment and other factors on inequality is likely to be one of the decade's most significant contributions to the debate in this area.

This book began while the authors were employees of the federal Office of Technology Assessment (OTA), an agency created in 1972 to conduct research as a resource for Congress on policy decisions about technical issues. Over the decades, the OTA issued hundreds of studies that proved to be immensely valuable not only to policymakers but also to the academic community and the public generally. In 1995 the agency was eliminated, ostensibly to help cut the federal deficit (although the tiny OTA budget made little difference one way or the other). The authors asked the Fund to help them finish the project. But those in Congress who eliminated the OTA because they suspected that the private and nonprofit sectors would supply the same kinds of reports in the agency's absence would be misguided if they cited this book's sponsorship as a case in point. While this particular project happened to fit the Fund's agenda, dozens of other studies that Congress had requested have been canceled because of lack of support from private or nonprofit institutions. Information that would have helped to guide lawmakers is no longer available. Policy is being designed in the dark.

Messrs. Herzenberg, Alic, and Wial demonstrate in this book that the government lost something valuable when it closed the OTA. On behalf of the Trustees of the Twentieth Century Fund / Century Foundation, I thank them for contributing to our understanding of American jobs and public policy.

RICHARD C. LEONE, President
The Twentieth Century Fund / Century Foundation
January 1998

Preface

Through the 1980s, public debate about American jobs and standards of living centered on manufacturing. As the United States continued to lose manufacturing jobs, scholars and pundits alike proclaimed that "manufacturing matters" and predicted "a future of lousy jobs" in the service sector. Underlying the preoccupation with manufacturing was the widely shared assumption that good jobs, at least for those without advanced levels of education, were to be found only in the likes of auto plants and steel mills. Few seemed willing to consider seriously whether the service sector could ever generate good jobs and rising living standards for most Americans.

Today more people appear ready to take a hard look at the services, which employ the vast majority of American workers. The "new economy" is suddenly the rage, viewed now with a sense of possibility and promise as well as continuing trepidation. In this book we hope to encourage that sense of possibility and promise. We seek to understand the dynamics of today's service industries and jobs and to use that understanding to map out a set of public policies that will benefit workers as well as businesses and consumers.

Our central conclusion is that too many policies still reflect the old manufacturing-centered economy. For this reason, they often fail to address the needs of today's workforce, while impeding the ability of businesses to respond to rapidly changing, uncertain markets. The policies we advocate are designed to preserve the benefits of a vibrant, competitive economy, at the same time softening the effects of low-wage competition on American workers and reversing the wage stagnation and heightened inequality that have characterized the last two decades. Achieving this goal requires a realigned policy system that addresses the needs of the great bulk of American workers, who do not have postgraduate degrees, rare skills and abilities, or supernormal drive and ambition. Reestablishing the sense of well-being common during the "Wonder Years" of the 1950s and 1960s requires public policies that will create better opportunities for the vast majority of workers, not just a narrow elite. We offer *New Rules for a New Economy* as a guide to a prosperous future, one that supports rather than destroys community, and makes work more rewarding in intangible ways as well as in terms of wages and benefits.

This book has its origins in a report for the congressional Office of Technology Assessment (OTA), uncompleted at the time OTA closed in the fall of 1995. The Twentieth Century Fund came to our rescue, providing support to complete the research and, more important, to extend it. What had begun as a government report could thus be turned into a book addressing a broader audience. For this, we are especially grateful; we knew from the beginning that an honest attempt to lay out policies capable of reversing two decades of wage stagnation and income polarization would push the boundaries of the OTA assessment process.

We owe thanks to Rob Atkinson, Ken Freeman, Frank Gallo, and Margaret Hilton for their work during the OTA portion of this study, and to OTA program director Audrey Buyrn for her faith in the project. Our great appreciation goes also to Rose Batt and Harley Shaiken, who reviewed the manuscript and provided helpful guidance. Marty Gottron, our Twentieth Century Fund editor, helped convert the original OTA manuscript into a book, struggling with it at a time when many of our ideas were fuzzy. Bev Goldberg and Greg Anrig of the Twentieth Century Fund gave us support when we needed it and showed great patience with both our delays and our unwillingness to see the book go to press until we were happy with it. Fran Benson, editor-in-chief of Cornell University Press, took an interest in the manuscript when it was not yet complete and gave us the time we needed to finish. Dave Webster, of the Economic Policy Institute, provided us with the data we used for the quantitative analyses in the book. Margaret Alic, Eileen Appelbaum, Jim Atleson, Paul Barton, Fred Block, Françoise Carre, Harry Freeman, Robert Gibbons, Dinah Jacobs, David Levine, Carla Lipsig-Mumme,

Ruth Milkman, Sara Nicholas, Steve Rose, Lucy Suchman, Edward Wolff, and Jim Wooten gave us helpful comments on earlier versions of the manuscript or portions of the book's argument. We also received helpful comments from seminar participants at the law school of the State University of New York at Buffalo and the management school of Case Western Reserve University. During much of our work, finally, John Alic was in residence at the Johns Hopkins School of Advanced International Studies and wishes to thank the many people at SAIS who made him feel at home there.

We conclude with a few words on our respective contributions. Steve Herzenberg directed the original OTA project. In light of their comparable but different contributions to the book, John Alic and Howard Wial are listed alphabetically. Howard, jointly with Steve, shaped the overall argument of the book and the major analytical and policy ideas.

STEPHEN A. HERZENBERG
Harrisburg, Pennsylvania

JOHN A. ALIC
Washington, D.C.

HOWARD WIAL
Philadelphia, Pennsylvania

New Rules for a New Economy

1 Recreating the Prosperity of the Past in the Economy of the Future

The U.S. economy has grown steadily in the 1990s. By 1998, inflation and the federal budget deficit had melted away. Despite occasional jitters, the stock market continued to reach historic peaks. But regardless of what the business page says about consumer confidence at the time you read this book, Americans' anxiety about the future remains below the surface. Wages for all but a fortunate few have stagnated or fallen. Health care costs are up and insurance coverage down. Unemployment is low, but many people still fear the next round of layoffs. With factories moving offshore, big companies downsizing, and the public sector shrinking, workers are asking where the good new jobs will come from.

There is good reason to worry. Automation and international competition continue to eat away at the manufacturing jobs that were once plentiful. Service industries now employ about three-quarters of the workforce, with many workers trapped in low-wage, dead-end jobs. This book is about the reasons and the remedies for stagnation and decline in American living standards, for growing wage inequality and employment instability. Both causes and cures are to be found in the service economy; that is where the bulk of the jobs are and where the jobs of the future will be created.

Our starting point is the breakdown of the national economic system that generated prosperity for three decades after World War II, a period we call the Wonder Years. For a decade or more after the breakdown began, people clung to a past that could not be recovered. Now most Americans recognize that the past has gone for good. Yet no vision of the future has crystallized to take the place of people's past understandings of the economic world and their place in it: the old ideas of a job and career; how individuals and families achieve economic security; how employers, communities, and the nation prosper.

In this book we outline a reconstruction of the contemporary economy that could generate a new sense of confidence and a new era of widely shared prosperity. We argue that many elements of a reconstructed U.S. economic system have already begun to appear. We try to put the pieces together, showing how they might yield better performance as well as greater economic security.

The system we believe attainable would not be economic and social nirvana. Drudgery and hard physical labor would remain. Some Americans would still perform much more of this work, and earn much less, than others. Even if consumer price indices adequately accounted for new products and improved quality, we would not expect another period of quantitative growth—of more and more "stuff" every year—like the 1950s and 1960s. Still, the potential for qualitative improvements in services, for making work itself more rewarding, and for enjoying the fruits of growth in the form of shorter work time suggests an attainable future that Americans could look toward with optimism rather than unease.

Services Matter

Ever since Adam Smith wrote *The Wealth of Nations* in 1776, economic development has been virtually synonymous with manufacturing.[1] Many people continue to regard production of services as subsidiary to production of goods, even a parasitic drag on economic performance. Although services have accounted for more than half of U.S. employment for more than fifty years (Figure 1), policymakers, economists, and business writers continue to focus on manufacturing. After all, for a quarter-century after World War II, productivity increases in manufacturing stimulated a virtuous circle of rising wages and growing consumer demand, corporate profits, more investment, job creation, and higher living standards. That era has ended.

When public attention belatedly turned to service industries, powerful rhetorical images portrayed the service worker as a hamburger flipper or window washer, producing nothing lasting or solid. Pundits and politicians asked how Americans could expect to get along, much less prosper, taking in each other's laundry.

Goods-producing industries still matter, of course. But the simple fact is that services now account for most of U.S. employment, while manu-

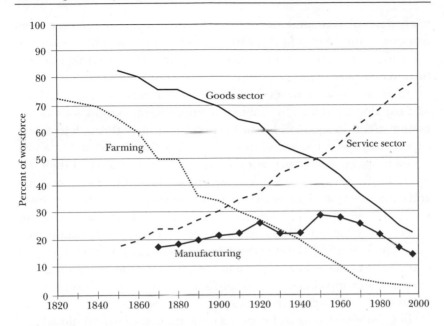

Note: The goods sector is made up of farming, forestry, fishing, manufacturing, construction, and mining. The ser vice sector includes the rest of the economy

Sources: U.S. Department of Labor, Bureau of Labor Statistics, Current Employment Statistics Survey and Current Population Survey, U.S. Department of Commerce, Bureau of the Census, *Historical Statistics of the United States, Colonial Times to 1970*, Part 1 (Washington, D.C.: U.S. Department of Commerce, September 1975), p. 138.

Figure 1. Growth of the service sector

facturing has fallen to around 15 percent and continues drifting down-ward. More Americans now work in physicians' offices than in auto plants, in laundries and dry cleaners than in steel mills. Services, as a re-sult, matter more than manufacturing when it comes to job quality. They also increasingly account for the rate at which living standards rise. But dependence on service jobs leaves many uneasy; say "dead-end job," and the image that comes to mind is McDonald's, not McDonnell Douglas.

It is wrong to assume that the majority of service workers will neces-sarily be stuck in low-wage jobs with poor benefits and little security. The services offer millions of good jobs, as well as millions of bad ones. And though a large share of service jobs pay little more than the minimum wage, this is a consequence of particular features of the U.S. economy and its labor market, especially the spread of wage-based competition.

With deregulation and new competition in sectors ranging from trucking to retailing to health care, employers have sought to cut labor costs, treating workers as interchangeable parts and accepting the high turnover and low commitment to the job that result.

In earlier decades, in service industries such as telecommunications and banking as well as in manufacturing, workers could start at the bottom of a firm's job ladder and expect to advance through learning, experience, and seniority. They could look forward to a career, a progression rather than a succession of jobs. Those who worked their way up in the 1970s and 1980s now confront an ongoing wave of mergers and corporate restructuring. These go by many names, including downsizing (or "rightsizing") and reengineering. Whatever the label, the consequences include layoffs, lateral transfers that may foreclose advancement opportunities, and, for those who keep their jobs this time, fear that the next wave will catch them too. At the same time, a shrunken social safety net and the decline of nuclear and extended families mean that those out of work have fewer resources to fall back on.

In goods-producing industries, a combination of international and domestic competition drives restructuring. In services, the direct impact of international competition has been minor compared with deregulation and other new sources of domestic competition: unlike goods, only a few service products can be shipped or stored; most must be produced at the point of sale.

When competitive forces lead to new and better service products, Americans benefit as consumers. But when competition leads to downward pressure on wages and benefits, Americans suffer as workers. And as wages below the top slice of the income distribution fall, workers can buy fewer goods and services. The loss of the opportunities that made the Wonder Years so promising for earlier generations also heightens social divisions.

This book shows how to reverse recent labor market trends and the poor economic performance that has accompanied wage-based competition in many service industries. We argue, in our last two chapters, for a new set of institutions that will support higher wages for middle- and low-income workers and create more opportunities for those who seek to advance. These same institutions will also improve economic performance and service quality. The job for public policy, in short, is to catch up with the changes in the economy since the 1970s (indeed, since the last round of major U.S. labor policy innovation in the 1930s).

The Wonder Years were wonderful not only because many workers could expect steady advances in pay and benefits but because the economy delivered in ways that people experienced every day—cars, boats, TVs, bigger homes, basic health care. (In some other respects, of course, the Wonder Years, a time of cold war and conformity, were anything but wonderful.) The reforms we propose should also contribute to tangible improvements in people's lives: child and elder care that enrich life rather than exacerbate guilt, better education, more responsive customer service, a revival of family and community life once wage increases for the many make the struggle to survive less consuming.

This book is rooted in an analysis of work and business in the services. We use mostly service examples because we are trying to reorient debate away from the old economy and old concepts—away from manufacturing. Even so, the concepts we develop to make sense of the huge and diverse service sector also shed light on goods-producing industries. For this reason, as well as because the services now make up the bulk of employment, we see our last two chapters as a prescription for economywide renewal.

The Past: The Origins and Decay of the Wonder Years

The core features of the Wonder Years provide a basis of comparison for our analysis of the services today, a gauge of how the world has changed since white bread and bland beer gave way to microbakeries and microbreweries, and a historical and analytical starting point for asking how to construct a new period of prosperity.[2]

During the one hundred years beginning in 1870, real gross domestic product (GDP) per labor-hour in the United States rose more than tenfold, an astounding increase. On a per capita basis, real GDP rose almost seven times between 1870 and 1973.[3]

Mechanization and automation in manufacturing powered the American economic engine. The technological basis was laid after the Civil War, with the rise of the steel industry—initially to provide railroad rails—and the development of the "American system" of manufactures. The American system of assembling standardized interchangeable components was spawned in armories and factories that made axes, firearms, and clocks. It led to affordable mass-produced sewing machines and bicycles, later to automobiles and many other consumer goods. Railroads, telephone, and telegraph helped manufacturers coordinate their growing purchasing and distribution networks.

Engineers and managers refined the American system in mass production industries, developing the methods still known as "scientific management."[4] Organizations capable of administering high-volume standardized production also emerged. Alfred Chandler has documented with painstaking detail the creation of new administrative giants in a long list of industries.[5]

The big corporations that dominated major industries became vehicles for spreading mass production technologies through the economy. They had the capital and the control over markets necessary to invest in expensive, single-purpose equipment. Productive capacity rose at an unprecedented rate.

No mechanism existed, however, to ensure that wages and purchasing power would rise in parallel with the economy's newfound capacity to produce. When the Great Depression brought a prolonged period of stagnant demand and corporate losses, there was nothing to stop massive layoffs and real wage cuts from building to a vicious circle in which falling demand pushed the entire economy into deep decline.

Widely shared perceptions that inadequate consumer demand had helped trigger the Depression added to support for New Deal labor and social welfare reforms. Congress passed legislation that helped create the institutional pillars of the Wonder Years, buttressing the economy against a future downward spiral fed by declining wages.

(1) The National Labor Relations Act of 1935 (also known as the Wagner Act) protected workers' rights to organize and bargain collectively. It contributed to the rise of labor unions in the steel, auto, rubber, electrical equipment, and other manufacturing industries. After World War II unions and collective bargaining established industrywide wage and benefit standards in core manufacturing industries. Postwar union contracts linked annual increases in real wages to the roughly 3 percent annual rate of national productivity growth.[6]

(2) The Fair Labor Standards Act of 1938 established national standards for the minimum wage, overtime pay, and restrictions on child labor. In the next thirty years periodic increases kept the national minimum wage above 40 percent of the average manufacturing wage. The federal minimum wage ensured that workers in many low-wage, nonunion industries also shared in the benefits of productivity growth.

(3) The Social Security Act of 1935, the foundation of the current social security system, established national contributory old-age pensions. The same legislation established a federal unemployment insurance tax and incentives that induced states to create unemployment insurance systems. When older or unemployed workers dropped out of the labor force, their consumption would no longer fall precipitously.

After World War II the United States entered the Wonder Years. The nation emerged from the war with unmatched industrial power. Not only were U.S. industries undamaged, but they had in many ways been strengthened by government investments in technology and production capacity. Conversion from military production proved less disruptive than many had feared. As other economies rebuilt, American industry in 1953 accounted for 45 percent of world manufacturing output.[7] With foreign competition a minor concern, major firms settled into generally comfortable domestic accommodations. Union contracts, minimum wage increases, and unemployment insurance payments joined Keynesian fiscal and monetary policy to dampen the business cycle, complementing mass production by sustaining consumer demand. Jobs were plentiful and so were profits.

This pattern could not last. It was easier for Europe and Japan to catch up than for the United States to stay ahead.[8] The big American steelmakers were complaining of "unfair" foreign competition by the end of the 1950s. Japan improved its manufacturing capabilities fast enough to become the world's low-cost supplier of goods ranging from ships to television sets in the 1960s. By the late 1970s imports accounted for almost 30 percent of U.S. automobile sales. No longer could U.S. Steel and General Motors function as price leaders, ensuring handsome margins for themselves and adequate, if usually smaller, profits for their domestic rivals and suppliers.

During the 1960s productivity rose at an average annual rate of 2.8 percent. The rate of increase fell below 2 percent in the 1970s and has since been even lower, around 1 percent a year. Low productivity growth put a damper on wage growth; without rising wages, demand growth slowed.

While international competition buffeted and broke the old oligopolies in manufacturing, deregulation, beginning under President Jimmy Carter in the late 1970s, contributed to steadily growing competitive pressures in a wide range of domestically oriented industries, including financial services, transportation, and telecommunications. At the same time, new entrants and changing consumer preferences brought new competitive pressures to industries such as retailing. In the 1990s attempts to contain rising costs brought competition even to the health care sector.

Manufacturing and service firms alike sought to reduce costs and improve quality and flexibility by automating and reorganizing their workplaces, closing off many internal job ladders, and cutting into well-paying jobs that had earlier been open to less-educated workers. Some manufacturers moved low-skilled, labor-intensive production to Asia and Mexico. In the 1980s Fortune 500 firms began to downsize, computers showed up on desktops, and employers merged, consolidated, and began to rely more heavily on part-time and temporary workers.

Meanwhile, the institutional framework of U.S. labor relations had been fraying. Male-dominated industrial unions adapted poorly to the rising percentage of women in the labor force and an expanding service sector. Advising corporations on how to remain "union-free" became a thriving cottage industry. Union coverage declined steadily to today's pre–Wagner Act levels—11 percent of the private nonagricultural labor force.

With the decline of unions came the erosion of the social policies supported by labor. The minimum wage roughly tracked productivity for the two decades after 1947, then lost half its value relative to productivity over the next three decades (see Figure 5, Chapter 8). The share of unemployed workers receiving unemployment insurance benefits fell.[9] By the end of President Bush's term most people understood that the old days were gone, even if they weren't quite sure why.

Making Sense of the New (and Old) Economy

The narrative above is familiar. This book goes beyond it to develop an analytical framework that describes the economy of the Wonder Years and of today. We then use that framework to define policies designed to point the nation toward a new era of prosperity.

We describe the economy using three concepts: work systems, business organization, and career paths. Each type of *work system* relies on a different basic approach to organize production and motivate or control how hard and well people work. Examples range from assembly lines, to janitorial labor with mop and broom, to the bureaucratic incentives of promotion and pay found in banks and insurance companies, to professions such as medicine and the law. Work systems emerge from a complex interaction among firms, employees, and technological and other contextual influences.

By *business organization* we mean the ways that firms structure their operations. To a majority of Americans, the most familiar forms of business organization are still the giant corporations—GM, Sears, AT&T (and newer firms such as Microsoft on which the media shower equal attention)—and the small establishments that consumers pass by and deal with daily. Within these organizations, managers decide which goods or services to offer and how to produce or distribute them. Relationships between firms, in turn, are coordinated through the market, that is, through "arm's-length" buying and selling between firms that have no enduring ties and will buy from someone else if they can get a better deal. Patterns of business organization in the services have always differed from those in manufacturing because of the smaller average size of service establishments and the prevalence of franchise agreements. In both services and manufacturing, recent trends in business organization include the creation of more enduring and cooperative links between separate firms (as, for example, in health care alliances).

Career paths structure the movement over time of workers through the labor market. These paths are shaped by the decisions of individual workers, groups of workers (informal communities, professional associations, labor unions), and owners and managers. The job ladders within large firms illustrate one kind of career path (e.g., from file clerk to secretary to office administrator). Another example is the movement of skilled craft workers in the construction trades from one worksite to another. As we define them, career paths do not necessarily imply that workers have "good" jobs. Nor does movement always lead to advancement in pay, skill, or responsibility.

Public policy affects economic outcomes not only directly but indirectly through its influence on work systems, business organization, and career paths (Figure 2). An obvious direct effect comes from the legally

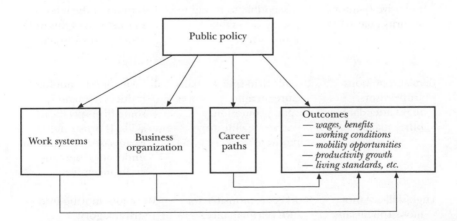

Figure 2. Relationships between public policy and employment
outcomes

mandated minimum wage. Examples of indirect impacts include antitrust laws that affect business organization and antidiscrimination laws that affect work systems and career paths.

The Wonder Years Revisited

Table 1 provides a brief comparison of the four work systems analyzed in detail in Chapters 3 and 4. The core of the middle class in the Wonder Years enjoyed one-company careers in vertically integrated firms. One major group consisted of blue-collar workers, many with "tightly constrained" jobs (including assembly-line jobs, although there

Table 1. Four work systems

Work system and examples	Defining characteristics	Major changes, 1960s–1990s
Tightly constrained (telephone operators, fast food workers)	Jobs narrowly defined, undemanding in terms of skills. Production paced by machine technology, customer pressure, or flow of work.	Some tasks and jobs automated out of existence, while automation and rationalization move other tasks and jobs into this work system.
Unrationalized labor-intensive (janitors, security guards)	Low wages. Work not susceptible to machine pacing or quality monitoring.	Declining pay at the bottom of the labor market makes this work system more attractive to employers.
Semiautonomous (supervisors, flight attendants, office managers)	Usually firm-specific skills. Bureaucratic incentives (pay, promotion, corporate culture) motivate workers.	Information technology reduces demand for some firm-specific skills. Downsizing, wage-based competition undermine bureaucratic incentives.
High-skill autonomous (physicians, electricians, teachers)	Workers responsible for own performance.	More jobs moving into this category.

were never as many as in the popular imagination). During the Wonder Years large numbers of middle-class Americans also found employment (as secretaries, middle managers, factory quality inspectors, and supervisors) in a work system we call semiautonomous. In this system, good wages, seniority-based pensions and promotion opportunities, and other bureaucratic incentives tied workers to firms and elicited effort and commitment. Since they generally stayed with one employer a long time, workers could acquire and apply firm-specific know-how. They learned the company's products, its "standard operating procedures," how to work effectively with others in the organization whose cooperation they needed. Most of those in tightly constrained blue-collar and semiautonomous white-collar jobs did not work for GM or AT&T. They worked for the GM supplier or dealer, the community hospital, the local bank or supermarket. But rapid economywide growth translated into promotion opportunities and security even in smaller firms.

The top of the labor market, in the Wonder Years as today, consisted of employees in the high-skill autonomous work system. This category includes professionals, upper-level managers, craft workers, and many technicians. In the high-skill autonomous system, employees, not their bosses, take primary responsibility for performance. Professional and craft pride, reinforced by career incentives, motivates effort and performance. Some high-skill autonomous workers during the Wonder Years spent their entire careers in one or a few organizations. Others, such as skilled construction workers, had careers that spanned many employers. Formal institutions (e.g., professional associations and hiring halls, portable credentials and benefits) supported informal networks of professional and craft workers, reducing the social and economic cost to the worker of moving to a new employer.

At the bottom of the labor market were "unskilled" labor-intensive jobs: janitors and gardeners, waiters and waitresses in all but elite restaurants, nurses' aides and hospital orderlies. In these jobs, the nature of the tasks prevents continuous, close supervision. Neither employers nor employees systematically analyze the work process to improve efficiency or quality. Low wages and the modest cost of capital equipment discourage employers from attempting the type of rationalization typical of capital-intensive production processes. For this reason, we term this category of work system "unrationalized labor-intensive." In the Wonder Years some people in unrationalized labor-intensive jobs moved up by moving out—into other work systems with other employers. For workers in both unrationalized and tightly constrained work systems, collective bargaining and the minimum wage kept pay rising roughly in step with salaries in the other two work systems.

Many Americans see the post–World War II period as wonderful in hindsight because, unlike today, workers' aspirations and opportunities were more or less in balance. White men, at least, could take for granted that they would make it into a well-paid tightly constrained or semiautonomous job by some time in their twenties. Others were not so fortunate. African Americans, emboldened by the civil rights movement in the 1960s, challenged their relegation to the most arduous and mind-numbing work. The women's movement took issue with female segregation into unrationalized jobs and bureaucratic, semiautonomous occupations that paid less than male-dominated job categories. Since the 1960s, aspirations have risen. Since the 1970s, opportunities, especially for those with modest educational credentials, have narrowed. Widening gaps between aspirations and opportunities have left many Americans anxious, uncertain, confused.

The New Economy: The Origins of Economic Anxiety

Table 2 summarizes wage and employment changes by work system between 1979 and 1996. (Changes in occupational definitions make comparisons for years before 1979 treacherous.) Employment in the unrationalized labor-intensive work system remains at about a quarter of the total, as in 1979, while growth in professional and technical jobs has increased the share of the high-skill autonomous work system. Semiautonomous jobs have declined relative to other categories. Some semiautonomous jobs have migrated to the high-skill category. In other cases, employers competing on the basis of low wages have replaced semiautonomous jobs with unrationalized labor-intensive work. Retailing illustrates the substitution. In department stores facing competition from both discounters and specialty outlets, many nonprofessional positions that once paid decent wages and benefits and offered advancement opportunities—classic semiautonomous jobs—have been transformed into low-paying, high-turnover positions.

The wage picture is even grimmer. Since 1979 pay in the unrationalized labor-intensive and tightly constrained work systems has fallen relative to the high-skill system. The decline of unions and the real value of the minimum wage contributed to the widening gap. Part of the drop in

Table 2. Changes in wages, mobility, and employment, by work system, 1979–1996

Work system	Relative size (as a share of economywide employment)	Real median wage	Prospects for individual advancement	Job security
Tightly constrained	Slight decline (from 6 to 5 percent)	Down 18 percent	Poorer: more dead-end jobs with no prospect of internal advance-ment	Poorer: more out-sourcing, permanent layoffs
Unration-alized labor-intensive	Stable, at about 25 percent	Down 11–12 percent	Still poor: low-wage jobs unconnected to better ones	Little change: some dead-end jobs are secure
Semi-autonomous	Down, from about 35 to 30 percent	Down roughly 6 percent	Worse: many skills of value only to current em-ployer but firm-specific job ladders breaking down	Worse: more reengi-neering, permanent layoffs
High-skill autonomous	Up, from 34 to about 40 percent	Down 6 percent	Still good in most cases	Little change: skills widely recognized and valued by many employers

Note: Chapters 3 and 4 document the changes summarized in this table.

union coverage reflects the difficulty of organizing service workers, many of whom work in small establishments spread across large industries such as retailing.

Within firms where the semiautonomous work system still predominates, career trajectories have become less predictable, in part because fewer of these jobs are in large firms with well-marked career paths.

With deregulation, companies such as AT&T have reduced payrolls and dismantled their internal hierarchies. Wage inequality has grown as firms have contracted out work once performed by their own employees. Janitorial, food-service, and security jobs that once paid big-company wages and benefits are more often isolated in low-cost suppliers that rely on low-paid contingent workers.

The analysis summarized above and explored in detail in later chapters points to three underlying roots of economic anxiety. The first is low pay and lack of upward mobility for those stuck in unrationalized labor-intensive jobs, as well as in a few expanding, tightly constrained settings such as telephone call centers. These kinds of jobs rarely lead to a step up on a big-firm job ladder. A second cause is the insecurity that troubles those with good jobs. Office workers, managers, and sales employees, lacking specialized skills in high demand or portable credentials, fear the loss of income and status that may follow from a forced change of employer.

A third root of economic anxiety is the apparently stagnant economic performance of the services, which limits the fruits available to distribute. We trace low measured productivity growth in part to the nature of service sector work processes. In unrationalized labor-intensive jobs, exemplified by nursing homes and other low-wage social services, employers don't care about improving performance because workers are so cheap. Workers do not have the training, knowledge, or power to improve performance on their own. Even in some tightly constrained and semiautonomous service work, low or stagnant wages and the high turnover they generate discourage firms from investing in workers or more energetically seeking performance improvement. Indeed, managerial approaches to performance improvement in the services to a surprising extent reflect preoccupation with the "deskilled" jobs of the mass manufacturing era, even though the tightly constrained work system has never been very prominent in the service sector.

Imagining Some Solutions: A Policy Preview

The policies proposed at the end of this book directly attack the low wages, rising job insecurity, and lackluster economic performance that we see as the roots of economic anxiety.

Since wages are too low in the poorest-paying work systems, they should be raised. This will not happen by relying on the market as it now operates. Public policy can support wage levels in two basic ways: by raising the hourly minimum and by encouraging collective bargaining. The federal minimum wage (now $5.15) remains about 25 percent below its real value in 1968 (which would be about $7 today) and less than half what it was in 1968 relative to labor productivity. The minimum wage should be raised substantially. This would also push up wages for workers paid somewhat above the minimum.

The one-employer career may not have disappeared, but even the largest firms make it plain today that there are no guarantees. With declining employment attachments, firms are less likely to support the skill development needed both for improved economic performance and for career advancement. (In Chapter 5 we explain why workers' skills and experience are the key to achieving large improvements in performance in many services.)

There is no point in wishing for an end to downsizing and reengineering (which in some cases make their own contributions to performance improvement). The only practical way to address the mismatch between worker aspirations and actual prospects for security and mobility is to construct career paths that cut across firms. That way workers can look forward to "staircase" careers in which they can move up by moving to another employer. Public policies to encourage staircase careers include support for developing skill standards, training institutions, and job referral systems coordinated by multifirm labor and management groups.

The third leg of our policy stool is an expansion of "reinvented," more craftlike unions. These are critical for raising wages, building new career ladders, and improving workers' performance in many service occupations. Current policies, however, effectively deny representation to many workers who move among small firms. Framed in the 1930s, U.S. laws were designed to encourage unionization at big factories. These laws are poorly suited to an era of small service establishments and transient employment attachments. Labor law reform should support union formation and bargaining across multiple employers (e.g., in retailing or office work). Employers would benefit through access to better prepared, more capable workers.

Taken together, these and other policies discussed in Chapters 7 and 8 would create conditions that foster better economic performance within firms, clusters of firms, and occupational groups. Our policies would limit "destructive" competition, based on working harder and for less, in favor of "constructive" competition. They would allow public

policy and institutions to catch up with the changes that have accumulated in work systems, business organization, and career paths since the
1930s.

We anticipate three sets of responses to the policy proposals summarized above. Some oppose wage-setting policies, maintaining that they
raise unemployment and undermine economic efficiency. But as we
argue in Chapter 8, allowing the minimum wage to fall erodes efficiency
gains over time because firms need not improve performance to stay in
business. There is, in addition, little evidence that recent hikes in the
minimum wage have cut into job creation. And even with a big increase
in the minimum wage, we suggest in Chapter 8 that the reinvention of
social policy could keep unemployment low.

Second, some may object that low-wage foreign competition in a
global economy must eventually prove overwhelming. Regardless of
one's view of the consequences of wage-based foreign competition for
U.S. manufacturing, only about 10 percent of the service workforce
holds jobs directly exposed to international competition. Adding manufacturing and agricultural jobs would roughly triple the number of jobs
potentially exposed to foreign competition, but even this total represents less than 30 percent of the labor force.[10]

The great bulk of service products are nontradable and will remain
so. It is true that information technologies, low-cost transportation, and
reductions in trade barriers may increase cross-border services trade
(e.g., back offices moved to Ireland or the Caribbean, software up-
grades produced in India). But it is domestic competition, in which
American workers compete only with one another, that holds down
wages and benefits for those without highly specialized skills and knowledge. In the less mobile parts of the services, states and localities, as well
as the national government, can set rules for competition without worrying that they will be undercut by others outside U.S. borders.

Finally, some might suggest that the best solutions to wage disper-
sion and dead-end jobs are found in education and training. Education
is a good in itself. But education, standing alone, cannot make low-wage
jobs disappear. As we argue in Chapter 4, low-wage jobs exist because
some work systems are not organized to raise performance in ways that
might lead to higher wages. Unless those work systems are reorganized,
jobs for those in the lower part of the wage distribution will not pay
better or offer greater career opportunities. More education will not automatically prompt reorganization, because low-wage work systems have

little place for higher skills. Indeed, more education and training absent other policies could simply make worker frustration more widespread. Rising numbers of Americans would face opportunities that fall short of their aspirations.

Building a Postindustrial System

In the next chapter we compare jobs and productivity performance (to the extent it can be measured) in the services with those in manufacturing. The organization of the rest of the book follows our three main analytical constructs. Chapters 3 through 5 deal with work systems. Chapter 6 turns to business organization. Chapter 7 examines career paths. Chapter 8 considers how work systems, business organization, and career paths might be reshaped by public policy to generate more good jobs and better economic performance.

Our book is also organized to help readers envision a "system-building" process parallel to the one that created the manufacturing-centered prosperity of the Wonder Years. As we saw, three distinct but intertwined developments combined to create that prosperity. In stage 1, technological and organizational innovations—new products, rationalization, mechanization, and scientific management—led to dramatic rises in productivity. Stage 2 saw the creation of institutions that helped spread mass production methods and related innovations through the economy. The key institutions were corporations with enough market power to be confident that, after making large-scale investments, they would be able to profit from a correspondingly large volume of sales. Stage 3, completed in the 1930s and 1940s, ensured the purchasing power necessary to keep the national economy expanding. It involved the creation of demand-sustaining labor market institutions (industrial unions, pattern bargaining, the minimum wage) and social policies (unemployment insurance and social security).

Over the next generation or so the United States can choose to emulate the three-stage evolution that led to the Wonder Years.

Stage 1: Recent innovations in service sector work processes have begun to suggest new ways of improving performance. In Chapter 5 we argue that learning by workers, individually and collectively, can generate performance gains sufficient to support better jobs and better pay.

Stage 2: As the technological and organizational basis for performance improvement in services develops, the nation will need mechanisms that can propagate the new approaches, much as big corporations and labor market policy spread mass production methods. In Chapter 6 we suggest that recent changes in corporate strategy and structure are not enough to diffuse more productive approaches throughout the service economy. Although fluid and fragmented forms of business organization make corporations more nimble, they undercut the capacity of individual firms to support the training, learning, and employment security essential to high-quality, high-productivity strategies. In Chapter 7, therefore, we examine multifirm structures that could foster adoption of the new approaches to performance improvement and simultaneously give workers a wider range of employment and learning opportunities.

Stage 3: In the creation of the old industrial system, the final step was the resolution of the problem of aggregate demand and unemployment. We discuss the manifestation of this issue in the new economy briefly in Chapter 8. Today, there must be enough paid jobs and social support that vulnerable workers are not forced to take subsistence jobs in the low-wage unrationalized labor-intensive work system. We speculate that creative social policy could make it easier to move among paid work, education, family responsibilities, and community service. Harking back to the preindustrial era, people would always have useful activity to perform in one of these realms. And the ability to move among them could keep the need for paid work in balance with the available jobs.

The analysis of particular firms, industries, and work systems in the chapters that follow shows that competition can operate in constructive or destructive ways. That argument would likely be taken for granted if we were talking about the world of sports, where the game is a more obviously artificial construct. Basketball's competition committee, for example, modifies the rules periodically to maintain audience appeal. Why? Because coaches and players keep trying to beat the old rules. Several years ago the committee instituted severe penalties for flagrant fouls and prohibited hand checking. The new rules help ensure that fluidity and athletic skill, rather than brute force and barely contained violence, remain the keys to success on the court. The competition committee, in other words, acted to discourage destructive competition.

The economic world is also a human construct, not a state of nature. It is based on competition guided by rules. The issue is the type of economic competition and organization that the rules, from property rights to labor laws, encourage. Today they encourage widespread low-wage, low-skill competition and fail to encourage widespread improvement of service sector economic performance. Better economic and social outcomes require better rules.

2 The Service Economy and the Service Worker

Work is life, you know, and without it, there's nothing but fear and insecurity.
—*John Lennon, BBC-TV, December 15, 1969*

In 1996 about three-quarters of all employed Americans worked in service industries, up from two-thirds in 1979. Retail and wholesale trade together employ more people than manufacturing. Wal-Mart, now the fourth-largest U.S. corporation measured by revenues, created more than half a million new jobs over the past dozen years.[1] General Electric, the fourth-largest U.S. manufacturing firm (and sixth-largest overall), gets more than half its revenues from service businesses—a sign of the shift of old-line manufacturers toward financial and other services. In acknowledgment of these changes, *Fortune* magazine in 1995 redefined its Fortune 500 list, which previously included only manufacturing companies, to include service firms.[2] Around the same time, though with less fanfare, the Department of Commerce began to report trade in services monthly, as it long had done for goods, rather than quarterly, and redefined what it calls the trade balance to include services.

In this chapter we set the stage for our analysis of jobs and economic performance in the service sector and how they might be changed for the better. We begin by highlighting common features of service industries. The bulk of the chapter deals with employment. Many Americans' anxieties about their working lives center on perceptions that wages are falling, that wage disparities between rich and poor are growing, and that jobs are becoming less secure. To what extent are these perceptions true? Are they more true of the services than of manufacturing? We conclude with a discussion of economic performance in the services. Measured productivity growth in most service industries has been low. Because long-term wage increases depend on productivity improvements, the productivity measures, if they can be believed, imply that the shift of employment to the services bodes ill for the wages and benefits of American workers.

Can You Drop It on Your Foot?

The teenager serving hamburgers and french fries at a local fast-food restaurant may be the stereotype of the service worker, but everyone knows that Michael Jordan and Michael Jackson are service workers too, along with investment bankers and computer professionals. Conventionally defined as a residual category, the service sector includes all parts of the economy other than farming, resource extraction (mining, forestry, fishing), construction, and manufacturing. Table 3 gives service sector employment by major industry.

For all their diversity, the services have a number of common characteristics. The great bulk of services cannot be produced in advance, shipped, and then stored until a customer comes along. Examples include not only retail sales and retail banking but also health care and transportation. It is true that a growing volume of services can be produced remotely for delivery via computer network or other electronic medium. Rather than telling her stockbroker over the phone to buy AT&T and sell gold, a customer may place orders with the aid of a touchtone phone or personal computer, never speaking to an employee of the brokerage firm. Nonetheless, if home shopping via mail order, telephone, and the Internet displaces some in-store sales, people still deliver the package or the pizza, and if computers help physicians diagnose diseases, robot surgeons (although not robot assistance) remain well in the future. Most services are still produced by workers who deal directly with customers.

Most service products are also intangible: you can't drop them on your foot. And even if you can—a legal brief, a movie—most of the value of the product stems from the know-how and skills going into the original production, not the physical artifact. The value in the legal brief reflects knowledge of the law; the value in the movie is in the writing, directing, and acting.[3]

These characteristics make services much less footloose than manufacturing. The services have become more important in the nation's trade balance, contributing a surplus of nearly $75 billion in 1996 and offsetting more than half the deficit in manufacturing. Still, many service products cannot be easily traded (although when a foreign national travels to the Mayo Clinic for surgery, his expenditures count as a U.S. service export). Financial services firms may have shipped back-office work overseas, as well as to Iowa and South Dakota. But before too long automation is likely to take over much of this work. The costs of the few workers still needed will be too small to have great influence over the location of facilities.

Table 3 suggests that government statistics in the United States (and elsewhere) lump service industries together with little obvious or satisfying logic. For example, real estate is conventionally grouped with insurance and banking, utilities with transportation. Moreover, the term "services" is sometimes used to refer to a smaller set of industries that includes business and repair services, professional services, and per-

Table 3. Employment in manufacturing and major service industries

	Annual average employment (millions)			
	1979	1989	1996	% change, 1979–96
Manufacturing	22.0	20.8	19.7	−10
All Services	58.3	74.6	83.8	44
Transportation, communications, and utilities	6.2	6.8	7.3	18
Wholesale trade	3.3	3.9	4.4	33
Retail trade	13.9	17.3	19.3	39
Finance, insurance, and real estate	5.3	7.0	7.0	32
Business and repair services	2.8	5.6	6.2	121
Personal services	2.9	3.6	3.5	21
Entertainment and recreation	0.9	1.1	2.0	122
Professional services	17.9	22.7	27.4	53
Public administration	5.2	6.5	6.6	27

Source: Calculated based on combined outgoing rotation groups of the Bureau of Labor Statistics' Current Population Survey for years given. Includes only workers age 16 and older who had positive earnings and were not self-employed. Major service industry figures may not add to "all services" totals because of rounding.

sonal services. (As distinct from professional services, business services include mostly low-wage industries such as building maintenance and cleaning, security, and temporary help.) And sometimes "services" means personal services alone (dry cleaning, barber and beauty shops, and so on). This casual approach dates from a time when government agencies viewed the nongoods residual as having minor significance for the economy.

Not only the government's industrial classifications but the way most Americans think about the economy reflects the continuing hold of manufacturing, especially high-volume standardized manufacturing, on the collective imagination. Gross national product (GNP) and gross domestic product (GDP), for example, emerged as measures of national output only in the first third of the twentieth century, with the development of technical methods for national income accounting. GDP quickly took on a life of its own. It functions well as a measure of output in an economy dominated by standardized goods: it is easy to count bushels of corn, Model T's in black, men's shirts in white. But GDP functions less well in an economy composed mostly of less standardized services. Inputs can be measured easily enough (e.g., an hour with a lawyer or an astrologer). But what is the output and what is it worth? How should heart surgery be valued in computing the GDP? Yet when technocrats produce a figure for GDP based on more or less arbitrary assumptions, the public more or less automatically accepts the result, taking it to be an "objective" measure of national economic welfare. As the service economy comes into better focus, it will be easier to see the GDP as an accounting convention and there will be more room for debating alternative measures of national well-being (as environmentalists and others have been urging for years).

As with GDP, so other economic terms emerged or took on meanings linked to the manufacturing economy. "Productivity" meant making more Model T's with fewer workers.[4] A job meant a full-time permanent position. Unemployment was understood to mean the loss of such a job. Although they also expanded alongside mass manufacturing, project-based industries such as construction and entertainment, in which employment was temporary and crews were hired anew for each office building or movie, were somehow seen as exceptional. Similarly, the growth of part-time, temporary, and other forms of contingent employment has been seen as anomalous, like the underground economy, which has always been characterized by transient employment relationships (for example, when a householder pays cash to a handyman who paints the garage).

There are many other cases in which words and images from the past hinder our ability to understand the present and shape the future. "Trade association," in the American context, connotes a political and lobbying organization, despite the productive role in human resource development and the diffusion of new technologies and organizational practices that such organizations play in other countries and might play here. "Union" brings to mind the old industrial unions that defended workers slotted into narrowly defined jobs. Many people assume, in consequence, that associations of workers exist primarily to do battle with employers, that unions have sought and will continue to seek to restrict output levels and effort, hinder flexibility, and resist new technology. None of these generalizations is historically true even in manufacturing.

Any view of worker organizations less tied to mass manufacturing would include craft unions in construction, Actors' Equity, and professional associations of nurses, accountants, engineers, and physicians. Such groups have long had a major role in skill formation, quality assurance, and the organization and management of production. It could hardly be otherwise when those who do the work are the only ones who fully understand its intricacies.

Service Jobs: What the Numbers Show

A glance at Table 3 suggests how misleading it is to generalize from hamburger flippers to other service workers. Most fast-food jobs fall under retail trade, the second-largest service industry, with more than 19 million employees (23 percent of nearly 84 million service workers). But retail workers fill a wide range of jobs, from cashiers and stock clerks to buyers in department stores. Retail trade has grown rapidly, but other services even more so. Entertainment and recreation and business and repair services have been the fastest growing since 1979, each more than doubling in employment. All service industries, though, have expanded since the late 1970s, while manufacturing has lost jobs.[5]

Women outnumber men in the services (55 percent to 45 percent in 1996), whereas most manufacturing workers are men (68 percent). These proportions have not changed much since the 1970s.[6] The racial/ethnic composition of service employment is not much different from that of manufacturing: the fraction of white workers has declined since the 1970s, from 82–83 percent to 75 percent in both sectors. (See Table A-1, in Appendix A, where we have placed some of the more detailed statistics extracted from the Current Population Survey.) Service workers have more education (but earn less, as we will see) than their counterparts in manufacturing (Table A-2). In 1996 nearly 60 percent of service workers had some post–high school education, compared with 44 percent in manufacturing. Nearly 30 percent of service workers, but only 19 percent of manufacturing workers, reported four or more years of college.

Sources of Anxiety I: Low Wages and Rising Inequality

In Chapter 1 we identified low-wage, dead-end jobs as one of three roots of economic anxiety. This section reports on two manifestations of low wages: median wage trends within major industries and a distribution of wages that has become more unequal since the 1970s.

Declining Wages

Real (inflation-adjusted) wages for most American workers have been falling for two decades. In both manufacturing and services, the median real wage dropped steadily from 1979 to 1989 to 1996 (Table 4).[7] Because the median service sector wage is lower than the median manufacturing wage, the shift of employment from manufacturing toward services has meant a shift from higher- to lower-wage employment. At the same time, because manufacturing wages have fallen more (in percentage terms) than service sector wages, the gap between the two sectors has narrowed.

For the major service industries, the story is much the same as in the aggregate. Only workers in professional services experienced steady real wage gains over the period 1979–96. Workers in finance-insurance-real estate (a higher-than-manufacturing-wage industry by 1996) and personal services (one of the lowest-wage service industries) were better off in 1996 than in 1979. Workers in all other service industries (including high-wage public administration) lost ground between 1979 and 1996. Transportation-communication-utilities, wholesale, and retail workers lost the most: their wages fell as much as or more than those of manufacturing workers in percentage terms.

Table 4. Median hourly wages in manufacturing
and major service industries (in 1996 dollars)

	1979	1989	1996	% change, 1979–1996
Manufacturing	$ 12.72	$ 12.24	$ 11.47	−10
All services	10.39	10.12	10.00	−4
Transportation, communications and utilities	15.12	14.15	12.50	−17
Wholesale trade	12.19	11.39	10.94	−10
Retail trade	7.42	6.33	6.50	−12
Finance, insurance, and real estate	10.60	11.84	11.64	10
Business and repair services	9.97	10.05	9.30	−7
Personal services	6.36	6.33	6.50	2
Entertainment and recreation	7.95	7.59	7.50	−6
Professional services	10.60	11.39	11.53	9
Public administration	14.46	14.55	14.01	−3

Source: Same as Table 3. Wages deflated using the CPI-U-X1. Hourly wages for nonhourly workers imputed by dividing usual weekly earnings by usual weekly hours. Hours imputed for variable-hour workers.

Table A-3 shows that union coverage remains high in transportation, communications, utilities, education, and government, where workers tend to be well paid. Many of these jobs have come under threat in recent years, and these threats show no signs of abating. Communication and utilities workers will probably lose ground as deregulation of local telephone service and electric power proceeds. Workers at all levels in health care may feel the consequences of efforts to reduce costs. Fiscal constraints and privatization put pressure on the jobs, wages, and benefits of federal, state, and local government workers.

Turning to worker demographics, we find that all groups of workers are worse off in services than in manufacturing and that only a few groups in either sector have escaped real wage losses since the 1970s. Men lost the same amount of ground in manufacturing and the services, some 15 percent in both sectors between 1979 and 1996 (Table A-4). Real wages for women changed relatively little in manufacturing (up 2 percent) and rose by 6 percent in services. Workers in all racial/

ethnic groups suffered losses in both manufacturing and services (Table A-5). Wage declines were smaller for all groups in the services. Blacks and Hispanics make less than whites in absolute terms in all cases. These gaps have widened since 1979. Wages for whites in the services fell by 2 percent between 1979 and 1996. For blacks, the decline was 7 percent; for Hispanics, 14 percent. All workers except those with a college diploma experienced losses in both manufacturing and services, but once again, the wage declines were smaller in the services (Table A-6). Those with the least schooling saw their wages fall the most. Wages for high school graduates fell by 11 percent in services from 1979 to 1996, compared with 19 percent in manufacturing. Four-year college graduates gained ground during the 1980s but slipped back during the early 1990s. In manufacturing, but not in services, college graduates were marginally worse off in 1996 than in 1979.

Increasing Wage Inequality

During the 1980s wage gaps between rich and poor workers widened and wage inequality grew among workers of every race, sex, educational background, and industry.[8] Some people worried that the United States was becoming a "winner-take-all" society, in which workers would compete for a limited number of high-status, high-paying jobs, with most remaining stuck in lower-status (and lower-paid) positions.[9]

The shift toward services has contributed to the rise in inequality. One way to measure wage inequality is to compare the wages of workers near the top of the wage distribution (the 90th percentile, say—those who earn more than 90 percent of all workers) with those near the bottom (the 10th percentile). As measured by this 90–10 ratio, the gap between the best-paid and poorest-paid Americans is wider in services than in manufacturing (Table 5). In 1996 a 90th percentile service worker made 4.6 times as much per hour as a 10th percentile worker. The 90–10 ratio was 3.96 in manufacturing.

Wage inequality varies greatly by industry (Table 5). In personal services, where almost all workers earn low wages, the 90–10 ratio is only 3.3. Transportation-communication-utilities, wholesale trade, retail trade, and public administration also have lower 90–10 wage ratios than manufacturing. In contrast, the professional services industry, of which health care is a part, includes both well-paid physicians and poorly paid hospital orderlies, and has a 90–10 ratio of 4.55.

Since the 1970s wage inequality has grown in both manufacturing and services and within every major service industry except personal

Table 5. Wage inequality in manufacturing and major service industries

	Ratio of wage of 90th percentile worker to wage of 10th percentile worker		
	1979	1989	1996
Manufacturing	3.20	3.75	3.96
All services	3.45	4.41	4.60[a]
Transportation, communications, and utilities	3.26	3.64	3.70
Wholesale trade	3.46	3.84	3.89
Retail trade	2.83	3.39	3.44
Finance, insurance, and real estate	3.59	4.15	4.31
Business and repair services	3.45	4.43	4.52
Personal services	6.00	4.00	3.30
Entertainment and recreational services	3.75	4.64	4.27
Professional services	3.45	4.22	4.55
Public administration	3.29	3.25	3.62

[a]The 90–10 ratio in services as a whole exceeds that in all individual service industries in 1996 because aggregating services can lead to a 90th percentile wage that is above that in individual industries and a 10th percentile wage that is below that in individual industries.

Source: See Table 4.

services. The 90–10 ratio increased between 1979 and 1996 in both manufacturing and services, but the increase was greater (in both absolute and percentage terms) in services.

Since the 1970s, wage differentials along educational and racial/ethnic dimensions have widened in both services and manufacturing, although they generally remain smaller in services (Tables A-5 and A-6). There was one bright spot in our examination of wage inequality: wages for women have improved relative to those for men, with the relative gains greater in services than in manufacturing. In most other respects, there is more inequality in services than in manufacturing and more in both sectors today than at the end of the 1970s.

Sources of Anxiety II: Declining Job Security

Many Americans, after surviving the Great Depression and World War II, began to believe they had a job for life if they wanted it. That sense of security is gone. Layoffs were a fact of working life for many Americans during the Wonder Years, but mostly as a consequence of the business cycle. Now, in a period of long-running economic expansion, people are losing jobs as a consequence of management fiat through downsizing, restructuring, mergers. With once-familiar names disappearing from banks, department stores, and airport terminals, nearly everyone knows people who have lost what seemed like a good job, even if they have not been fired themselves.

Even so, the available data show only small declines in measures of job stability, at least until quite recently.[10] Since 1993, consistent with common perceptions, worker displacement rates have increased. From 1993 to 1995, job loss affected 15 percent of the overall workforce, compared with 9 percent from 1987 to 1989, an earlier period of economic expansion.[11] For male high school graduates, displacement rates increased from 11 to 17 percent. For high school–educated women, the increase was from 9 to 15 percent. Roughly twice as many college-educated workers lost their jobs in the later period: 11.9 percent of men in 1993–96, compared with 6.5 percent in 1987–89, and 10.6 percent for college-educated women, compared with 5.2 percent.

Examining differences in job stability by industry and occupation shows that service jobs are less stable than those in manufacturing. Among major private service sector industries, only the highly unionized, heavily regulated transportation-communication-utilities industry shows stronger worker attachment to individual employers than does manufacturing. Separation rates rose during the 1980s in low-wage service industries (notably business and repair, entertainment and recreation, and personal services) and in nonprofessional, nonmanagerial service occupations.[12]

Other evidence shows that long-term employment relationships no longer function as they once did. Employers are more likely to dismiss workers permanently during economic downturns rather than laying them off temporarily.[13] When workers do hold onto jobs for lengthy periods, wages do not rise as swiftly as in the past.[14]

Two additional trends contribute to perceptions of declining job security. First, Americans who lose jobs have a harder time finding new work and more often suffer large wage declines than in the past.[15] Second, prime-age men who could once count on finding long-term jobs now face more competition for those jobs. Nearly 60 percent of women (sixteen years and older) are now in the labor force, compared with 43 percent as recently as 1970.[16] Before the 1970s many women moved in and out of the labor force as needed to supplement family income (or based on the number and age of children at home). Now the primary wage earners in many households, more women seek full-time jobs with employment security, decent wages and benefits, and career opportunities. Thus perceptions of a decline in job security may be due in part to the failure of the number of long-term jobs to keep pace with the rising share of workers who want them.

Reports of rapid growth in contingent, part-time, and temporary jobs as opposed to "regular" full-time jobs have added to the sense of instability and insecurity felt by many Americans. Most types of nonstandard employment are more prevalent in services than in manufacturing, with the somewhat unexpected exception of temporary employment.[17] For example, "alternative work arrangements"—which the Bureau of Labor Statistics (BLS) defines to include on-call and day laborers, independent contractors, and people employed by temporary help agencies and on a contract basis—cover about 10 percent of all service workers, nearly twice the level in manufacturing (Table A-7). The most prevalent form of alternative work arrangement, independent contracting, is more common in every major service industry, except public administration, than in manufacturing. But contrary to images of the "temp" as an office worker, temporaries account for a higher share of manufacturing (2 percent) than service (1 percent) jobs.

Part-time work, defined by BLS as anything less than thirty-five hours per week, is more common in every major service industry than in manufacturing (Table A-8). More than 30 percent of workers in retail trade, entertainment and recreation services, and personal services work part-time. The frequency of part-time work has changed little since the late 1970s in the service sector as a whole (or in manufacturing). Within the services, no industry has seen a substantial increase in part-time work, and perhaps surprisingly, industries including personal services have actually experienced considerable declines.

Sources of Economic Anxiety III: Low Productivity Growth

Labor productivity is calculated by dividing the output of a production process—making computers, processing an insurance claim—by the labor input to that process. More complicated measures, such as multifactor productivity, consider output changes in response to increases in inputs other than labor, such as capital. Labor productivity is the most straightforward and widely used measure. In the services, multifactor productivity series are available only for two capital-intensive industries, transportation and utilities.

When labor productivity growth is rapid, as it was during the Wonder Years, many workers enjoy rising wages, while consumers benefit through declining prices and product improvements resulting from technological innovation. But with productivity growth slow since the early 1970s, and the economy delivering fewer gains for workers and consumers, it is no surprise that Americans began worrying more about the distribution of income and wealth.

Although productivity growth declined throughout the industrial world at about the same time—for reasons that nobody understands—the slowdown has been especially long-lasting and severe in the United States. Moreover, apparent productivity performance has been especially poor in the nonmanufacturing sector of the economy. Although productivity growth fell in manufacturing during the 1970s, the decline was much greater for the nonfarm business economy as a whole (Table A-9).

Productivity in Service Industries

The two federal agencies that compile data related to labor productivity acknowledge that their measures are less accurate for services than for manufacturing. BLS reports output per worker-hour (and/or output per worker) for thirty-nine service industries, most of which are included in Table A-10. These thirty-nine industries account for less than half of private sector service employment, however, too small a portion of the service sector to be useful for exploring aggregate trends.[18]

The Bureau of Economic Analysis (BEA), part of the Department of Commerce, compiles real value-added for all industries by two-digit standard industrial classification (SIC) code (Table A-11). But BEA acknowledges serious biases in much of its data. Poor-quality data has led to possible underestimation of real output and productivity growth in industries responsible for about 38 percent of service sector output.[19] In some cases, output is not measured at all, and BEA bases outputs solely on inputs. (Government is one such case.) If "measured" output grows only in proportion to labor input, productivity growth is zero by definition. BLS and BEA have ongoing efforts to generate better measures of output in services.

Although poor data make it difficult to generalize, apparently slow productivity growth extends to many services in which measurement methods do not automatically bias the numbers downward. From 1977 to 1994, only in communications and wholesale trade did the annual rate of growth of value-added per hour in a service industry exceed that in manufacturing. From 1990 to 1994, average annual productivity growth climbed slightly above that in manufacturing (2.2 percent per year over this period) in two additional service industries, transportation (at 2.3 percent) and public utilities (at 2.8 percent). Productivity growth in fifteen of the seventeen service industries in Table A-10 remains below that in manufacturing. The question is why. Is productivity growth actually lower? Or are measures of output in services flawed in ways other than those already mentioned?

The Measurement Problem in Services

Estimating output and productivity is difficult in many goods-producing industries. It is even harder in services. The major problem common to both sectors is valuing changes in product attributes over time—the increase in real output when cars are safer, break down less often, and emit fewer pollutants, for example, or when recorded music sounds more like a concert hall, or when cash can be obtained from an ATM at any hour of the day or night.

Computers, because their speed, memory capacity, and other attributes have improved by orders of magnitude over several decades, represent a particularly challenging output measurement case in manufacturing even though on a conceptual level digital computers function much the same today as in the 1950s.[20] In services, deregulation and new entrants have led to rapid change (not always improvements) in quality and service features. Trucking has changed so much since deregulation in the late 1970s that BLS ended its series on output per employee after 1989. The accuracy of the figures reported by trucking companies (number of employees or miles driven, output in ton-miles) deteriorated, and it had become difficult to collect data from the many independent truckers entering and exiting the industry.[21] Recently, with more of their customers operating on a just-in-time basis, some trucking firms have begun to compete on service quality as well as price. This shift makes traditional indicators such as ton-miles per employee suspect, but no data are available on measures of service quality such as door-to-door transit times or adherence to schedules.

In telecommunications, services such as call waiting and voice mail purchased from the phone company have proliferated. Fundamentally new products such as wireless telephony are still more difficult to deal with. (Voice mail can replace an answering machine or answering service, but pagers and cellular telephones have no meaningful precedents.)

In insurance, BEA's value-added measure has been criticized for failing to account adequately for the value of new products.[22] Part of the flat or declining productivity shown in Tables A-10 and A-11 for the hotel industry may result from inadequate accounting for improvement in the standard of accommodation.

Even for simple-seeming services such as trash collection, productivity estimates have become problematic. Although no federal agency has tried to develop a series for trash collection, local governments could, until recently, track performance in terms of tons or cubic yards of waste collected. Today hazardous materials get much more careful handling than in the past, and trash may be sorted for recycling. Environmental controls on landfills have raised disposal costs relative to collection costs. Meanwhile, cities and municipalities under budgetary pressure have sought to restructure their trash collection systems, for instance by asking neighboring residents to put trash in common dumpsters. Without adjustments for changes in these dimensions of output— a nontrivial task—comparisons over time or across municipalities on some basis such as ton-miles per worker would be meaningless.

Changes in product attributes are daunting enough for economists and statisticians to try to untangle, but the intangible nature of many service outputs creates additional measurement problems that have no counterparts in goods-producing industries. Service products do not come in units that are boxed, stored, shipped, and counted. Unlike cars or computers, service products may not have well-defined attributes. Some services are produced to a "blueprint," but most are not.

In standardized retail services, worker-customer interaction may make each purchase unique, but in a trivial sense that can be disregarded. McDonald's, for example, standardizes interactions with its employees to the point that buying a hamburger at one store differs little from buying it at another. In cases where service varies more substantially, it might be possible to evaluate quality using customer surveys. The problem would thus reduce to a familiar one of tracking "customer service" and treating it as one of the product attributes.

In many other situations, however, the intangible, heterogeneous nature of output confounds measurement. Do rising prices in legal services in the 1980s reflect uncaptured improvements in quality? In all but routine legal work, no realistic prospect exists of defining real output over time in terms meaningful to customers. Customers could answer a survey asking whether they had gotten their money's worth. But they would not realistically know whether they had ended up with the lawyerly equivalent of steak or hamburger. Perhaps another attorney would have wrung a higher judgment from the civil defendant, perhaps not. In health care, practitioners are still at the earliest stages of trying to define outcome measures in terms of whether the patient got better and stayed better (although they may be able to tell you how many hours a new mother spent at the hospital or whether patients liked the chicken soup).

Intangibility causes measurement problems that may be more challenging in the highest-skill industries, but the problems are not limited to them. They are also endemic in industries such as home health care and temporary help services. A law firm may pay $20 an hour to an agency for a temporary receptionist. It may know it is taking some risk of alienating clients because a temporary, even with good interpersonal skills, cannot be expected to know much about the firm and its practice. As to the size of this risk, it has little clue.

An added difficulty, distinct from that of measuring output, arises when the customer participates in service production. If you can clearly explain what seems wrong with your car, the mechanic should be better able to diagnose and fix it. The capacity of a school to increase learning depends on what students know from outside as well as the attitudes they bring with them to the classroom. Unless you can correct for differences in the contribution of the customer to performance, or plausibly assume that customer contribution is unchanged over time, it is impossible to measure what the service provider has contributed to output. It is impossible, in sum, to measure productivity growth.

Still, even with all the caveats, there is ample evidence that performance in service industries over the past two decades has been mediocre. If not for efforts to account better for quality improvement, the productivity statistics would look even worse.[23] Moreover, there is no particular reason to believe that measuring output became harder in the 1970s. This suggests that productivity growth actually deteriorated in services about that time. Keep in mind also that new products and services tend to be consumed by the affluent; you must own securities to trade them over the Internet. If attributes undercounted in output figures benefit mostly the wealthy, then the recent rise in wage inequality understates the rise in the inequality of economic well-being. Most important for policy and for this book, when combined with the qualitative case studies presented later, the quantitative data strongly suggest that service industry performance could be much better than it is.

Although there are many good jobs in service industries, the shift of employment from manufacturing to services and the observed trends within the service sector over the last two decades provide ample reason for Americans to feel anxious. Real wages in both the services and manufacturing have been declining despite a long-running economic expansion. Service sector workers earn less on average than manufacturing workers. Wage inequality is greater in the services, and inequality has been rising in both sectors. The evidence on employment insecurity, though less clear-cut, suggests that long-term jobs are less common in services than in manufacturing, and the economy also seems less able to satisfy the demand for long-term jobs than a generation ago.

Although there are good reasons to be skeptical about the government's productivity statistics, the fact that the data are poor does not mean that actual productivity performance is better than reported. If companies and customers as well as economists have trouble assessing service value, they may be less inclined to improve or pay a premium for it, and the economy may fail to realize achievable performance gains. Unrealized performance gains in the services hold down service sector wages. The next four chapters explore the underlying causes of the inequality, insecurity, and mediocre performance of so much of the service economy.

3 Work Systems

It required, in fact, a man of Napoleon [ic] nerve and ambition to subdue
the refractory tempers of work-people accustomed to irregular paroxysms
of diligence.

—*Andrew Ure*, The Philosophy of Manufactures, *1835*

Imagine an enormous office that looks like a classroom during exam period. Desks face the front of the
room; the windows are blacked out. In "the cage" (an old banking term
for the money-handling area), workers slit open envelopes, remove
checks, and sort the remaining contents at the rate of three envelopes a
minute. At the desks, clerks enter the amount on each check into a
computer system. Clerks have a quota of eighty-five hundred keystrokes
an hour. Everyone's performance is monitored. A manager watches
from a platform elevated above the room that workers call "the
pedestal" or "the birdhouse." Other supervisors monitor workers from
the back of the room, and a black globe containing television cameras
hangs from the ceiling.

The office is Electronic Banking Systems, Inc. (EBS), in Hagerstown,
Maryland, which specializes in processing donations to charities and ad-
vocacy groups.[1] It is typical of the "lockbox" processing that is increasingly the province of firms specializing in "back office" operations. The
jobs are tightly constrained. At EBS, inexperienced workers start at the
minimum wage; most earned about $6 an hour in 1994.

"This is a controlled environment," says Ron Eden, the owner of
EBS. From his upstairs office, Eden can monitor video images from
eight cameras around the processing center. Using remote control he

can zoom in on a worker's desk. Tracking productivity, not only keystrokes but the number of errors each worker makes, helps him weed
out those who do not keep up.

"It's got to add stress when everyone knows their production is being
monitored. I don't apologize for that," Eden says. He is also unapolo-
getic about a rule forbidding talk unrelated to the task. "I'm not paying
people to chat. I'm paying them to open envelopes," he says. The windows are blackened, he adds, because "I don't want them looking out—
it's distracting. They'll make mistakes."

Some workers circumvent the silence rule. "If you don't turn your
head and sort of mumble out of the side of your mouth, supervisors
won't hear you most of the time," one worker explained. She said her fi-
ancé avoided her for a couple of hours after work "because I don't shut
up—I need to talk, talk, talk." Still others find it hard to leave the routine behind at the end of the day. One worker said her husband complained that she awakened him at night "shuffling my hands in my
sleep" as if still opening envelopes.

Now imagine a nursing home. Arianne, a nurses' aide, arrives at 6:20 A.M.
and begins to set aside a supply of clean towels and sheets.[2] Because several of her co-workers have called in sick, Arianne must care for an additional six residents this day, sixteen altogether. She starts waking residents, changing their diapers, and washing them. Half are lying in wet
or dirty sheets. Shortly after 7:30 Arianne wheels the eight residents she
has gotten dressed to breakfast and returns for the rest. She skips a ten-
minute scheduled break at 8:30 to answer two patient call lights. Later
that morning one of Arianne's patients has a cardiac arrest and is taken
to the hospital. Arianne is momentarily relieved that she has one fewer
person to care for during the rest of the day, then immediately feels
guilty.

After her own half-hour lunch break Arianne takes the fifteen residents to the dining room for their lunch and then changes diapers
again. She also has to take care of paperwork from the previous day. "If
it's not documented, it didn't happen," says the director of nursing. Arianne asks: "Isn't it better to take care of someone than to write down
that you did?" Now she is trying to remember who had a bowel movement, what they ate, and who had a bath. From 1:30 to 2:30 P.M. she
takes residents to activities and gives two baths, interrupted by resident

call lights. She asks the charge nurse for help, but no one is available. She is too busy to chat with residents, who like to hear about her children and talk about their own grandchildren. Leaving a little after 3:00 P.M., Arianne catches the bus for her second job, the dinner shift at another nursing home.

Arianne has more autonomy over her daily tasks than do the check processors at EBS, but her pay is low—$5.50 an hour—and she receives few benefits. She would like to get her high school equivalency diploma but cannot manage school on top of two jobs. Her family does not have health insurance because she cannot afford the co-payment. She has been looking for a promotion to rehabilitation aide, which pays $5.75 an hour and requires less lifting and running. But there are forty nurses' aides in the ninety-nine-bed home and only one rehabilitation aide.

Now imagine an ornate, nineteenth-century building connected by elevated walkways to others in a complex that spans three city blocks. You can visit any other office in the headquarters of this life insurance company without meeting anyone in the outside world.[3] The company pays well for the area and, so far, provides jobs for life.

Gloria, a senior service representative, works in a fifth-floor cubicle separated from others by a low divider in the open office layout. She came to the company out of high school twenty-one years ago when a friend of her mother's told her about an opening. Gloria started as a messenger in underwriting, then moved to filing. Soon she became a secretary in the investment department that manages the company's assets. Now, as one of a team of seventeen workers who service policies marketed by field agencies in six midwestern states, she has reached the top of the company's nonmanagerial job ladder. Gloria calls herself a cheerleader and she looks and acts the part.

Most of the time, Gloria and her colleagues deal with routine matters—address changes, tax-time questions, billings, reinstating lapsed policies. But she also handles complaints that customers have taken to the state insurance commission. On her team, members rotate between four-month stints on the phones answering questions and three-month stints off the phones.

Six workers in Gloria's team have more than six years of seniority. As Chris, their manager, says, "Since it takes two years to get up to speed, we don't want people leaving; it's only in the second year that the light bulb goes on." Indeed, formal training lasts almost a year. Workers must learn some eighty-five computer software application packages, each customized for a different function. In recent years the company has begun to require a college degree even for entry-level clerical positions. Still, when Chris asked other managers to imagine doing without two of their team members, then two more, they usually wanted to keep the most experienced workers over the college-educated—in some cases, to their own surprise.

The company tracks the number of cases handled by each worker, but Chris doesn't show these figures to new employees until their third year. Chris knows that some people deal with problems briskly while others may be slower but better at ferreting out a customer's underlying concerns. A labor organization represents the company's "nonexempt" employees. But with an open-shop agreement workers do not have to belong to the union, and only two members of Gloria's team have joined. In teams with older workers and less admired managers, a majority of workers belong to the union. Some employees and union officials have been complaining of work intensification. But even if that were the case, it's not clear what choice workers would have but to accept the pressures. What they know isn't worth much to another company, even in insurance. The only jobs older, less educated workers in this midwestern city could hope to find would pay perhaps half as much.

Finally, imagine a twenty-two-year-old, recently graduated from a prestigious business school, who has just been hired into the San Francisco branch of one of the best-known management consulting firms in the country. On his first day he flies to New York, where a colleague briefs him on fertilizer, the subject of a project he will be working on for an oil company. Two days later he flies to Calgary to assess Canadian supply and demand for agrichemicals.

As the years pass, this highly skilled employee takes on a variety of different projects, all of which require some degree of substantive learning, and advances up the ladder at the consulting firm. He receives top-notch technical assistance and office support as well as mentoring in the early years from the firm's more experienced consultants. Eventually, this employee leaves to set up his own consulting firm, the Tom Peters Group. Tom Peters may be exceptional, but the contacts, credentials, and education on and off the job that helped him develop and advance in his profession are present in all highly skilled work.[4]

These four vignettes illustrate the diversity of work in the service sector as well as four distinct work systems. Each of the four represents a fundamentally different way of organizing service production. The work systems vary by skill requirements and pay levels, the degree of autonomy workers have in performing their tasks, and the extent to which managerial and organizational constraints discipline and pace the production process (Table 6).

Each of the four work systems relies on a different basic mechanism or set of mechanisms to regulate how work is done and to induce workers to act in ways consistent with the employer's goals. In the *tightly constrained* work system, exemplified by EBS check processing, jobs are narrowly defined, much like on an assembly line. Each task is paced by some combination of technology, organizational constraints, and customer demand (e.g., the line of people waiting for Big Macs). In the *unrationalized labor-intensive* work system, employers regulate effort by such means as linking pay to output and, in low-wage social service work (like that performed by nurses' aides), counting on workers' socialized sense of obligation to those they serve. In the *semiautonomous* work system, illustrated by the insurance example, workers perform tasks that cannot be technically controlled or monitored. Managers rely on incentives, such as internal promotion ladders, along with organizational culture and peer pressure, to align worker behavior with organizational goals. In the *high-skill autonomous* work system, self-motivation reflects professional commitment and craft pride, reinforced by financial and career incentives.

Work is organized in an infinite variety of ways, but these four work systems capture the basic characteristics. Each work system could be subdivided, but none of the four could be folded into one of the others. Though focusing on services, we divide all jobs, including those in manufacturing, into these four work systems. The four systems should help the reader make sense of the range and variety of service work and its consequences, from piece-rate poodle washer to first-line office supervisor, hamburger flipper to master chef. The four work systems are central to our analysis of the consequences of service work from the points of view of employers, customers, and workers themselves.

Table 6. Work systems summarized

	Tightly constrained	Unrationalized labor-intensive	Semiautonomous	High-skill autonomous
Examples	Telephone operators, fast-food workers, check proofers	Some nurses' aides, hotel maids, domestics, long-distance truck drivers, child care workers, clerical home workers	Clerical and administrative jobs with relatively broad responsibilities, low-level managers, some sales workers, UPS truck drivers	Physicians, high-level managers, laboratory technicians, electricians, engineers
Business strategy/ markets served	High volume, low cost; standardized quality	Low cost, low volume; often low or uneven quality	Volume and quality vary	Low volume (each job may differ); quality often in the eye of the beholder
Extent of organizational rationalization	High (jobs designed by management)	Low	Moderate	Low to moderate
Task supervision	Tight	Loose	Moderate	Little
Output monitoring/ quantitative performance measurement	Machine or technological pacing common	Quantitative measurement in some cases	Quantitative measurement in some cases	Quantitative measurement rare

Table 6. (Continued)

Formal education/credentials	Low to moderate	Low to moderate (skill often unrecognized)	Moderate	High
Formal, firm-specific training	Minimal	Minimal	Significant for those who climb internal job ladders	Varies
On-the-job training	Limited	Some informal, unrecognized OJT from other workers	Limited to moderate	Substantial
Pay	Often flat hourly; some bonuses linked to output or profits	Sometimes piece rate; sometimes flat hourly	Often flat hourly; some bonuses linked to output or profits	Usually salary; salary or profit share may be linked to billing, attracting clients
Screening of job applicants	Limited	Little	Careful	Usually very careful
Internal job ladders	Limited except in some union firms	No	Important	Important for some workers
Mobility across firms	Lateral mobility in some cases	Lateral, no upward mobility	Most experience not portable	Lateral mobility, upward mobility in some professions

Work systems differ in knowledge and skill requirements and in the extent to which skill transfers across firms. The tightly constrained work system usually requires little in the way of skills. The skills it does require do not typically transfer across employers (e.g., knowing the location of food choices on the McDonald's cash register or how to find a phone number on an operator's terminal). The unrationalized labor-intensive work system consists of jobs requiring nonspecialized skills acquired during early socialization (e.g., cleaning, lifting, driving, caregiving) and easily transferred across firms. Semiautonomous jobs usually involve significant levels of skill that are relevant primarily to one employer. Examples include the administrative and reporting procedures of an organization, the intricacies of customized computer software packages (as used in insurance companies), or the idiosyncrasies of a particular company's product line. The high-skill autonomous work system requires specialized skills ordinarily useful to many employers and often recognized by professional credentials.

There are exceptions to these tendencies. Tightly constrained check proofers may take their skills to another bank for another dollar an hour. Semiautonomous legal secretaries can switch employers in search of a less imperious boss. Skill levels and skill portability are not determined by "technology" but depend on the design of jobs and on the industry and policy environment within which firms operate.

Before we discuss the four work systems in greater detail, a few more caveats are necessary. Some jobs fit squarely in one of the four categories. Others fit less neatly. Each work system, in addition, may supplement its defining mechanisms for shaping worker behavior with mechanisms identified with one of the other work systems. Even jobs not categorized as high-skill autonomous, for example, rely to some extent on worker self-motivation. Promotion, training, and financial incentives, to take a second example, influence many professional and tightly constrained workers as well as semiautonomous employees. (Think of the long hours put in by lawyers hoping to make partner.)

Different work systems may be used to accomplish similar tasks, as the case study of nursing homes at the end of this chapter illustrates. A firm chooses which work system (or systems) it will rely on depending on its history, goals, and business strategy; its choice of technology; and incentives in particular product and labor markets. A related point: traditional occupational categories often span work systems. Sales jobs, for instance, include clerks in low-wage, low-skill, high-turnover positions that might best be categorized as unrationalized labor-intensive (in some department stores, for example). They also include tightly constrained customer service representatives in telephone call centers, where sophisticated computer systems control the flow of work and channel calls ("Press 3 to speak to a representative about your account"). Some other salespeople fall into the semiautonomous work system. Examples include many of those who sell office equipment. Such workers typically get substantial training, earn commissions, and may be able to advance into management positions. Likewise, some workers who sell financial services receive a good deal of product training and develop a commitment to the job more typical of high-skill autonomous professionals.

Finally, many jobs include tasks that are incidental to the distinctive core of the work. Professionals, for example, spend much of their time on mundane tasks that do not draw on their specialized training and experience. They may do their own filing and sneak away after jamming the copying machine. It is the core of the job that determines the work system with which it should be identified.

For services and manufacturing, Table 7 gives our estimates of the share of employment in each work system as of 1996. Table 8 gives the median wage and several other characteristics of each work system. The occupational categories in the Current Population Survey can only be matched to work systems on the basis of somewhat arbitrary

Table 7. Employment in services and manufacturing, by work system, 1996 (as percentage of total employment within each work system)

Work system	All industries (%)	Services (%)	Manufacturing %
Tightly constrained	5	4	10
Unrationalized labor-intensive	25	26	15
Semiautonomous	30	29	34
High-skill autonomous	41	40	40

Source: Estimates based on Current Population Survey. Appendix B gives the assumptions on which the summary figures above are based.

Note: Totals may not add to 100 because of rounding.

Table 8. Wages and employment characteristics, by work system, 1996

	Services				Manufacturing			
	Tightly constrained	Unration-alized labor-intensive	Semi-autonomous	High-skill autonomous	Tightly constrained	Unration-alized labor intensive	Semi-autonomous	High-skill autonomous
Median hourly wage	$ 5.75	$ 6.00	$ 10.00	$ 15.00	$8.00	$6.40	$ 11.55	$ 16.00
Women (%)	80	54	63	46	47	40	36	22
Union members (%)	8	12	15	20	23	16	21	16
Workers with no more than high school education (%)	64	66	42	21	77	80	60	37
Workers with four years of college or more (%)	6	6	20	51	3	3	12	35

Source: Estimates based on Current Population Survey; see Appendix B.

choices. Therefore, the figures in the two tables are rough approximations. (Appendix B gives the basis for our estimates.)

The Tightly Constrained Work System

Tightly constrained jobs are circumscribed and controlled by a combination of technology and organizational practice. This category includes the jobs most influenced by the tradition of scientific management. Operations are broken down into simplified tasks performed by workers who are closely monitored, often today by computers as well as supervisors. Examples include telephone operators, fast-food workers, and data-entry clerks such as the check processors at EBS.

Training usually takes a few days or weeks, rarely more than a few months. Turnover tends to be high, particularly among lower-paid workers. Better-paid, longer-tenured workers in manufacturing are often represented by unions. The fast pace and high stress that accompany most jobs in the tightly constrained work system contribute to high turnover. Opportunities for promotion are limited.

In some tightly constrained service jobs, employees deal directly with customers, with possibilities for social interaction and change of pace. Growing use of part-time workers and sophisticated scheduling systems to "staff to demand" reduce fluctuations in work pace and load, however. In some banks, computer programs with more than one hundred variables predict hour-by-hour, day-by-day, branch-by-branch demand for tellers.

Only about 4 percent of U.S. service jobs fall into the tightly constrained category, including the hamburger flippers so closely identified in the public mind with low-paying, dead-end service jobs. In tightly constrained service sector jobs in 1996, the median hourly wage was $5.75, nearly 30 percent below the median wage in this work system in manufacturing.

The Unrationalized Labor-Intensive Work System

In unrationalized labor-intensive service work, capital costs are low compared with labor costs. In some cases, including clerical homeworkers paid by the keystroke and truckers paid by the mile, most costs consist of piece-rate payments. In other situations, such as child care, low-level retail sales, or janitorial services, at least some segments of the market do not reward quality. Labor-intensive firms that pay poorly (or by the piece) and are in markets insensitive to quality have little motivation to improve performance.[5] As a consequence, they neither systematically analyze work to enhance productivity and quality nor invest in training their employees. Work is, in this sense, unrationalized. About 26 percent of service workers hold unrationalized labor-intensive jobs, far above the manufacturing number of 15 percent.

Most people who do not work in unrationalized labor-intensive jobs probably perceive the skill and knowledge requirements of those jobs as low. It is true that training and opportunities for career advancement are limited. Still, furniture movers, uncredentialed short-order cooks, and many others in this work system often develop skills that make them much more productive than a novice would be. Workers generally develop such skills on their own and learn from co-workers; rarely do they receive substantive or problem-solving training that would help them build on informal know-how or develop innovative approaches to their tasks. Nor do employers spend much time and effort asking how technology might improve performance.

The 1996 median hourly wage for workers in unrationalized labor-intensive service jobs was $6.00. Job tenure tends to be low, but occupational tenure may be lengthy because many workers move from one employer to another doing basically the same thing.

Within the unrationalized labor-intensive category, we define three subcategories based on whether and how employers monitor output and quality and otherwise manage workers.

Quantitative Control

In some cases, employers can easily measure output and reject low quality. These employers usually pay a fixed amount per unit of output (i.e., a piece rate) or require workers to complete a fixed set of tasks in the work day. Hotel housekeepers we interviewed, for example, clean about seventeen rooms a day. At $6 an hour with an eight-hour day, this comes to a little less than $3 a room. Supervisors or quality inspectors check each room. After a little on-the-job training from a co-worker, hotel housekeepers are largely left to do the job as they see fit. Much the same is true for janitors and trash collectors.

Socialized/Customer Control

In unrationalized social service work, quality tends to be difficult to evaluate and the market fails to reward it. For example, in nursing homes dependent on Medicaid for much of their revenue, federal and state regulations effectively determine staffing levels and set payments independent of quality. Homes offer the lowest wage that will attract the staff required by law. Patient loads and loose supervision regulate the quantity of work. How well the job is accomplished depends on the workers themselves—their informally acquired know-how, their sense of obligation to patients, and their awareness that skipping or putting off some tasks may mean more work down the road.

Much child care also fits into the unrationalized labor-intensive category. Child care centers now look after nearly 30 percent of American children for at least part of the day. Labor accounts for 70 percent of costs.[6] The median wage of child day care workers was $6.00 per hour in 1996, the same as for the work system as a whole.[7] Low pay, few benefits, and difficult working conditions result in high rates of turnover; even workers who find the job rewarding often leave for better pay in other occupations.

Relatives and hired help care for even more American children in "family day care." A 1992 survey found that these providers earned from $3,000 to $16,000 a year.[8] Facing the same low wages and difficult conditions as employees of child care centers, family day care providers often have little long-term commitment to their work. The survey found that only 9 percent of family child care homes provided good quality care, 56 percent provided adequate care, and 35 percent were rated as "growth-harming."[9]

Working parents often lack both the knowledge and the financial resources to exert market pressure that could improve the quality of child care. As with nursing homes, monitoring quality is difficult.[10] (Young children may not be able to convey their unhappiness or the reasons for it, and language barriers sometimes exist between providers and parents.) Although workers in child care centers have higher average levels of education and formal training than nurses' aides, the quality of care again tends to reflect workers' attitudes plus whatever knowledge (and good or bad habits) workers acquire informally through their families, other providers, or experience.

Internalized commitment to the job as well as customer pressure contribute to high effort levels among some groups of workers in unrationalized social service work. Ironically, a strong work ethic among participants in the unrationalized work system creates a further disincentive for employers to consider other means of improving performance.

Simple Control

Employers resort to simple control in a wide range of other unrationalized settings in which wages are low and a perception exists that there is little potential to improve performance through technology or job redesign. In these settings, task variety impedes quantitative control, and worker commitment is usually weaker than in the socialized/customer control category. Simple control exists in much of independent retailing, in low-skill office clerical work (including some temporary work) when output is not machine-paced or closely regulated, in many (though by no means all) small businesses, and in much casual labor and nonprofessional self-employment. Here, performance varies widely and often depends on the personal relationship of supervisor to worker and on whether supervisors have carrots (a small raise, flexible hours) or sticks (inflexible, bad, or few hours; the worst assignments) that can be used to motivate or coerce workers.

The Semiautonomous Work System

Semiautonomous jobs, though nonprofessional, require material knowledge and skill, usually but not always firm-specific. Task variety or complexity or the movement of workers over wide areas makes it difficult for employers to monitor performance. About 29 percent of all service workers hold semiautonomous jobs. Examples include less routine administrative and secretarial work; low-level management; sales positions requiring significant training in selling techniques, product attributes, or both; customer service representatives whose jobs are not subject to machine pacing; flight attendants; and truck driving in service-oriented companies such as Federal Express or United Parcel Service.

The semiautonomous work system contrasts with the unrationalized labor-intensive system because firms recognize the skills required and systematize the transmission of working knowledge to inexperienced employees. Unlike tightly constrained jobs, semiautonomous jobs cannot easily be rationalized because of the variability and complexity of the tasks performed. (Parts of semiautonomous jobs may be broken off and tightly constrained, however.) Compared with high-skill autonomous work, skill levels and self-management responsibilities are

lower in the semiautonomous work system. Semiautonomous jobs also
instill less occupational pride than is typical in high-skill autonomous
jobs. Peer pressure and commitment to high-quality work nonetheless
motivate many semiautonomous workers.

Semiautonomous jobs often require substantial organization-spe-
cific skills, so that worker and employer share an interest in a long-term
relationship. Firms invest in their workers and lose productivity while
training replacements. Workers want to keep their jobs because much
of the knowledge and experience they have is valuable only to their current employer. To cement a long-term relationship with semiautonomous employees, firms use incentives, including pay and benefits
above what workers might be able to get elsewhere, internal job ladders,
and in some cases profit sharing or commissions.

Employers also motivate workers by creating "corporate cultures"
that encourage identification with the goals of the firm. Much employer-
provided training has this purpose. By encouraging "teamwork" and
showing employees how their jobs fit into the larger whole, companies
socialize them, increase their sense of belonging and commitment, and,
in the process, make workers more self-managing. Motivational training
often merges with the development of contextual knowledge that employees need if they are to understand how their work affects the rest of
the organization and its customers. This kind of subtle coercion is a
major objective of programs that go by names such as total quality management and continuous improvement.

Many employees in semiautonomous jobs have high seniority in the
firm but low tenure in their current position, consistent with movement
through a sequence of jobs with the same employer. Some semiautonomous workers, including sales representatives and secretaries,
along with some managers, acquire a combination of firm-specific and
occupational skills that permit them to move from one employer to another. Nonetheless, after a long stint at one organization, they may have
to take a pay cut at a new place of employment. Wages are comparatively
high (a median wage of $10.00 in services in 1996), the result of efforts
by employers to limit turnover and of the seniority of workers.

The High-Skill Autonomous Work System

At the core of the high-skill autonomous work system are those with substantial, recognized skills: professional and many craft and technical

workers. An estimated 40 percent of service workers fall into this work system, making it the largest of the four.[11] Despite the differences among occupations, workers have substantial autonomy on the job (even if, like nurses, they operate formally in a subordinate role to another professional or a manager). Personal commitment to the standards of the occupation plays a critical role in maintaining performance. Although some employers of professionals track output and quality (the number of times a scientist's work is cited, for example, or a surgeon's mortality rate), performance evaluation has a large subjective element usually based in part on peer judgment. In traditional professions such as law and the clergy, intraoccupational (and often intraorganizational) advancement opportunities hinge on a combination of formal but subjective review (before making partner or bishop) and personal social networks ("who you know").

In contrast to the unrationalized labor-intensive work system, employers of high-skill autonomous workers usually screen carefully and provide substantial formal and informal support for on-the-job learning and supplementary education and training. As in the case of the unrationalized labor-intensive work system, employers of high-skill workers may have little understanding of what determines worker performance and how it could be measured or improved. Indeed, the complex, nonroutine, and intangible nature of much craft and professional work makes defining, never mind evaluating, performance a sometimes insuperable task. Competence is in principle easier to judge for nurses' aides than physicians, even if nursing homes rarely make the effort. Workers themselves may develop a rough internal consensus about what constitutes good performance, but this may or may not coincide with the interests of their employers or customers.

Men are overrepresented among high-skill autonomous workers in both services (1996 median wage $15.00 per hour) and manufacturing (median wage $1 higher). Job turnover is comparatively low, and occupational tenure, high.

Nursing Homes: Alternative Choices about Work Systems

Firms that produce the same service may use different work systems, with different outcomes for employees and customers. Ordinarily, the choice reflects alternative business strategies. Most aides in nursing homes, for example, fall into the unrationalized labor-intensive work system. But some should be classed in the semiautonomous work system. The differences stem from organizational philosophy and objectives, which often reflect contrasts between profit-seeking nursing homes and those run by not-for-profit institutions (mostly religious groups). The economic incentives embedded in the way different homes are paid also contribute to the variations observed.[12]

In nearly all nursing homes, aides provide 80 to 90 percent of direct patient care. Federal law requires that aides have at least seventy-five hours of initial training and pass a short written test. Aides are directly supervised by licensed personnel, who usually have at least two years of training. For several reasons, most nursing homes operate close to capacity. The elderly population is growing. People are less able and willing to care for aging parents. Hospitals are shifting patients to nursing homes. Finally, state regulations typically restrict the supply of new beds.

About 75 percent of nursing homes are owned by private, for-profit firms. Many primarily serve Medicaid recipients, relying on a guaranteed supply of residents, each of whom earns them reimbursement on a fixed-fee schedule independent of the quality of care. To maximize their profits, many of these homes staff to minimal levels and pay aides poorly. State-regulated staffing levels can then become de facto ceilings, with homes slipping below the legal minimum because of absences, vacations, or vacant positions. Penalties for violating the standard are trivial to mild. In California, for example, the maximum fine for repeated understaffing is eight hundred dollars, and even this penalty is automatically waived following a written notice of intent to improve.

Medicaid-dependent homes rarely encounter direct customer pressure to improve quality. Half the residents in these homes are too ill to respond to questions or explain what they want. Relatives, feeling guilty, may wish to know almost as little about what really happens inside the nursing home as the home wants them to know. Family members who seek to evaluate quality may find it difficult even in the best of circumstances. Moving to another home is disruptive at the very least. Even when a bed elsewhere can be found, it may be impossible to know that care will be any better.

Most nurses' aides say they cannot finish all their assigned tasks. In interviews, managers, resident advocates, and union officials agree that minimum staffing requirements (typically less than three hours per patient per day, counting all nursing staff) are too low. Two studies found that patients receive an average of thirty-six and twenty-one minutes of care per day, respectively.[13] "It's a job," one young aide in a Wisconsin home told a reporter. "But there's nothing to look forward to. You come to work. It's a heavy workload, and you try to get through." "I went to school to be a nurse," a licensed practical nurse said, "and I end up treating people worse than I treat my dog."[14]

Low compensation and difficult working conditions lead to turnover rates that exceed 100 percent on average.[15] Turnover can raise costs. According to nursing home sources, hiring and training a new aide costs four thousand dollars on average. A home with annual turnover of 100 percent will spend one-third as much each year in turnover costs as it pays out directly in wages.[16]

Still, many aides do the best they can in a difficult situation. That is partly a result of customer pressure (from the roughly 50 percent of residents who are well enough to turn on their call lights). Many workers also get satisfaction from caring for the elderly, satisfaction derived in part from the socialization of women as caregivers. Aides at one home were insulted when an irate nursing director told them that if they didn't like the way they were being treated, they could get a job at McDonald's. These nurses' aides saw their work as being far more socially valuable than serving hamburgers.

Labor accounts for about 70 percent of nursing home costs, but managers rarely explore options for reorganizing work that might affect those costs. Many do not believe that reorganization, even if it improved patient care, would have any impact on revenues or profits. Some deny that any potential for improvement exists; for most this is simply an unexamined assumption.

The jobs of aides in homes that fit the description above fall within the unrationalized labor-intensive work system. At the same time, a minority of nursing homes pursue higher-quality strategies. Some of them offer better care and higher staffing levels to attract larger fractions of private-pay and Medicare (rather than Medicaid) patients. The best homes have sought to break with a series of mutually reinforcing assumptions: that higher quality necessarily costs more (something no longer taken for granted in manufacturing), that nursing homes cannot be organized any differently, and that the decline of residents is irreversible. These homes have reconceived the work of aides to be more than custodial. They aim to enhance residents' quality of life as much as possible given their infirmities. Aide jobs in these homes fit into the semiautonomous work system.

Unlike homes with unrationalized jobs and high rates of turnover, the innovative homes seek to retain high-tenure aides who come to know their patients well.[17] Nurses' aides in these homes typically receive higher wages, better benefits, and more training. Institutionalized cooperation among nurses' aides and between aides and medical personnel accelerates diffusion of know-how to less-experienced workers. The best homes provide a level of support and opportunity for learning and development that give nurses' aide jobs a paraprofessional flavor.

As this example demonstrates, similar jobs can be organized in ways that fit into different work systems. The system used may change, often at management initiative, in response to factors such as product market conditions, public policies, and the availability of workers with particular skills. In the next chapter we look in more depth at the dynamics of change within work systems.

4

The Dynamics of Change
in Work Systems

Finally, we begin in our own day to observe the swelling energies of a third wave.... By now, it is plain, a new world has come into existence; but it exists only in fragments.

—*Lewis Mumford,* Technics and Civilization, *1934*

In Chapter 3 we gave a static view of work systems. In this chapter we examine changes in work systems resulting from new technology, organizational restructuring, and shifts in business strategy. The consequences for job quality, productivity, and other indicators of economic performance vary by industry, occupation, and in some cases by firm or establishment. Even so, one conclusion stands out: the changes under way in the U.S. service economy will not automatically generate substantial improvements in either productivity or job quality.

The dynamics in most of the services differ from those that prevailed in mass manufacturing and that continue to shape conventional views of economic performance. In such views, product and process innovations are the twin engines of economic progress. Product innovations, in an earlier era associated with entrepreneurial invention, today come in considerable part from organized research and development. Process innovations come both from technological innovation (labor-saving machines, automation) and from tight technical control over work processes. In mass manufacturing, managers, relying on scientific management and industrial engineering, improve the fortunes of their companies and of the economy as a whole, by breaking work down into narrow, repetitive tasks that people with no special skills can perform with the aid of special-purpose machines. Automation is applied where technological possibilities permit and cost calculations predict it will pay off.

Over time, fewer workers produce more output. With reduced labor costs, firms lower prices. The market for the product expands. As firms grow, they continue the process, breaking down jobs into ever more minute pieces and using ever more specialized machines and equipment. This view of work rationalization stems directly from Adam Smith's famous pin factory example. It reaches its apotheosis with Henry Ford's Model T and the huge factories that today churn out Corn Flakes and computer chips. Consumers benefit through more abundant goods and services. Some workers (e.g., those who had earlier built cars by hand) lose through deskilling (as tasks are standardized) and reductions in autonomy (as tasks become more tightly coupled in large-scale production systems).

Since long before the "invention" of the vertical file, work has been simplified, standardized, and rationalized in services as well as manufacturing, in offices as well as workshops. The dynamic of automation and job standardization sketched above applies in the services today to the 4 percent of jobs that are tightly constrained. The check-processing case discussed later in this chapter provides an illustration. Computer technology has also made it easier to automate elements of some jobs in other work systems, even though these jobs may not resemble tightly constrained work in their overall characteristics. Semiautonomous clerical workers, administrators, and lower-level managers continue to be responsible for tasks such as bookkeeping, accounting, payrolls, ordering, and inventory control. But today they do their work with the aid of computer-based communications, information processing, and decision support systems. Technological change alters elements of the job but not the work system.

Outside tightly constrained and pockets of semiautonomous work, technological change has had less dramatic effects. The lack of standardization of unrationalized labor-intensive work, the variability of most semiautonomous jobs, and the complexity of much high-skill autonomous work mean that technology—the janitor's backpack vacuum, the trucker's on-board telephone, the financial analyst's spreadsheet—is generally a supplemental tool with incremental rather than transforming effects. In such cases, technological change typically has only modest potential to improve performance or alter job quality.

Organizational restructuring, a second source of change in work systems, reflects, in part, the impact of deregulation and new competition in many service industries. Whatever the cost savings of mergers, downsizing, and reengineering, the case studies in this chapter show that one of the side effects has been to undermine the career incentives that made the semiautonomous work system effective in industries such as banking and telecommunications.

Finally, when companies compete primarily through low-wage business strategies—as in the retailing, trucking, and janitorial cases reviewed below—they may profit without raising performance.

Technology and Work Systems

In the near future, as in the past, technological change will likely have its most pervasive impacts on tightly constrained service jobs; automation is easiest where people already perform machinelike tasks. Elevator operators have disappeared; computerized voice-recognition systems promise to make telephone operators all but obsolete.

Although technological change plays some role in the evolution of all work systems, for most high-skill autonomous and unrationalized labor-intensive jobs that role is incremental. Surgeons operate under microscopes and with the aid of lasers, with robotic assistance on the way. But like the trucker with her on-board phone, the surgeon remains queen of the operating room; full automation of such jobs is decades if not generations away.

In three cases explored in more detail below, technological change has had substantial impact. As noted above, check processing illustrates the familiar dynamic of automation and rationalization. When each bank branch handled its own processing, the doors closed in the afternoon while tellers totaled the day's transactions and reconciled accounts. Today the branch sends its checks to a processing center, perhaps run by an independent firm, where "proofers" work through the night in tightly constrained settings that function much like assembly lines.

In trucking, information technologies, primarily in the form of software programs used for planning routes and scheduling pickups and deliveries, improve efficiency while decreasing the autonomy of semiautonomous drivers. At the same time, the high-skill autonomous workers who use this software must learn new skills and sales personnel must be able to explain the advantages to customers.

In the insurance industry, information technologies have facilitated the transformation of some tightly constrained clerical jobs into semiautonomous work. The number of these semiautonomous jobs may ultimately decline, limiting opportunities for workers to move into higher-skilled, better-paying positions.

Check Processing

Americans write nearly sixty-five billion checks per year, a number that is growing at 2 to 3 percent annually despite the spread of automatic teller machines (ATMs) and other forms of electronic banking.[1] Half of all bank employees spend some of their time handling checks. Processing costs about $8 billion a year, half for proof-of-deposit processing and half for posting to customer accounts and preparing statements.[2] Technology offers two quite different ways to reduce the costs of processing checks, as well as credit-card billings and other consumer financial transactions: automation of paper processing and replacement of paper with electronic transactions.

Since the 1970s magnetic ink characters on each check have identified the bank of origin and the account. Machines can read this information, but human proofers keypunch the handwritten dollar amounts into a "proof machine," which then prints the amount on the check and automatically totals the value of all checks in a batch. If this total does not agree with the cover sheet submitted with the batch, the checks go to a separate tracing and adjustment department. Proofing is a classic example of a tightly constrained job. Proof operators work at a pace approaching two thousand checks an hour.[3] They do nothing else. Compensation schemes often include incentive rates and deductions for errors.

Optical imaging equipment speeds processing. Imagers blow up each check on an eye-level screen, making the dollar amounts easier to read and minimizing the amount of paper proofers have to shuffle. Optical character recognition (OCR) systems are now good enough to read some handwritten figures. Managers at one credit card center we visited said their system handles about 20 percent of payments received without operator intervention.[4] OCR accuracy is increasing, which will permit more efficient processing of paper-based transactions, but it may plateau at levels well under 100 percent.

Electronic funds transfers (EFT), by eliminating paper, cut processing costs by up to 90 percent. When they are combined with other computerized transactions, such as ordering and invoicing, the savings multiply. As a result, the use of EFT is growing, especially among businesses (which account for about one-quarter of the paper checks written). Electronic commerce will spread less rapidly among households but even so will cut into semiautonomous and tightly constrained jobs for processing orders, invoices, shipping notices, accounts payable and receivable, and other data entry tasks. For example, the cost to a catalog firm for a mail or telephone order is $10 to $15.[5] Electronic ordering over the Internet promises to reduce this cost to less than $5, while permitting customers to check on the status of orders electronically and submit queries via electronic mail (rather than telephoning).

Self-Service

ATMs and self-service gas pumps are familiar examples of "labor-saving" technologies in which customers coproduce the service, doing some of the work for themselves (and, in cases such as ATMs, benefiting through greater convenience). Many of the jobs replaced fall into the tightly constrained or semiautonomous categories. For instance, the number of telephone operators has declined steadily since 1950 as people began dialing more of their own calls.[6]

Self-service technologies continue to spread. For several years, Amtrak and a number of airlines have offered electronic tickets, which have processing costs of about $1, compared with $8 for a paper ticket.[7] Banks are beginning to install ATMs that can cash checks to the penny, print a statement, even sell stamps and movie tickets.[8] First Union, based in Charlotte, North Carolina, is experimenting with lightly staffed branches in which bank personnel spend most of their time helping customers learn to use advanced ATMs. Huntington Bancshares, in Columbus, Ohio, is replacing some of its branches with fully automated kiosks that provide a broad range of retail services, including loans, aided by two-way video links with bank employees stationed elsewhere. At least one insurance company has tested automated systems that enable customers to fill out and file their own claim forms.

Over the past several years the Internet has emerged as an alternative delivery mechanism for many financial and other services. By mid-1996, more than 10 percent of American homes had Internet connections, and since around 40 percent of households have personal computers, the numbers can be expected to rise.[9] Home banking, although limited by the inability to handle deposits and withdrawals, appears to be growing. Brokerage houses, including Charles Schwab and a number of small, specialized firms, have introduced Internet services that permit individual investors to manage their accounts directly. Something like a million Americans already use their home computers to buy and sell securities, bypassing both high-skill autonomous brokers and tightly constrained or semiautonomous customer service representatives.[10]

Governments, too, have begun to embrace self-service.[11] Several states permit motorists to renew their drivers' licenses from remote terminals. In Tulare County, California, applicants can apply for welfare using a multilingual audio/video system. Taxpayers can now download federal and many state tax forms from agency web sites. Although an Internal Revenue Service computer automation project planned to replace thousands of back-office jobs has been declared a failure, in Australia some 70 percent of income tax filings already take place electronically.[12]

Trucking

In capital-intensive industries such as airlines and trucking, firms must make efficient use of equipment. A major trucking company, which we call Nationwide, relies on a semicustom computer software package, Superspin II, to route and schedule its trucks and their "less-than-truckload" consignments.[13] (Firms in the less-than-truckload segment of the industry specialize in shipments that fill only part of a truck and must be combined with others to make a full truckload.) Before the advent of software such as Superspin, scheduling and routing were much more difficult tasks. Now the computer helps optimize operations.

Superspin is a sophisticated piece of software that costs about half a million dollars and requires considerable training to apply effectively. The program can model a distribution network with up to twelve thousand pairs of origins and destinations. Shipments headed for different destinations can be broken down at terminals and repackaged with other goods headed in the same direction. A given shipment might pass through several terminals as loads are consolidated to keep trucks filled. Routing and scheduling problems of this type are so complex that in many cases the computer model serves not so much as a tool for automated decision making—because that is in fact impossible—but as a decision support system for use by clever, informed, and experienced workers.

Each Nationwide driver carries a hand-held data-entry device, a "wand." At every stop, the driver records pickup and delivery information, along with his truck's odometer reading. (Most drivers are men.) For deliveries, the driver simply scans a bar code from the Nationwide freight bill. For pickups, he must record the name of the shipper, city and zip code, the content of the shipment, and other particulars. The wand's internal clock records times, including those for the driver's breaks.

Superspin provides information for cost control as well as scheduling. According to William Rodgers, president of Pioneer Trucking (another pseudonym), one of Nationwide's subsidiaries, after deregulation trucking firms had to answer the basic question of how much it cost them to handle each shipment. This was a matter of little concern to some when rates were fixed by the Interstate Commerce Commission. Pioneer now employs five times as many people in pricing as it did before deregulation. With carriers freed to compete on service as well as price, to go anywhere and do anything, Pioneer's customers have come to expect on-time pickup and delivery, real-time tracking of their shipments, and one-stop shopping—all at low prices. As a result, Pioneer's salespeople have had to become analysts as much as relationship builders.

Despite the changes in the business, Rodgers claims that "it still all boils down to a human being loading, unloading, and driving a truck." Pickup and delivery drivers, he says, are 90 percent unsupervised and line drivers 99 percent unsupervised; their hustle, attitude, and route-specific knowledge (where to drop off a load, whom they need to talk to, the best back route when there is traffic), especially in pickup and delivery, are the keys to productivity and service quality. With its semi-autonomous work system, Nationwide stands in contrast to some other trucking firms, who base their competitive strategies on low rates achieved through low wages (discussed below).

Technology in an Insurance Company

The insurance industry was one of the earliest users of mainframe computers and, more recently, of distributed systems that put terminals on the desk of each worker. Today insurance companies are moving rapidly into decentralized computing, electronic data interchange and funds transfer, imaging, computer-based personal financial planning tools, and knowledge-based computer systems that, for instance, permit experienced clerical workers to handle routine underwriting. (Knowledge-based systems embody a simple form of artificial intelligence.) We focus here on the way one company's use of technology induced it to reorganize its work structure.

Mount Rushmore Mutual (MRM), a pseudonym, markets life and disability insurance and annuity products to groups and to individuals, primarily upper-middle-income professionals.[14] The company is noted for the quality of its underwriting—assessing risks and assigning premiums—and for a lapsed policy rate of less than half the industry average. MRM sells policies through a network of seven thousand "tied" but self-employed agents, organized into one hundred general agencies that handle only MRM products. Managers encourage the thirty-five hundred headquarters workers to view the general agencies as their "customers."

Until the 1980s MRM, like most of its competitors, used computers primarily for bulk operations, such as billing. Clerical jobs were narrow and highly specialized. The policy services division, for example, had eight job families, including administration of premium collections and reinstatement of lapsed policies. In 1981 the company abolished the job-families structure and converted most of the policy services staff into customer service representatives (CSRs), each of whom handled cases from start to finish. Senior CSRs took the more difficult cases, including complaints (e.g., from customers who felt that an agent had misled them). Over a year-long startup period MRM gave CSRs training in their new, broader jobs and organized them into work groups with members drawn from each of the former job families.

Initially, the CSRs worked with MRM's mainframe computer system. Later they were given personal computers, and the company eliminated its typing pools, archival clerks, and many data entry workers. In addition to handling their own correspondence, CSRs use personal computers as terminals to download databases, track cases and keep records, and communicate within headquarters and with their customers in the general agencies.

Before they were merged in 1981, the applications processing and underwriting departments were separate and often at odds with each other. The work flow was basically from applications processing, where clerical workers prepared files for risk assessment, to underwriting. Each department blamed the other for delays and lost information. With the merger, each underwriter was assigned a CSR to handle "paperwork." Eventually, the CSR job was split into a "field service representative" and an "underwriter assistant," largely because the volume of communications with agents had ballooned. Underwriters also began doing more of their own data entry and back-and-forth with agents.

Newer software provides a daily status report, accessible by agents as well as headquarters staff, on each pending application and routes questions via electronic mail in preference to the telephone. MRM has not yet installed knowledge-based systems, choosing instead to split off routine policies for rate setting by lower-paid junior underwriters. At the time of our interviews the company was engaged in a reengineering study aimed at cutting the time needed to prepare a new policy. The underwriting process averaged thirteen days but took up to sixty days for complicated policies. MRM managers anticipated that reengineering analysis would show that application processing should be shifted to the agencies. With more underwriting in the field, perhaps in conjunction with knowledge-based systems for decision support, MRM could then expect to reduce the size of its headquarters staff, particularly the ranks of junior underwriters and underwriter assistants.

Agents, who pay a fee for access to the MRM computer network, rely on a growing range of software tools in their sales and policy conversion work. Recently, MRM gave each agent a free customer planning package that can chart a customer's anticipated financial needs and the contributions that disability and life insurance could make; half the agents quickly became active users of the software. MRM's marketing department also provides agents with a client management package that helps them maintain updated records of existing policies. In the future the company hopes to handle application fees and premium payments through EFT.

At MRM, networked personal computers facilitated reorganization of tightly constrained clerical work into broader semiautonomous jobs. But it also seems likely that at least some of those semiautonomous jobs will be eliminated as agents and senior underwriters make greater use of information technologies for tasks now delegated to their assistants. Other insurance companies have detached processing centers from the home office, locating these centers in regions with ample supplies of workers willing to accept relatively low wages (often reasonably well educated women who lack other local job opportunities). Geographical separation, made possible by wide-area computer and telecommunications networks, drastically reduces mobility from higher-level clerical positions to junior professional and lower-level managerial jobs.

Like other companies, MRM has developed proprietary computer applications with the help of hardware and software vendors and consulting firms. Older "legacy" computer systems, in particular, have been hard for new employees to learn. Companies in many industries have begun replacing portions of their older systems with "intranets," networks based on universal or open-system technologies like those of the Internet, which provide the equivalent of web sites, hyperlinks, and other now-familiar features. Intranets are quite flexible and indefinitely expandable but remain simple to navigate. Companies can link computer systems that were previously separate and incompatible. Workers need little incremental training because intranets use web browsers already familiar to many. Intranets promise to speed learning and in many cases will reduce the value of experienced workers to the firm. This could destabilize semiautonomous jobs predicated on developing and retaining experienced workers.

Organizational Restructuring

Telecommunications and banking provide examples of both successful and failed attempts to rationalize and automate semiautonomous jobs in large service bureaucracies. But perhaps the most important effect of restructuring in these industries has been to undermine the firm-specific career paths that provided semiautonomous workers with opportunities for economic advancement and generated the organizational commitment on which the semiautonomous work system depends. These career paths often spanned more than one work system, so that a telephone operator or a bank teller could move from a tightly constrained job into a semiautonomous lower-level management position. By weakening the core mechanism that generated motivation and organizational commitment among such workers, shrinkage and truncation of career paths not only reduces the quality of the work and the productivity of the worker; it calls into question the continued viability of the semiautonomous work system in these industries.

Telecommunications

Technological change and the court-ordered breakup of the largest telephone company in the nation combined to trigger a rapid and ongoing series of changes in the three major work systems at AT&T and its descendants.[15] Telephone operators epitomize the tightly constrained, machine-paced service worker. Computer automation has reduced the need for operators and constrained the jobs of the remaining operators even more than in the past. Customer service representatives and lower-level managers belong to the semiautonomous work system, but in recent years computer monitoring has constrained some CSR jobs, while restructuring has collapsed the career ladders once open to lower-level managers. Craft positions, classified as high-skill autonomous, have probably changed the least, but they too are threatened by technological developments that make some tasks obsolete while creating new work for software specialists.

Operators. Historically, the AT&T Traffic Department consisted of thousands of operators working at huge banks of switchboards. Supervisors behind each row of operators monitored their activities and helped resolve problems. Thanks to steadily more sophisticated monitoring, AT&T was able to double the ratio of operators to supervisors from ten to one in 1910 to twenty to one in 1980 (compared with six to one in craft jobs in 1980 and ten to one for CSRs).

In the early years operators were responsible for a wide range of tasks. They had to watch for signal lights and talk with both customers and operators at other offices while working switchboards festooned with plugs and cords. They also kept billing records for the long-distance calls they placed. Technological change made it possible for customers to dial their own local calls in the 1920s, long-distance calls in the 1950s, and credit card calls in the 1970s. These same innovations eliminated the diagnostic work performed by operators, who once helped locate system faults by identifying the characteristic sounds of bad connections and defective equipment. The overall result has been steadily to reduce task variety.

Since divestiture in 1984 split AT&T into a long-distance carrier and seven regional operating companies, automated call distribution systems have come into widespread use. These systems cover large geographical areas, feeding a steady flow of calls to each operator and putting an end to call loads that varied widely during the course of a shift. With "automated response systems," an information operator can take a second call while a computer recites the number requested by the first caller. Better voice recognition systems will further reduce the number of operators, as may up-to-date directory listings available over the World Wide Web. And with operators geographically separated from business offices, pathways to more varied and better-paid clerical and administrative jobs have been largely closed off.

Customer Service Representatives. CSRs handle sales, service orders, service or billing questions, and overdue accounts. Before divestiture an AT&T operator or a low-level employee in a business or repair office could work her way up a job ladder to become a "universal" CSR. In the latter job, she would enjoy considerable autonomy, control her own work pace, and deal with a wide range of customer problems and queries. After divestiture the Bell operating companies generally split these jobs into collections representatives, who deal with "negative" customer interactions such as overdue bills (and who are paid 10 percent less than CSRs), and CSRs who are responsible for selling not only basic phone services but an increasingly complex and varied array of household and business services (such as call waiting, voice mail, and optional billing plans). Collections representatives and CSRs now work in phone banks linked to automated call distribution systems.

Craft Jobs. Technology and restructuring are also affecting the high-skilled craft workers responsible for installing and repairing telephone lines and equipment. For years, telephone companies tried and failed to find ways to monitor the performance of craft workers closely. Too many supervisors were needed, quantitative performance measures were hard to devise, and grievance loads were heavy. Cable pullers and other field workers retained considerable autonomy and decision-making discretion.

Technological improvements have changed the nature of some telecommunication crafts jobs. For example, reliable computer-based switching systems have replaced trouble-prone electromechanical cross-bar switches. Maintenance and repair require a new set of skills. In recent years a few well-paid systems analysts and software specialists, assisted by a much larger number of clerical workers who handle simple remote diagnostic and repair tasks, have taken over from workers whose experience-based skills in maintaining and repairing cross-bar switches are now obsolete.

Banking

In the 1980s, as financial services firms battled one another for consumer deposits, the corner gas station gave way to the corner bank branch. In the 1990s banks began closing many of those offices, for two primary reasons. First, automation and self-service allow banks to provide similar services with lower staffing levels, often at hours more convenient for the customer. Second, a wave of mergers and acquisitions in banking brought under common ownership many branches in close proximity that once competed, with some then closing. In 1985 branches handled 70 percent of retail bank transactions; a decade later their share had fallen to around 50 percent. Forty percent of branch banks may be gone in a decade, with ATMs, kiosks, telephone service centers, and the Internet picking up the slack.[16]

In earlier years branch offices typically operated on a quasi-independent basis; they processed checks and prepared statements, and their officers had loan authority for local business and household customers. As described earlier, banks began moving back-office processing out of their branches and into centralized facilities to take advantage of scale economies offered by automation. One large Los Angeles bank with hundreds of branches first consolidated its check-processing operations into eighty-five proofing centers. By the early 1990s it had only sixteen centers and was planning to cut the number to two.[17]

At the same time, CSRs working in call centers have begun to take over tasks that were once the province of tellers and platform workers in branch offices. (Platform workers handle new accounts, lending, and other services not available at the "window.") With regulators permitting banks to enter new markets, some of these centers deal with many more products (such as individual retirement accounts and mutual funds) than the old branch offices. Computer-based customer scoring, used for assessing creditworthiness, has permitted banks to centralize financial analysis and loan authority. Skilled clerical staff now perform such work under the supervision of managers and professionals who provide depth and breadth of backup that few branches were big enough to afford.

Because branches typically hired locally, these changes have cut into the number of full-time, entry-level jobs available in many urban neighborhoods and also knocked the rungs out of internal job ladders. In Los Angeles, clerical workers accounted for two-thirds of branch employment in 1970. About half were tellers. Particularly in retail banking, people without a college degree could enter as tellers or check processors and advance on the job. Demonstrated competence and experience-based learning were enough to earn promotions to lead teller, assistant operations officer (monitoring tellers and paper processing), and operations officer—and then to lending responsibilities.[18]

By the mid-1990s Los Angeles bank branches were smaller, with strictly limited functional responsibilities, and staffed mostly with part-time workers and temporaries (on fixed-term contracts). In 1970, in five of nine Los Angeles banks, part-time and temporary workers accounted for less than 10 percent of the workforce (and less than 25 percent in two others). By 1990 95 to 100 percent of tellers in four of the banks were part-time or temporary. Job structures and workplace demographics became much like those in retail trade. (In two other banks, however, the share of part-time and temporary workers remained below 10 percent.) For example, 63 percent of tellers were under age twenty-five or over age fifty-five in 1990, up from 44 percent in 1970.

At the same time, hourly compensation improved. Real median wages in Los Angeles banks rose by 18 percent during the 1980s (19 percent for women, 4 percent for men), compared with 3 percent for all industries in Los Angeles. Clerical, managerial, professional, and sales workers received wage hikes of 11 to 29 percent. Still, low-wage, part-time work with little prospect of advancement generates the same kinds of problems as in retailing: high turnover, absenteeism, low morale, and poor service. In response, banks have redesigned teller jobs so that they can be performed with minimal training. That has the effect of making it still harder for tellers to advance.

Banks now fill many of their higher-level jobs by hiring from outside, typically requiring a college degree. New internal job ladders may be created in consolidated processing and teleservice operations, so that proofers can advance to read-and-sort machine operators, and CSRs to jobs offering more variety and better pay. At a vertically integrated, 2,800-employee credit card processing center we visited, workers without a college degree can advance from data entry or mail sorting to machine monitoring; customer service jobs of various degrees of responsibility; and better-paid and more specialized jobs, such as tracking down potential fraud cases and authorizing increases in customer credit limits. One reason is location; the center is in a small midwestern city that has less than 3 percent unemployment and the company has had difficulty attracting college graduates. (Managerial and specialized technical jobs, such as systems professionals, remain closed to internal advancement.) In any event, not all processing centers have as many job categories as this large, centralized facility. And even this facility does not offer as much upward mobility as the old branch banks.

Business Strategies and Work Systems

In many markets one of the fundamental strategic choices for employers is whether to compete on price or on quality (or on a combination of the two). Companies that seek to be the lowest-priced provider of a relatively standardized product gain their competitive advantage by finding ways to reduce costs, including labor costs, and thereby reduce prices. The alternative requires differentiating one's products from those of competitors so that consumers will be willing to pay a premium. Companies that choose this second strategy seek competitive advantage through product attributes that increase the value perceived by at least some customers; higher costs are acceptable if offset by higher revenues.

A firm's work system(s) will depend in part on its business strategy. A low-cost strategy often leads to reliance on unrationalized labor-intensive rather than semiautonomous workers (together with some minimal number of high-paid, high-skill autonomous managers and professionals). Firms pursuing the product-differentiation or high-quality strategy often prefer semiautonomous (or high-skill) workers. Pioneer Trucking, discussed earlier, depends on semiautonomous workers to implement its quality-based strategy. In parts of the industry in which low-cost strategies predominate, employers rely on unrationalized labor-intensive drivers, who need to do little more than take a truck from one city to another. In retail department stores (see below), reactive cost cutting in response to new competition contributed to a switch from the semiautonomous to the unrationalized labor-intensive work system (and an erosion of service). For some large retailers, this change proved a failure. Low-paid workers may feel little obligation to customers, the work is too varied for effective after-the-fact quality inspections, and the personal relations critical to simple control do not exist in large retailers. Workers may slip away when customers approach (or simply ignore them), in turn demoralizing other, more committed workers.

Long-Distance Trucking

Low-wage competition and an absence of incentives to improve efficiency characterize parts of the truckload industry, leading to unrationalized labor-intensive jobs.[19] Truckload companies haul single-customer shipments that fill most or all of a truck. Unlike less-than-truckload carriers, they do not need terminals to sort and reload consignments by destination.

Especially when the goods to be shipped are of low value, the name of the game in the truckload business is low labor costs. (What is the minimum the driver can be paid for taking a load of chicken feed from Tulsa to Tucumcari?) Labor costs make up about a third of shipping costs for truckload companies, half of this paying for drivers and helpers. Most nonlabor costs are either fixed in the short run (payments on the truck) or determined in competitive markets (fuel costs and, within broader limits, truck maintenance). Most truckload companies pay drivers by the mile. They often do not pay for loading, unloading, or waiting time. Only rarely do they cover meals or lodging on the road. A flat mileage fee shifts the risks of bad weather, mechanical problems, and inefficient loading operations onto the driver. It also creates incentives for drivers to speed, take few breaks, and conduct only cursory safety checks before embarking.

Neither unions, now a minor presence in the truckload part of the industry, nor legislated labor standards have much influence on wages or working conditions. Truckers are not covered by the overtime provisions of the Fair Labor Standards Act. Regulations issued by the Department of Transportation limit the work week to sixty hours for seven-day weeks and seventy hours for eight-day weeks, but drivers can log off duty during waiting periods. Counting waiting time, some truckload drivers (including owner-operators) put in ninety hours or more a week. Hours regulations and the minimum wage are difficult to enforce because drivers seek to raise their weekly income by working more hours and because of the ease of falsifying logs.[20]

With few constraints on lowering labor standards, and declining alternative opportunities for less-educated males, wages have eroded and driving hours expanded in long-haul trucking since deregulation. Real annual earnings of all trucking employees (including many unionized less-than-truckload drivers) dropped by nearly 30 percent from 1978 to 1990. Real earnings declined almost 50 percent for truckload drivers over this period.

Aspiring truckers can earn the required federal commercial driver's license with a few weeks of training. Truckload firms prefer to hire experienced drivers, but like nursing home administrators they usually assume that neophytes can pick up most of what they need to know with a brief on-the-job demonstration from a more experienced employee. Few firms make systematic efforts to develop safety skills. The intrinsic rewards of over-the-road driving for many men—the masculine, even cowboy, image; sometimes the exclusive use of their "own" truck—contribute to willingness to work long hours.

A few truckload companies have begun to take a different approach. Following in the footsteps of some less-than-truckload firms, these truckload carriers have invested in technology such as satellite tracking and logistics software that optimize routings (and also help them monitor drivers). They have also trained drivers to work within their more integrated systems. A three-tiered wage structure appears to be emerging, with package delivery and less than-truckload firms (where service quality is most important) paying the highest wages, sophisticated truckload firms paying the next level, and low-quality truckload firms at the bottom.

Janitorial Services

Although quality-oriented strategies have taken hold in parts of trucking, no such trends are visible in janitorial and building services, an industry that has expanded rapidly as building owners seeking to cut costs have contracted out services previously provided by their own employees.[21] Some of the larger firms now offer integrated packages including janitorial, elevator, engineering, lighting, parking, and security services. But even if they cater to "prestige" office buildings, these companies, like the many small, local firms in the industry, stress costs over quality. One manager stated that even the most quality-conscious customers would be unlikely to pay a 1 or 2 percent premium to retain a contractor with a record demonstrating superior performance.

As in other low-wage, low-productivity work, capital intensity is low in janitorial services and thus provides little incentive for rationalization. Technology has had almost no impact. A 1994 survey found that the average janitorial service contractor spent two cents for powered cleaning equipment and one cent for nonpowered equipment for every dollar spent on wages and benefits.[22] Costs depend on wages, and janitorial firms compete primarily on the basis of labor costs. Small janitorial firms rely heavily on part-time workers. They may hire undocumented immigrants, pay employees "off the books," label employees independent contractors to circumvent payroll taxes, or "subcontract" to workers and their families, who end up working for less than the minimum wage.

Rough estimates suggest that annual turnover runs around 200 per-cent. Employers accept high turnover because, with little training as-sumed necessary, new people can be put to work quickly. Larger firms pay slightly better and can attract and retain more reliable and experi-enced workers. A senior executive of a national firm said his company would prefer a higher-wage, low-turnover, full-time workforce to in-crease efficiency and customer satisfaction. But he said his firm was able to pursue that strategy only where high levels of unionization precluded wage-based competition. In those settings his firm had turnover rates as low as 5 percent. In the absence of widespread unionization, then, this is an industry where only one type of business strategy, based on low labor costs, appears viable.

Retailing

Today few retail workers can hope to advance in the industry. It was not always this way. Two generations ago retailing had a reputation for pro-viding good career opportunities. A department store sales worker could advance to buyer or assistant buyer within his or her department and then into managerial ranks. In the 1960s competition from low-overhead discounters put new pressure on established chains such as Macy's.[23] Kmart could cut prices because its payroll costs amounted to 6 or 7 percent of sales, compared with 18 to 20 percent for old-line de-partment stores. In response, Macy's, like most of the other traditional retailers, centralized the buying function above the store level. The company also began to require a four-year college degree for entry on a management track. To staff evening and weekend hours and to cut costs among nonsupervisory workers, Macy's began to hire part-time workers. In the mid-1960s nearly two-thirds of Macy's workforce was full-time; by the late 1970s nearly two-thirds worked part-time.

Over time, retailers found it more difficult to attract workers from their traditional labor source—middle-class white women with children at home and husbands earning enough to support the family. They therefore hired more young people and minorities. Turnover rose, in part because, with a shrinking fraction of managers and administrators (currently around 8 percent), most sales personnel could no longer re-alistically expect to advance into a better job. By the 1980s Macy's man-agement realized that a high-turnover sales force, with little attachment to the company, was alienating customers. One executive said, "We used to promise upward mobility, but we do not any longer. We need much greater involvement of sales clerks. There is a malaise ... [P]eople are bored with their jobs and with the prospect of staying thirty years in the same jobs."[24] Macy's considered moving away from part-time employment to alleviate these problems, but a new wave of competitive pressures, from Wal-Mart on the low end and specialty apparel and other stores at the high end, intensified pressure to control labor costs.

Wages declined along with promotion opportunities. In 1960 workers in retail earned 76 percent as much as those in insurance and 81 percent as much as workers in banking. By 1996 the median wage in retail had fallen to only 50 percent of the level in insurance and about 62 percent of that in banking.[25] With falling wages and rising turnover, the semiautonomous work system at Macy's and other established chains functioned less effectively. In retailing, however, there are no clear alternatives, such as technical monitoring of work or payment of piece rates. (Commissions have traditionally been reserved for expensive goods, such as furniture, appliances, and tailored clothing.) Unable to structure work beyond the cash register effectively, firms let the ranks of floor personnel thin, leaving customers on their own to find and select merchandise. Declining morale among sales workers contributes to what has been called a "cycle of failure." Low wages and lack of opportunity lead to poor service, thereby eroding sales, intensifying cost pressures and market-share problems that keep wages and promotion opportunities low.[26]

Chain discounters have constructed semiautonomous jobs on terms less generous than those once offered by the established chains. Rapid expansion has permitted some to sustain the commitment of a critical mass (albeit perhaps still a minority) of workers by offering the prospect of promotion or profit sharing. Wal-Mart alone employed over 725,000 workers in 1997, more than half of them full time. "The jobs [discounters] offer, mostly at $5 to $9 an hour, would have been unappealing in another era," Louis Uchitelle reported in the *New York Times*. "But in these hard times, the low hourly pay—sweetened with health insurance and profit sharing—is turning out to be one of the best deals that corporate America is offering to the mass of Americans looking for 'good' jobs."[27]

Trends in Service Work Systems

Table 9 summarizes the work system dynamics that the examples in this chapter illustrate. To shed further light on changes over time, we esti-

Table 9. Work system dynamics

Work system	Major forces of change	Likely impacts (within the work system)
Tightly constrained	Continuing rationalization, computer-based automation	• Declining number of jobs • Wages, benefits already low in most cases—little change • Generally positive implications for productivity and service quality
Unrationalized labor-intensive	Spread of low-cost business strategies, wage-based competition	• Growing number of jobs • Downward pressure on wages and benefits • Negative implications for productivity and service quality
Semiautonomous	Reengineering, spread and growing sophistication of information technologies	• Declining share of jobs • Greater dispersion in wages and benefits as compensation rises for those with skills in high demand relative to those with more generic skills • Employment instability tends to erode productivity and service quality • Information technology raises productivity
High-skill autonomous	Technological change permitting lower-skilled employees to replace some high-skill autonomous workers, accompanied by continued growth in demand for new types of skills (e.g., for electronic commerce)	• Continued growth in number of jobs likely, but some high-skill autonomous jobs may come to resemble unrationalized labor-intensive • Wages likely to rise for new and scarce skills, decline for some traditional professions (e.g., physicians, lawyers)

mated employment by work system in 1979 and compared it with the 1996 figures given in Chapter 3. Table 10 presents the comparisons, including two alternative estimates for 1979. In one we assigned occupations to the four work systems using the same proportions as for 1996. In the other we took explicit account of the most quantitatively important changes in work systems that our case studies suggest. This second estimate assigns a higher proportion of retail sales workers and clerical and administrative workers to the semiautonomous work system in 1979 than in 1996. It also places more truck drivers in the semiautonomous work system in 1979, since deregulation had barely begun at that point.

In combination with our case studies, Table 10 suggests that the employment share of the tightly constrained work system is declining slightly. Most of the service jobs that could easily be redesigned on this basis already have been. Examples include telephone operators and fast-food preparation. Although there is increasing monitoring and tracking of jobs such as less-than-truckload trucking, comprehensive tightening of the constraints on such jobs is difficult to imagine. In these and many other cases the production process varies with demand, and customers value accommodation to their particular needs. Thus,

Table 10. Employment, by work system, 1979 and 1996
(as percentage of total employment)

Work system	1979 Allocating occupations into work systems in the same proportions as in 1996 (%)	1979 Allocating occupations into work systems to take account of major changes in work systems since 1979 (%)	1996 (%)
Tightly constrained	6	6	5
Unrationalized labor-intensive	28	23	25
Semiautonomous	32	37	30
High-skill autonomous	34	34	41

Source: Calculations based on the CPS for the entire economy. See Appendix B for more detail on estimation methods.

employers cannot travel very far down the route of automation and scientific management.

In jobs that are already tightly constrained, on the other hand, further automation is proceeding apace. The net result is to reduce the number of jobs in categories such as data entry. Although job quality is generally low, the tightly constrained work system typically produces combinations of cost and quality that consumers value (within the limits set by standardization). But the likely inability to rationalize large parts of the service sector in traditional ways means that we cannot count on widespread and sustained improvements in economic performance through rationalization and automation.

Our calculations show no clear trends in the employment share of unrationalized labor-intensive jobs. But case studies suggest that this work system has been expanding and will continue to do so. With cost-based competition widespread, firms continue to look to low wages, and hence to the unrationalized labor-intensive work system, as a source of competitive advantage. Moreover, as long as underemployment is substantial, the unrationalized labor-intensive work system will likely flourish, in part within the underground economy and self-employment (off-the-books cleaning, lawn, and repair services and street retail sales). No doubt the information age will bring forth new ways of absorbing "surplus" labor, as in the growth of telephone commission sales by minimally trained telemarketers—"virtual begging."

Semiautonomous jobs appear to be shrinking as a share of the total. By contrast, employment in the high-skill autonomous work system shows rapid growth.

This chapter presents a mixed picture with respect to performance improvement. The large number of unrationalized labor-intensive jobs in services continues to drag down performance. Some tightly constrained and semiautonomous service jobs are being rationalized (or further rationalized) and automated, with increases in productivity. Other semiautonomous jobs, however, are shifting in the direction of unrationalized labor-intensive work. And organizational restructuring has sometimes upset the bureaucratic career incentives that induced loyalty among semiautonomous workers. Even some high-skill autonomous workers, we suggest below, face cost pressures that may weaken performance over time. Overall, the service economy does not appear to be on a path that will generate pervasive and sustained performance improvement. In the next chapter we explore an alternative that might do so.

Work Systems and Wage Inequality

Rising wage inequality in the United States reflects the combined effect of wage dynamics within each work system and the changing distribution of employment among the four systems (Table 11). Stable or growing employment in the inherently low-wage unrationalized labor-intensive work system has held down the bottom of the earnings distribution. Also pulling down the lower end of the wage distribution, tightly constrained jobs have experienced the largest fall in wages since 1979, in part because of deunionization. Tightly constrained service jobs still pay less than those in manufacturing (see Table 8). In part because tightly constrained service work processes tend to be less capital-intensive, employers rarely seem willing to pay a premium for better workers; because of the absence of labor unions, they rarely have to pay more.

In the middle of the wage distribution, the reliance of the semiautonomous work system on a strong tie between worker and firm limits how far wages can be cut. Nonetheless, wages in some semiautonomous jobs have declined because employers believe they need only maintain a large enough differential with the lower end of the labor market to

Table 11. Median wage, by work system, 1979 and 1996 (in 1996 dollars)

Work system	1979 Method 1 (assuming no changes in work systems by occupation)	1979 Method 2 (accounting for major changes in work systems by occupation)	1996	% change, 1979 (Method 1) to 1996	% change, 1979 (Method 2) to 1996
Tightly constrained	$7.95	$7.95	$6.50	−18	−18
Unrationalized labor-intensive	$6.78	$6.74	$6.00	−12	−11
Semiautonomous	$11.87	$10.60	$10.50	−12	−1
High-skill autonomous	$15.90	$15.90	$15.00	−6	−6

Source: Calculations based on the CPS for the entire economy. See Appendix B for more detail on estimation methods.

deter turnover. Falling wages at the bottom, therefore, enable employers to cut the wages of semiautonomous workers.[28] Until quite recently, at the top end of the labor market, high-skill autonomous professionals and managers did well (and their growing number contributed to the overall polarization of income).

In recent years high-skill autonomous workers have experienced diverging fortunes. Some now find their wages behaving like those in the other work systems. One source of economic vulnerability for high-skill workers (as lower-status technical and blue-collar craft workers have long understood) is precisely the professional pride and knowledge that enables self-direction. Freelance writers and musicians know that if you love what you do, employers have less need to pay you decently for it. Newly minted scientists stuck in a series of postdoctoral positions are learning the same lesson. Wages for physicians have slid enough that some of those who persevered through medical school for the money no doubt regret their choice of careers (while those who truly care about medicine are more likely to see managed care as a threat to quality than a threat to wages).[29]

There is another problem, one that mostly affects the nonprofessional occupations in the high-skill autonomous work system. As the construction example in Chapter 7 shows, taking workers' existing knowledge and commitment for granted can deplete those resources over time. When it does, performance suffers, and the line between high-skill and unrationalized work begins to blur. The more pervasive this process, the more likely it becomes that income gains in the future will be restricted to a narrow band of elite professionals and managers at the top.

Economists normally explain wage inequality as a consequence of the returns to education: more educated workers are more productive, allowing them to command higher wages. Examining wage and employment trends by work system suggests that inequality is driven just as much by institutional developments linked with decisions about how to organize work. So far, those with more education have done better because their credentials have become the necessary ticket to the two highest-paying work systems. That does not necessarily mean that actual skill requirements of positions in banks and department stores that now require a college degree have increased significantly since the days when a high-school diploma was enough.

The conventional interpretation of labor market inequality leads to policy prescriptions emphasizing education and training; inequality can be reduced by giving more schooling or training to the less skilled. But if entry requirements for the better jobs simply ratchet upward as more people gain credentials, economywide wage differentials will not change much.[30] Our case studies provide no reason to expect that higher average levels of education and training will, by themselves, cause employers to change their business strategies and thereby lead to alterations in the structure of work systems.

In the absence of policies to change the composition of employment by work system, more education and training is a recipe for further frustrating workers' aspirations. In the next chapter, we suggest a path that promises to diminish the number of unrationalized labor-intensive jobs and further increase the number of high-skill autonomous ones without necessitating large increases in formal education. This would create better opportunities for workers while also improving economic performance.

5

Reorganizing Work:
Using Knowledge and Skill
to Improve Economic Performance

> But our already highly mechanized and organized world community, if it is
> to develop further and sustain an efficient common life, requires before
> everything else interested and participating workers.
> —*H. G. Wells,* Experiment in Autobiography, *1934*

If current trends do not suggest a path leading to long-term performance improvement across a broad range of service industries, how might such a trajectory be initiated? Because many U.S. manufacturing firms have, since the early 1980s, reorganized their operations under the pressure of international competition to reduce costs, improve quality, and increase adaptability to changing markets, one possibility might be to borrow from these reforms. Some manufacturing companies, for example, train workers in statistical process control (SPC). Although the ostensible purpose is to reduce defects, training in the rudiments of SPC also, and more important, serves as a motivational tool. By persuading workers that their tasks, no matter how mundane, are vital to the firm's business—that profits and jobs depend on working hard and working well—SPC seeks to align employee behavior with management objectives. Total quality management (TQM) has similar goals but takes a more comprehensive approach to motivation and training. Just-in-time (JIT) production minimizes in-process inventories while exposing bottlenecks in the manufacturing process. JIT creates conditions under which engineers, managers, and production workers can identify and solve shopfloor problems that may have been hidden for years. Quality circles and self-managed work groups permit employees to evaluate and perhaps redefine their role in the larger production system. Workers may be given discretion in assigning tasks to individuals and sometimes in altering the design of jobs. In nearly all cases, the new forms of work organization place a higher value on the skills and knowledge of workers than older models associated with scientific management and the industrial engineering tradition.

Some service sector firms have adapted innovative work practices from manufacturing. TQM, in particular, has attracted service firms because of its rhetoric stressing customer satisfaction. Nonetheless, the diffusion of work teams, quality circles, and related reforms has been noticeably slower in the services than in manufacturing.[1] A principal goal in manufacturing has been to improve performance in tightly constrained settings. For instance, by slightly loosening the constraints, manufacturers have found that they can improve quality and also gain more flexibility in responding to changing demand. But tightly constrained jobs are less prevalent in services, limiting the scope for direct emulation of innovations in tightly constrained manufacturing work. More important, tightly constrained production processes tend to be simpler in the services than in manufacturing (hamburgers or bank checks rather than automobiles or semiconductors). When production involves hundreds or thousands of operations and products are periodically redesigned, there are ample opportunities to pursue "continuous improvement." But the relative simplicity of production processes in tightly constrained service work makes big gains unlikely through either small, cumulative improvements or more radical innovations.

On the other hand, unrationalized labor-intensive jobs, often viewed (rightly or wrongly) as poor candidates for improved performance, are much more common in the services. For this reason, reforms that have been demonstrated in manufacturing may have limited relevance in services. Finally, a number of reforms that are truly innovative in manufacturing have been standard practice in some high-skill autonomous and semiautonomous service jobs. Long before work groups became fashionable in factories, teamwork was taken for granted among physicians and nurses in surgical wards, among actors and musicians, in advertising agencies and architectural practices.

There is room in the service sector for further diffusion of work reforms from manufacturing. But it is unlikely that emulation or extension of these practices will lead to widespread, sustained performance improvement. In this chapter we explore the reasons why and develop an approach better suited to the characteristics of production processes in services.

The Engineering and Interpretive Models

The scientific management tradition, like the more recent reforms in work organization mentioned above, originated in industries where the output is a tangible product with well-defined attributes. These attributes are specified before production begins, typically by engineers who design both product and process. Developing a new car, for example, takes several thousand engineers about three years at a cost of several billion dollars. Once factory production begins, workers follow product and process specifications, most simply a "blueprint." The primary objective is to make products that conform to design specifications, and to do so as cheaply as possible.[2]

Manufacture, therefore, can be viewed as the solution of a technical or engineering problem, one that has unambiguous objectives (functional performance, cost, quality). The technical problem has two parts: product design and process design. The product design problem may be relatively simple, as for apparel or furniture. More generally, it is multifaceted and technically very complex, as for automobiles. Process design often poses vexing problems even for simple products. In apparel production, for example, some tasks (stitching collars) take much longer than others (attaching pockets); part of the problem is then to balance the flow of production, taking account of the differing times required for tasks performed sequentially. More complex products bring more complex process design problems. A typical automobile axle, for example, can be put together in hundreds of different ways, no one of which may be obviously best. This is one reason scientific management leads to the breaking down of production processes into simple, repetitive tasks (which can be rearranged through trial and error to improve performance).

Scientific management is not, in fact, very "scientific." Rather, it depends heavily on rules of thumb, the most fundamental of which is to keep each task simple as a response to system-level complexity.[3] A few of the recent reforms in manufacturing represent a significant break with scientific management (as in Volvo's famous, and now abandoned, team-based auto factories, which dispensed with assembly lines). More often, work reorganization is an extension of the basic approach. In any case, the intent is to solve the technical problem of making a well-defined product in accord with a predetermined design, and to do so as cheaply as possible. The principle behind TQM, for example, is that, with better trained and motivated workers, the discrepancy between the product as designed and the product as manufactured can be reduced. TQM and similar reforms deviate from traditional scientific management primarily in acknowledging that production workers, as well as engineers and managers, can contribute to improvement in the outcomes of the production process. But workers (or engineers or managers) do not "redefine" and redesign the product each time they make it, as is the case in production of many services.

Fast-food preparation and telephone directory assistance both have well-defined outputs. Because these come in a limited number of varieties that can be specified in advance, the production process can be conceived in engineering terms, and indeed planners and managers do so. In much of the service sector, though, the engineering model applies poorly or not at all (or to only part of the production process). Intangible service outputs—health, a legal brief, even a clean hotel room—are, to begin with, difficult to define and measure in ways that would enable production to be viewed purely in engineering terms. It is possible first to define the attributes of an automobile or a hamburger, then to evaluate the quality, or conformance to design, of autos or hamburgers as they are made. But judgments made by workers, managers, and/or customers are part of the definition of a healthy patient, a good legal brief, or a clean hotel room. There is inevitably an element of subjective interpretation in determining what is "good enough" or "clean enough."

A second problem in applying the engineering model is that the attributes of service products may be partly or wholly inseparable from the process of production, as illustrated by table service in a restaurant. Customers care about how services are delivered as well as what is delivered.

A third problem arises when the customer takes part in the provision of the service but does not know, or knows only vaguely, what she wants. Workers and customers can jointly plan a haircut or an advertising campaign, but in health care or auto repair the customer normally lacks the expertise to diagnose the problem. In all these cases, the definition or "design" of the product is part of the process of production.

Finally, some services (including child care, education, and much of health care) vary too much with the situation to permit application of the engineering model. These products are tailored to needs that may be unique. In principle, one might envision child care workers, teachers, or nurses and physicians as consulting "rulebooks" or "manuals" that tell them what to do in every contingency. But there are simply too many contingencies to enable this approach to be implemented in full. (As we see later, even the technicians who repair photocopy machines—and confront a limited range of contingencies—find that the manuals their employers provide are of little use.) Moreover, reducing the number of contingencies by reducing the extent to which the service is customized is often unacceptable to customers, many of whom want and are willing to pay for such services. (What would a rulebook for a real estate agent look like?)

Where the engineering model of production is inapplicable or only partially applicable, it must be replaced or supplemented by an alternative model that we call interpretive.[4] The interpretive model takes as problematic what the engineering model takes as given: the prior definition of the product and the independence of the production process from the design of the product. In the interpretive model, workers develop skills in understanding customer wants and needs. They then translate those wants and needs into the services they provide. If the worker finds that the service and method of provision he has initially chosen are not producing the intended or desired effects, he modifies the service or method of delivery or his interpretation of what the customer wants or needs.[5] The worker continues to adjust his interpretation of customer needs until he perceives that they match the customer's expectations.[6]

The process of medical diagnosis and treatment illustrates the interpretive model in its most complete form. Through dialogue with the patient, examination, and sometimes a battery of specialized tests, the physician explores symptoms, elicits a medical history, develops a tentative understanding of the patient's condition, and seeks to verify and, if necessary, correct that diagnosis. Treatment may lead to further detective work, perhaps a change in diagnosis and an altered treatment regimen. In difficult cases, the physician calls in specialists. The goal, sometimes achieved and sometimes not, is to bring symptoms and treatment into congruence. Auto mechanics and copier repair technicians use similar interpretive processes, in which diagnosis and treatment are intertwined. So, in their own ways, do teachers.

As the illustrations above suggest, high-skill autonomous workers are most likely to follow some version of the interpretive model, but service workers in the semiautonomous and unrationalized labor-intensive work systems also apply it. Aides in a nursing home must engage in a process of diagnosis and treatment, in this case directed at the everyday needs of residents. Nurses' aides deal with a narrow range of choices compared with that of physicians, but the framework is similar. And the interpretive problems can be baffling: what, for instance, might calm a patient suffering the disorientation of Alzheimer's? Waiters, customer service representatives, and salespeople must likewise develop skills in interpretation.

The engineering and interpretive models represent distinct approaches to product design and development and the organization of work. As a result, they have different implications for performance improvement. In the engineering model, product design comes first. In the interpretive model, product and process design are intertwined and interdependent. In both, work processes should make the product and its "design" resemble each other as closely as possible. But in the interpretive model, product design emerges from the process rather than being specified in advance.

In the engineering model, performance can be improved along three nominally independent dimensions: product design, conformance, and cost. Improvement can result from configuring a product that better meets customer needs (design), producing each unit to reflect the idealized design as closely as possible (conformance), and reducing unit costs (without sacrificing conformance).

In the interpretive model, workers, individually or as part of a group, both interpret needs and execute tasks (e.g., they diagnose a balky copier and begin a repair, help diners select a wine to go with their meal and decant it). The worker may also seek to influence, subtly or not, the expression of needs. Performance improvement follows from improvement in the worker's ability to elicit, understand, and respond to the situation, to select and follow work practices from an available repertoire, and perhaps to learn or invent new practices.

When design and conformance are addressed simultaneously through a process of mutual adjustment, it is misleading to speak of independent dimensions of improvement. Rather, it is the process as a whole that improves. Of course, many service products are partly de-signed in deliberate fashion, much like manufactured goods. Still, the insurance agent may customize a policy or discount the premium for a valued client, the theater director take liberties with the playwright's text.

In some cases, improvement in service performance takes the form of more rapid production (fast service). Costs may decline, as when the copier repair technician improves her diagnostic skills and can find and fix the problem more quickly (or develops shortcuts in carrying out common repairs). Alternatively, performance improvement may take the form of an increase in choice or variety of services, as when the cook learns how to make a new dish. There are many other possibilities. The copier technician may learn to anticipate problems, replacing a part be-fore it fails; the machine does not break down, and the customer does not have to pay for another visit. And a technician who fixes the ma-chine so it stays fixed is delivering a functionally better product.

Performance improvement, then, typically results from some combi-nation of greater speed, greater variety, and a functionally superior out-come. Regardless of the ways in which performance improvement man-ifests itself, only sometimes does it result from making work more routine (as in the production of fast foods). In this way, much service production contrasts with the engineering model, in which standardiza-tion is central to productivity improvement.

We have sharply distinguished between the engineering and inter-pretive models in order to demonstrate that they embody alternative ways of thinking about work organization and performance improve-ment. Some processes are better viewed in terms of the engineering model, others in terms of the interpretive model. Many work processes, perhaps most, combine features of both. We noted above that the con-ceptual design of manufactured goods has a strongly interpretive cast. Likewise, a group of factory workers diagnosing quality problems will proceed somewhat in the same way as the copier repair technician. Even where interpretation is paramount, the subsequent choice of tasks can sometimes be viewed in engineering terms. After diagnosing a pa-tient's condition, the physician prescribes the medication that is most likely to be effective—and, in a managed care setting, the cheapest. After deciding what a "clean" room means, and in what respects a par-ticular room is not clean, the housekeeper selects methods to do the job most quickly and effectively.

When engineering and interpretive aspects coexist, performance gains in both realms may be possible within the same work process. For example, a lawyer's efficiency may be improved by using a standard text for a routine legal document (such as a simple will), even though the customization of a will for particular clients remains fundamentally interpretive, not reducible to a set of rules.

Work reform practitioners have barely begun to think about performance gains on the interpretive dimension. Although TQM, for instance, puts a high priority on customer satisfaction, formalized TQM programs have little to say about how to *elicit* customer needs. Even recent engineering model work reforms thus neglect a source of potential gains. And in the service sector, where the interpretive model predominates, its neglect has limited improvements in performance.

Economies of Depth and Coordination

In the traditional engineering model, many production jobs are defined narrowly. In the interpretive model, jobs must be broad enough to allow leeway in responding to the needs of the situation. The interpretive model is irrelevant if the job is to prepare hamburgers according to a fixed recipe. On the other hand, the model becomes relevant if a worker has discretion to cook hamburgers in response to customer requests.

Although substantial job breadth is a precondition for the interpretive model, adding breadth will not necessarily lead to better performance. Indeed, if a cook also waits on tables, both cooking and table service may deteriorate. But if jobs include an appropriately broad and related range of tasks, performance can be improved by making workers better at what they do. We call this route "economies of depth."[7]

Economies of depth are attained through deeper understanding of work processes and greater skill in executing them. They result when a worker improves his ability to interpret situational needs and respond appropriately. Customers benefit because the work goes faster, because the worker can grasp and respond to a greater variety of needs, or because those responses are more effective (or some combination of the three). Learning is cumulative: there are always new situations, new lessons to be retained in one's personal stock of know-how. Therefore, economies of depth contribute to sustained performance improvement, just as rationalization and automation in the engineering model led to sustained improvement in manufacturing productivity.

When the lessons of experience can be passed on to others, benefits multiply. Whether people work alone, as copier technicians do, or in teams, as is common in health care, communication of knowledge accelerates the achievement of economies of depth. Knowledge can be diffused within occupations (e.g., among copier technicians) and across occupational boundaries (e.g., between physicians and nurses).

The significance of the interpersonal transmission of knowledge is easy to see for schooling, organized apprenticeship, or other training but is by no means limited to formal settings. Workers accumulate differing stocks of know-how even if they begin with the same education and training. Some technicians are better at diagnosing copier problems, others at executing repairs. Some physicians have seen hundreds of cases of appendicitis, others dozens. If workers can communicate their knowledge both within and across work settings, the know-how and skills of those in an occupation improve. Workers may also reach an implicit or perhaps explicit consensus on occupational "best practices." If unable to find consensus on what is best—not uncommon in medicine, for example—the occupational group may still be able to agree on "worst practices" to be eliminated. Even if there is no agreement about best or worst practices, individual workers or work groups might improve their performance by rethinking their own taken-for-granted work practices. Such rethinking is often stimulated by workers learning about different taken-for-granted practices (e.g., at another software company, school, or office).

Transfer and sharing of knowledge hold considerable untapped potential for performance gains because interpersonal modes are underdeveloped in many occupations and industries. In contrast, individual learning through repeated practice takes place more or less automatically, although this, too, can be accelerated.

Scientific research exemplifies the process of creating economies of depth. The reward system in science is based on open communication of results, with the greatest rewards for those who are first to publish. Occupational norms foster broad advances in scientific knowledge and also help guide research, as working scientists observe what others are doing and how the community responds to new results.

Economies of depth are relatively straightforward in science because much of scientific knowledge is "knowing that" rather than "knowing how."[8] Understanding the physical principles that make it possible to balance a bicycle is "knowing that." Knowing how to ride a bicycle is an entirely different kind of knowledge (or better, skill). The physical principles of bicycle riding, such as the gyroscopic effect, can be made explicit and communicated in words or via mathematics. Anyone who has the necessary background can learn them by reading or listening to an explanation. The knowledge and skill of actually riding a bicycle, however, cannot be made fully explicit. Novices learn through practice, often with the aid of coaching by an experienced rider, not by following written instructions. Although there are rules that can help—look ahead, not down; watch for gravel in the road—transmitting knowledge of how to ride a bicycle calls for less formal and more context-dependent communication than transmitting knowledge of the physics of bicycle riding.

Economies of depth in the services, especially where the interpretive model applies, depend heavily on "knowing how." Diagnosing a patient's illness or a copier's malfunctioning, caring for a nursing-home resident, helping a shopper pick a dress, teaching a child to read are all skills of "knowing how" (even though performance may also depend on explicit knowledge). Formulating a scientific hypothesis or designing an experiment to test it are also skills of knowing how. Perhaps for this reason, scientists have not developed methods for transmitting these skills that rival those for diffusing the formalized knowledge of science. Novices continue to pick up the tacit skills of doing science through apprenticeships in research, just as physicians and copier technicians learn through guided practice (and must demonstrate acceptable levels of competence before working independently).

The creation of economies of depth, then, is not solely a matter of transmitting codified knowledge. It may also require people to trade stories about how they handle work situations (as do writing teachers and members of Professional Secretaries International) or to work together in teams (as do scientists).[9] Promoting systematic communication among workers can thus contribute to economies of depth.

In contrast to economies of depth, which at bottom depend on the knowledge of individual workers, "economies of coordination" operate when people work in groups and coordinate their efforts through mutual adjustment. Where the interpretive model applies, workers must coordinate both their efforts to achieve a common goal and their efforts to define that goal. In a hospital, for example, physicians, nurses, laboratory technicians, and others contribute to both diagnosis and treatment of patients. With "reciprocal interdependence," each worker depends on the outputs of others, and workers need to recognize what they do not understand as well as what they do, so that they recognize when and how to get help. Coordination requires a greater degree of communication and joint decision making in situations of reciprocal interdependence than with nonreciprocal interdependence. This leads to correspondingly large opportunities for performance improvement.[10]

As with economies of depth, economies of coordination may appear to the customer as gains in speed, variety of service output, or functional effectiveness. Economies of coordination may result when workers in the same occupation cooperate, as when engineers design a new car. They may be cross-functional, involving different occupations, as when pilots, flight attendants, baggage handlers, gate agents, and mechanics work together to prepare an airplane for takeoff. Economies of coordination may also be cross-worksite, as when nurses from a hospital and a home health care agency cooperate to plan the continuing care of a patient scheduled for discharge.

Some readers may feel that economies of coordination are entirely the responsibility of managers and supervisors. That is not the case. When several thousand engineers work for several years to design an automobile, there is no way managers can closely supervise each step in the work. In simpler settings, too, as in the case studies below, coordination through mutual adjustment requires workers engaged in related tasks to communicate actively and solve problems collectively. Indeed, a recent study of the airline flight departure process found that cross-functional coordination by nonsupervisory personnel contributed substantially to performance improvement, whereas efforts by supervisors to enhance cross-functional coordination either had no effect or actually degraded performance.[11]

One way to achieve economies of coordination is to create teams that stay together over time, so members can learn which tasks each person is best at, develop a common interpretive framework, and create shortcuts for anticipating what needs to be done. Much of this again has to do with "knowing how": how to work with others, how to act within the set of common understandings that makes up a work culture. Performance depends on informal, context-dependent communication. When workers differ in status or world view (physicians and nurses, pilots and flight attendants), considerable time may be needed to develop collaborative relationships.

Practices that contribute to economics of coordination include performance evaluations that hold teams rather than individuals accountable for performance, "coaching" to improve teamwork skills, and selecting people for teams who enjoy and have aptitude for work that requires coordination through mutual adjustment.[12] Each of these practices can contribute to a dynamic of performance improvement and innovation sustainable over long periods of time.

Depth and Coordination in the Four Work Systems

The importance of economies of depth and economies of coordination varies with work system and setting. Depth is important in copier repair because the essence of the job is the often puzzling matter of diagnosis. Coordination is less important because technicians generally work alone. In some of the jobs associated with the airline flight departure process, such as gate agent, depth is a minor consideration whereas coordination with pilots, flight attendants, and others is paramount. For surgical nurses, both depth and coordination are important. Fast-food restaurants have limited scope for either depth or coordination economies because work is organized on the engineering model with managers doing much of the coordination.

The examples that follow, grouped by work system, illustrate situations in which economies of depth or coordination arise through either conscious planning or long-standing practice. In some of the cases, both interpretive and engineering models apply. Indeed, managers and workers may be uncertain or confused about whether they are following one model or the other (or elements of both) or whether they are pursuing economies of depth or of coordination. It is no surprise when the gains achieved fall short of the potential.

High-Skill Autonomous Work

Teachers. In Long Island's Shoreham–Wading River school district, writing was traditionally a subject that each teacher taught in his or her own way.[13] Teachers, part of the high-skill autonomous work system, chose their own methods and materials. Most developed a style of teaching early in their careers and continued thereafter with little self-conscious reflection. They rarely discussed how they taught writing or solicited feedback from students.

During several summers, instructor-researchers from the New York City Writing Project, based at the City University of New York, conducted writing workshops in which participating Shoreham–Wading

River teachers were asked to write essays on topics of interest to them and to keep journals in which they reflected on their own writing processes. They read both their essays and their journals aloud. Participants learned to listen actively to one another's work and to deliver useful feedback. The participating teachers were asked not only to revise their writing in response to the workshop's reactions but to reflect in their journals on the process. The instructor-researchers, teachers themselves, participated more as peers than as leaders, writing their own essays and offering them for comment.

After the summer workshops Shoreham–Wading River participants adopted the Writing Project methods in their own classes, which ranged from first through twelfth grade. Teachers wrote alongside their students, keeping journals, participating in small-group discussions, and seeking to act like mentors. As the process of writing, reading, reflecting, and revising continued, each student was asked to produce a piece that he or she, the teacher, and the rest of the class would find satisfying.

Some teachers had an easy time transferring the Writing Project methods to their classes. More instructive for our purposes are the experiences of teachers who had trouble. They found it necessary to engage in more reflection on their teaching styles and on student's reactions than did colleagues who took quickly to the workshop process.

Ross Burkhardt, an eighth-grade teacher for twenty years, saw that his students resented the questions he asked and the way he asked them. He began to doubt his abilities as a teacher. After talking over the situation with his instructor-researcher, Ross asked his students to write about what he was doing wrong as a teacher. Gradually, Ross came to understand that a need to be the center of attention in the classroom had prevented him from using the Writing Project methods successfully. Over the next several years he was able to alter his classroom style.

Ross's wife, Diane Burkhardt, also taught eighth grade. Her students complained constantly about keeping journals. She found that many had had unpleasant experiences the year before with a seventh-grade teacher who had been struggling with the Writing Project approach. Diane attempted to show her class, by example, that their journals did not have to conform to the format forced on them the year before, but most students remained skeptical. Both Diane and her instructor-researcher felt that students were not writing about what mattered to them. After rereading her own journal entries and some of the relevant professional literature, Diane raised this issue with her students, who said they were afraid to share writing that was "too personal." As Diane discussed how to resolve this issue with the class, her students slowly began to place more trust in one another and to write more honestly.

The Writing Project example illustrates the interpretive nature of teaching. Following their summer workshops the Shoreham–Wading River teachers began the school term with a commitment to a new method of instruction. But their ability to apply it varied. More learning was required, along with adaptation to grade levels and to the needs of particular students and groups of students. The process required them to experiment and to move iteratively toward a style with which they, as teachers, would be comfortable.

This example involves economies of depth. The Shoreham–Wading River teachers did not learn "cookbook" methods for teaching writing. Rather, as their interpretive skills improved—through repeated discussion with students, colleagues, and instructor-researchers—they became better at the "knowing how" of teaching writing.

In this case, communication was essential, not for coordination but for feedback and learning. This kind of communication with students was new to most of the teachers. Outside a few experimental programs such as the Writing Project, teachers today get little encouragement to reflect on their classroom style with the help of colleagues or students.

Technicians. It might seem to casual observers that copier technicians, computer support workers, and even emergency medical technicians follow standard procedures that cover virtually all contingencies. This image is far from accurate.

Xerox, like other companies that make or service copiers, gives its technicians repair manuals that are intended to provide solutions for all foreseeable problems.[14] These manuals reflect an engineering view of the machine. They include elaborate flowcharts that lead the technician through a series of diagnostic tests and conclude with a prescribed remedy. Xerox technicians have found, however, that except for the simplest malfunctions, the manuals and flowcharts cannot be used as intended. In many cases, they are incomplete, inaccurate, or simply too confusing to follow (unless the technician already understands the problem, in which case they may not be needed at all).[15] Lacking the prior knowledge of the technical writers who prepared the manuals, for instance, it is easy to trace the wrong branch on a flowchart. Diagnosing and repairing copiers thus remains an interpretive problem. Xerox technicians must rely on their own know-how, which reflects their understanding of the models and individual machines they work on. When baffled, a technician may refer to the manual but typically begins by trying to understand the purpose of the prescribed procedures rather than following them blindly.

Xerox technicians develop their knowledge and skills through company-provided training (e.g., on new models), through their own experience, and from the "war stories" they tell one another. These stories are a major source of economies of depth. Not all tell of heroic solutions to puzzling problems. Some are descriptions of failure. In such cases, a technician may describe the situation to her peers, possibly offering a tentative diagnosis while seeking alternative interpretations. She may describe the problem and rule out potential diagnoses in order to distinguish this case from others, seemingly similar, that are well understood. The stories relate specific experiences but may also serve as warnings or reminders—for example, of unexpected cause-effect relationships. Such cautions have more weight when presented in the context of a concrete situation (rather than as abstract exhortations of the sort that managers lacking recent field experience might issue). Sometimes a technician relates a case he has solved, minus the outcome, to challenge or test his peers.

Emergency medical technicians (EMTs) are required by law to follow specified protocols unless a physician directs them otherwise.[16] Even so, this requirement does not rule out interpretation and does not mean EMTs rigidly obey the protocols. Rather, EMTs conform to norms shared with others in work cultures that may include sympathetic physicians, nurses, firefighters, and police officers, as well as other EMTs. Among other things, these norms require them to take the initiative in asking for guidance from physicians. Thus if an EMT believes a patient needs a certain drug, she will ask for permission to administer it rather than simply wait for instructions. Furthermore, although EMTs accept the fact that physicians have expertise to which they should defer, they occasionally deviate from protocols without seeking permission. This is not nearly so common as television viewers may suppose, but EMTs do "break the rules" when they believe someone's life is at risk. In one instance, an EMT team performed an emergency tracheotomy after exhausting all the mandated procedures without success. Although the EMTs had been trained in this procedure, it was not part of their practice protocol and they knew they could lose their licenses. Despite the law's attempt to write a rulebook, EMTs understand—and so do those who write the rules—that protocols do not and cannot cover every possibility.

If the world of the EMT is one of contingency, uncertainty, and ambiguity, the world of computers would seem to be one of algorithms, an engineered world.[17] Computers have zero tolerance for ambiguity. Software—the computer's rulebook—tells them precisely what to do and how to do it. These instructions change only when programmers deliberately alter the code. Software support workers, on the other hand, must help harried users who may be under pressure from clients or bosses, may have no idea what created their problem (or may misremember), and may have mistaken ideas about how the system functions. Moreover, if computer systems are well defined in an engineering sense, they are also very complex, much more so than Xerox machines. Programs may have millions of lines of code, many unknown bugs, and poor documentation. That there is in theory a rational explanation and a precise solution for every possible problem does nothing to make the jobs of software support workers easier. They confront problems that cannot always be identified, explained, or even reproduced. They may have to find a "fix" that works for a user without knowing exactly why it works and reassure the user that the machine will now be okay.

The work is especially difficult for large mainframe programs and for software that is frequently updated. Revised code often comes with new bugs; indeed, a "repair" of faulty code may itself prove faulty. (Large programs can never be completely verified.) Support jobs call for a wide range of practical judgments that draw both on knowledge of users and what they need and on an understanding of the technical attributes of the computer system. Software support workers learn from their own experience and from one another, sharing knowledge much as do copier repair technicians.

These three examples suggest the range of interpretive work in which technicians engage and the sources of economies of depth. In many cases, considerably greater economies should be possible. In all three cases, communication among technicians is local and oral, limited to the work setting and whatever socializing takes place off the job. Although Xerox sends frequent repair bulletins to its technicians, as do software firms, this information flows mostly from the top down. In none of the three cases does the experience of technicians diffuse outside the local community. Nor do technicians write down the lessons embodied in their stories. But they could: it is easy to imagine, for instance, electronic (or printed) newsletters or bulletin boards where stories could be posted.[18] With the Internet and corporate intranets, this may begin to happen spontaneously. Smart employers will encourage it.

Unrationalized Labor-Intensive Work

When it comes to unrationalized labor-intensive work, the central problem is that employers do not see it as in their interest to improve performance. Managers often believe that such work cannot be done differently than it is done today. The examples that follow refute such preconceptions. They show that there is considerable potential for performance improvement through the transformation of unrationalized labor-intensive work into paraprofessional jobs that more closely resemble those of semiautonomous or high-skill autonomous workers.

Home Health Aides. Home health aides typically visit two to five housebound clients per day, assisting them with activities such as toileting, bathing, and buying groceries.[19] Aides are part of a team responsible for care. The aide, for example, may weigh the client and record his temperature and blood pressure, while a nurse visits to administer drugs or chemotherapy.

Home health aides face varied and unpredictable situations. Working alone, they may have to deal with obstinate clients, a sudden health crisis, or irate relatives. As in nursing homes, "performance" also means providing companionship for people who may be lonely and disoriented. Nonetheless, most home health agencies train their aides only to the legal minimum, provide wages and benefits at the bottom end of the local labor market, offer only irregular part-time work, and accept the high rates of turnover that result (commonly 40 to 100 percent).

As in the better nursing homes mentioned in Chapter 3, managers at worker-owned Cooperative Home Care Associates (CHCA) seek to improve standards of care by improving job quality for workers. The company pays $6.85 to $7.40 an hour, provides free health insurance and free transit passes, and offers an LPN (licensed practical nurse) program that aides can pursue. Because CHCA distributes hours based in part on seniority, aides who stay with the company can work full-time if they wish. Annual turnover is less than 20 percent.

CHCA hires one in five applicants, screening not only for empathy and caregiving disposition but for self-reliance and problem-solving and communications skills. More than half the company's aides are former welfare recipients. CHCA has found little relationship between formal schooling and the qualities that make for a good aide. Successful applicants average an eighth-grade education, with functional levels of English and arithmetic typically at fourth- to sixth-grade levels.

Most training programs for home health aides attempt, in an average of three weeks, to impart a body of knowledge and skills based on an engineering model. The aides are taught a set of rules to be followed for common tasks. In contrast, CHCA seeks quite deliberately to develop interpretive capacities. CHCA begins its training with a six-week program intended to help new employees think critically and learn to solve job-related problems on their own. As a manager put it, "We teach them to take charge of the situation—and their own lives." Aides are told that there is no one right way to solve a problem, that each problem should be viewed from multiple perspectives, and that choices should be openly discussed with clients. More concretely, CHCA seeks to build reflection and knowledge transmission into its organizational culture through means such as the "4 *P*s" mnemonic: "Pull-Back," "Paraphrase," "Present Choices," and "Pass It On." "Pull-Back" means that aides should acknowledge their emotions and put them aside as part of becoming a professional. "Paraphrase" means that aides should summarize and repeat back what a client has told them, to confirm or clarify their interpretation. "Present Choices" means that aides are to discuss alternatives with the client, making it more likely that a full range of options will be considered and that the client gets what he wants. "Pass It On" reminds aides to include necessary information in their written reports and to discuss their client visits with others who may need to know.

Rather than lecture to trainees in a classroom setting (in which workers may have a history of failure), CHCA uses educational games, simulations, and hands-on demonstrations. After their initial training, aides get three months of intensive on-the-job coaching. "Coordinators" talk through work situations with aides, engaging in an ongoing dialogue aimed at teaching aides to reflect on their experiences as a means of broadening and deepening their skills. Coordinators serve as collective memory for CHCA. For the aide, coordinators act as a mirror and a second set of eyes in situations that a trainee is seeing for the first time.

During the three-month coaching period aides also get structured feed-back from clients.

During the coaching period coordinator and trainee put together a "learning contract" that lists skills and knowledge to be developed (e.g., communicating with a supervisor) and spells out how the aide is to acquire them (e.g., shadowing an experienced aide). The learning contract includes performance goals, how they are to be measured, and a schedule for meeting them.

Hotel Housekeepers. Hotel housekeeping is another unrationalized labor-intensive job with unexplored potential for performance improvement (of both the engineering and interpretive kinds; on the latter, see the San Francisco Hotels Partnership example in Chapter 7). Hotel managements have generally been content so long as rooms were clean, which was easy enough to check. New recruits got little or no training; either they had done the work before or could learn on the job. Nonetheless, when Interstate Properties (a pseudonym) planned to expand its two low-cost chains aimed at business travelers, the firm sought improvements in work practices for housekeeping staff.[20] A high-level human resource manager said, "It's simply not true that cleaning rooms is a stagnant function with limited possibilities for greater productivity." She rattled off a long list of engineering-type improvements, some based on suggestions from housekeepers, that Interstate had already implemented. The company purchased lighter carts and vacuum cleaners, replaced hot polyester uniforms with cooler cotton versions, and bought supplies that reduced cleaning time even if they cost more. Additional productivity-enhancing engineering gains may be possible in economy business chains that have near-identical hotel and room architecture.

Semiautonomous Work

Insurance. At Mount Rushmore Mutual (MRM), the pseudonymous insurance company discussed in Chapter 4, newly hired clerical workers need about eighteen months to reach "proficiency," attesting to the importance of economies of depth.[21] Economies of coordination come from efficient processing of complex flows of information between field offices and headquarters and among the headquarters staff. Before the reengineering program mentioned in Chapter 4, putting a new policy in force meant thirty-plus "handoffs" between initial sale and delivery of the final contract to the customer. After reengineering (in progress) at least a half-dozen will remain. Each is a possible source of error.

A team-based structure provides for task-level coordination and helps deepen and diffuse interpretive capacities. Since a reorganization of policy service work in the late 1980s, groups of fifteen to twenty workers handle case management for general agencies. Previously, each clerical worker had maintained a backlog of as many as one hundred fifty cases. Now a team "work flow coordinator" assigns cases to workers whenever their backlog drops below ten. Teams meet, sometimes several times a week, to discuss difficult or unusual cases. Some maintain binders of sample cases and letters to customers. In interviews even senior workers noted that they benefit from this kind of pooled experience.

Air Travel. Southwest Airlines turns around its aircraft in an average of seventeen minutes, compared with an industry figure of forty-three minutes.[22] Economies of coordination enable Southwest to reduce capital expenses, keeping its planes in the air eleven hours a day rather than the more typical nine hours. Southwest also enjoys a 20 percent advantage in productivity measured as ton-miles per employee, while remaining at or near the top of the industry in on-time arrivals, fewest complaints per customer, and baggage handling performance.

Much of the credit can be traced to Southwest's work organization and human resource practices. A dozen different functional groups must cooperate to unload passengers, luggage, and cargo from a plane, then prepare it for another flight. An operations agent serves as case manager for each flight, tracking it from an hour before arrival to thirty minutes after departure and planning and coordinating the "attack" on the plane. The company's pilots have even been known to help clean a plane if needed.

Southwest hires and trains with an eye to developing workers who can communicate and cooperate across functional boundaries. Optional short-term job trading helps ramp, reservations, and operations agents understand one another's responsibilities. When delays occur, Southwest analyzes them less to penalize those responsible than to understand the problem and avoid repeating it. The most common code is "team delay," meaning that the station takes collective responsibility. At American Airlines, by contrast, when a delay means missed connections, the CEO "wants to see the corpse" (the individual responsible). The consequences include coverups that reduce opportunities for organizational learning and improvement.

Retailing. Home Depot operates more than two hundred fifty stores stocking some thirty thousand products, including building materials, hardware, and lawn and garden supplies.[23] When it can, the company hires people with experience in plumbing, carpentry, electrical work, and other home building and repair skills—the so-called Bernie's Boys, after one of the company's founders, Bernie Marcus—who can advise customers on installation and repair techniques as well as on product selection.

By hiring former construction workers, Home Depot is able to draw on interpretive abilities developed in high-skill autonomous work. A customer may not know what she needs, but after hearing about the job to be done or the problem to be solved, a Home Depot sales worker may be able to ask "diagnostic" questions and offer guidance on what to buy and how to use it.

Home Depot is unusual in incorporating former high-skill autonomous workers into the semiautonomous work system. But there are other segments of retail trade in which customers benefit from interpretive skills based on detailed product knowledge. An experienced salesperson of men's clothing can tell at a glance whether a customer has the right suit size and how much tailoring will be needed. Much the same is true in shoe sales, where the question may be how much the leather will stretch with break-in. The clerk at a fish counter may be able to help shoppers choose what they want for a dinner party and pass on tips for cooking shark or tilapia.

Package Delivery. Seeking efficiency and high levels of customer service in a competitive business, United Parcel Service (UPS) structures work based on the engineering model and scientific management.[24] There are standard times for each part of a driver's job, from starting the engine to greeting customers. Time-and-motion analysts ride each route every two years or so to estimate standard times. Of course, drivers may not actually follow the prescribed methods, and there is no one on hand to see whether they do. The veneer of scientific management is in part a way to legitimize work standards that call for high and consistent levels of effort.

UPS has been proud of its engineering-model approach, presenting it to the world as a sign of the firm's efficiency. At the same time, the company presents another face to the world: the collective face of its drivers. UPS puts a good deal of pressure on drivers, yet it also relies heavily on the knowledge of the men and women who visit the same offices day after day, cruise residential neighborhoods looking for hidden street numbers, know which neighbor will take a package or that it is not worth stopping because a homeowner's car is not in its usual place. At UPS, as in much semiautonomous work, engineering-model and interpretive skills must be married to achieve high levels of performance.

Tightly Constrained Work

Although the tightly constrained service work system adheres to the engineering model and workers have little freedom to deviate from their prescribed tasks, depth of knowledge still matters. Customer service representatives (CSRs), for example, may need to navigate complicated computer systems while identifying the underlying source of confusion over a bill or calming an angry customer. Economies of depth nonetheless appear to be minor in routine call-center work, and the interpretive dimension is limited by pressure to keep each call short. Employers could choose to define CSR jobs more broadly for reasons of "one-stop shopping" or more effective resolution of customer problems. But it seems at least as likely that firms will seek to reduce labor costs by replacing more of this work with electronic response systems. Customers may be asked—and some may prefer—to solve their own problems by querying a database over the telephone or Internet.

Fast-food firms have sometimes experimented with work reorganization. McDonald's employees are now permitted to replace a spilled cup of coffee without asking the manager, even to deviate occasionally from the script when taking orders.[25] Many Taco Bell outlets now operate without a full-time store manager. Crew members, working in teams, have been trained and given responsibility for ordering food, scheduling their hours, and even hiring. Taco Bell's measures of customer satisfaction increased over the several-year period during which these changes were instituted, although it is impossible to know how much of this increase, if any, was due to team-based management as opposed to, say, menu changes.[26]

Compared with the cases examined earlier, these tightly constrained examples depart only slightly from scientific management. Indeed, work reform in tightly constrained service jobs is minimal even by contrast with tightly constrained manufacturing work. This appears to be a matter of process complexity. Although tightly constrained jobs are relatively simple by definition, manufacturing, as noted earlier, tends to be much more complex at the system level than tightly constrained service work. Engineering-type reforms have less to offer in many kinds of tightly constrained service work because existing forms of work organization already provide acceptable solutions to the problem of organizing and managing production. Work reform of the interpretive type is relevant to tightly constrained service work mainly to the extent that management decides to vary the nature of the service, making the job, in the process, less tightly constrained.

Prospects for Performance Improvement

The examples in this chapter suggest potential in much of the service sector for performance improvement through economies of depth and coordination. Only in tightly constrained work is the interpretive model of limited applicability, with performance improvement more likely to occur via continued rationalization and automation.

Interpretive-model work reforms, along with engineering-model reforms where the latter are relevant, will alter the distribution of employment among work systems and, to some extent, the nature of the work systems themselves. Some tightly constrained jobs will no doubt remain, but as suggested in Chapter 4, continued rationalization and automation will probably reduce the relative number of such jobs. The unrationalized labor-intensive work system could shrink if jobs such as those of home health aides begin to look more like semiautonomous or high-skill autonomous work than they do today.

Managers and workers in the semiautonomous work system are generally more concerned with coordination than with depth, as suggested by the emphasis on creating a bond between worker and employer and on making workers experts in firm-specific ways of working. In high-skill autonomous work, depth is usually more important than coordination, as suggested by the emphasis on occupational, rather than firm- or workgroup-specific learning. But if semiautonomous workers begin to pay more attention to depth, and high-skill autonomous workers start to become more concerned about coordination, the difference between these two work systems could narrow.

There are major obstacles to the diffusion of interpretive-model work reforms, beginning with the prevalence of wage-based competition, which discourages skill-based performance improvement. But even in the absence of wage-based competition, not many firms seem likely to risk pioneering interpretive models for performance improvement, especially where this would require more communication between their employees and workers in other firms. By design, the hierarchical organization of most American businesses channels and limits communication inside the firm and discourages interfirm cooperation. Although patterns of business organization are changing in ways that may be more conducive to interpretive-model reforms, in the next chapter we suggest that changes in business organization by themselves will not stimulate the kinds of communication needed for performance improvement. But associations of workers, such as professional groups and "reinvented" unions, can effectively promote communication across firms. The absence of these associations from many parts of the U.S. economy is, therefore, an obstacle to interpretive-model performance improvement. Public policy to spread the interpretive model will have to promote broad-based worker associations as well as discourage wage-based competition.

6

Business Organization

In Chapter 1 we described the role of business organization in generating the productivity improvements of the Wonder Years. After the turn of the century large, hierarchical corporations systematically pursued engineering-model performance improvements. Their market power enabled them to invest in single-purpose capital equipment with confidence that demand for new capacity would materialize. Business shared the productivity gains with consumers and workers.

Could business organization play an analogous role in disseminating the interpretive model in today's service-dominated economy? If, as we argue in Chapter 5, untapped potential exists for performance improvement in the services, might we expect corporate forms to evolve in directions that realize the potential? To address this question, we examine emerging forms of business organization in services.

Trends in Business Organization

For a century, in services as in manufacturing, large service firms such as Sears and AT&T coexisted with small, local businesses. In services, smaller firms and establishments have always been more prevalent; in 1993 establishments in services employed fourteen workers on average versus forty-seven in manufacturing.[1]

Both large, hierarchical service firms and small, local providers have come under new competitive pressures since the 1970s. In response, business organization in the services is and will remain in flux, with firms and industries reorganizing in contradictory and uncoordinated ways. We focus here on three major developments: rising concentration, outsourcing, and the emergence of business networks.

Although service firms still tend to be small, concentration has been rising in some services. The four largest grocery wholesalers increased their share of the national market from 17 to 35 percent from 1982 to 1992. In the grocery store industry, the largest four firms in major metropolitan areas accounted for 45 percent of sales on average in 1954 and 58 percent in 1982.[2] In banking, accounting, and health care, concentration has increased recently as a result of mergers and acquisitions. The number of U.S. banks has fallen by five thousand since 1980, to about nine thousand.[3] The big six accounting firms will become the big five as a result of a merger between Coopers & Lybrand and Price Waterhouse.[4]

Even when concentration rises in services, it does not necessarily lead to the types of vertically integrated structures (and firm-specific job ladders) familiar from manufacturing.[5] One reason is the flexibility of capital in services; another is the prevalence in services of franchising arrangements, which leave individual outlets (or groups of outlets) in the hands of independent entrepreneurs who purchase services from the franchisor.

In manufacturing, the inflexible capital predominant early in the century created powerful incentives for firms to stabilize demand for their goods so that dedicated equipment would not remain idle. In services today, capital often has alternative applications if demand declines or its composition changes. A truck fleet, a computer, a storefront, even an optical scanning machine can be redeployed easily. With less of an imperative to stabilize demand, service firms have less tendency to stabilize employment.

Franchise operations have also gained at the expense of totally independent operations. For example, franchised outlets accounted for about one-quarter of all restaurant sales in 1970 and nearly half two decades later.[6] Franchised hotels had a little over half the market in 1980, two-thirds by the early 1990s.[7] Smaller budget hotels and motels are often owner-operated under a franchise agreement with a national marketing-reservations company such as Best Western. Firms such as Hilton, Marriott, and Sheraton operate some of their own hotels and also handle management, marketing, and reservations for franchisees under contract. Job ladders tend to be limited in franchise operations because each franchisee maintains an independent employment policy, as well as because the franchisees may be small and geographically dispersed.

Alongside increasing concentration, competitive pressures have led large firms to outsource services spanning the range from security guards and cafeteria workers to data processing specialists. After real estate values plummeted and recession cut into occupancy levels, hotels in the early 1990s began to cut costs by contracting out the operation of bars and restaurants (which typically remain open for long hours but may serve few guests). Today upscale hotels may rent space to well-known chefs who can attract diners while enhancing the hotel's image. Others have sought to cut costs by outsourcing preparation of desserts or precut vegetables. Hotels are contracting with local restaurants or pizza chains to deliver "room service," with parking-lot operators to run their garages, and with commercial laundries to handle linens.

In a third development, service firms in a number of industries are forging closer, more cooperative relations with favored customers and/or suppliers. Department stores that once bought from thousands of suppliers now deal with hundreds, seeking to match their stocks of merchandise better with day-to-day demands. Large corporations that had parceled out legal work to many law firms, paying their hourly rates without much scrutiny, now work more closely with a few and at the same time have downsized their internal legal departments. They may negotiate fees on a per-case (rather than hourly) basis and take a more active role in deciding the services they actually need.[8]

Outsourcing is normally an arm's-length transaction (e.g., when a building owner contracts with the janitorial firm that offers the lowest price). In contrast, mutually cooperating firms seek joint advantages through risk sharing, greater flexibility or innovative capacity, or the ability to offer a more attractive package of services than possible separately. (For example, airlines now make rental car reservations for passengers; they may also coordinate their flight schedules with commuter airlines so that passengers can make connections easily.) We use the term "business network" to describe such relationships.[9]

In networked firms, employees in one firm may spend much of their time working with those in others. Better communication and coordination (for instance, between an insurance company and independent agents, or between organizations in a health care network) promise performance improvements based on both engineering and interpretive models. But other changes in business organization create obstacles to performance improvement. Looser ties between workers and firms, one consequence of outsourcing and more fluid organizational forms, reduce incentives for training. Shorter job tenures can limit experiential learning and effective mentoring. (They can also spread good ideas across firm boundaries.) Outsourcing, moreover, creates islands of unrationalized labor-intensive and tightly constrained work while dissolving the institutional and social forces that contain wage inequality. The cases in the next section illustrate the evolution of firm size, outsourcing, and network formation.

Business Organization in Service Industries

Health Care

Traditionally, health care in the United States was delivered by independent actors, each of which provided a separate bundle of services (Figure 3).[10] For many patients, the first point of contact with the health care system was the office of a general practitioner. Specialized practices and clinics dealt with pediatrics or ophthalmology. Hospitals, the largest organizations in the health care industry, provided a broad range of services including surgery, obstetrics, radiology, and emergency care. They also provided care for recovering patients. Nursing homes cared for those

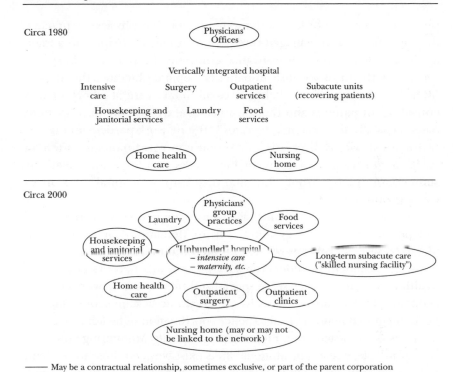

Figure 3. Network forms of business organization in health care

no longer able to live on their own. Insurance companies, Medicare, and Medicaid reimbursed providers on a fee-for-service or per diem basis.

With health care costs rising, payers began to push for cost containment. The major recent trends have been a gradual shift toward payment on a capitation basis (a fixed annual payment per patient) and the expansion of managed care (i.e., the coordination and control, by insurance companies or health maintenance organizations [HMOs], of consumption of health care services by patients). Cost pressures and overcapacity have led the highest-wage and most capital-intensive health care providers, the hospitals, to close some units while forming closer ties with physicians' practices, specialized clinics, and other service providers. The goal is to ensure a steady, predictable flow of patients, hence revenues, while reducing the combined costs of the package of services through better coordination.

Emerging health care networks take a variety of forms. A hospital may own or have a share in individual or group practices. A group of physicians may own or have a share in a hospital. A physicians' practice may operate its own managed-care plan or it may participate in a managed-care plan run by an insurance company. Increasingly, hospitals serve only the most seriously ill patients. Separate facilities that do not offer the full range of hospital services often take care of others, such as convalescent patients and those who can be treated on an outpatient basis. Typically, the "system integrator" (the network participant that coordinates service delivery) is a firm that controls financing, often an HMO or insurance company, or has access to a large and relatively stable patient base (from a hospital or group of hospitals or a physicians' group practice).

As more providers join in managed-care arrangements, the remaining independents must worry about future demand. Not all will join managed-care networks or be incorporated within hierarchical organizations. Independent providers can survive even in a network-dominated health care system if they serve specialized needs that networks cannot economically provide for themselves (an orthopedic clinic, for example).

If integrated networks lead to better coordination of health care across the units of the system, they might improve quality. Monitoring outcomes is, in principle, easier if institutional links exist between those who attend to patients, from an initial doctor's visit to a hospital procedure to subsequent care at home. Networks and large firms also have the potential to accelerate the introduction of computerized medical records. Once the bugs are worked out—which is likely to take decades rather than years—electronic records could improve the quality of care, for instance, by providing more reliable access to more complete medical histories.

Efforts to cut costs, however, may work against cooperation within and across sites in health care networks. Cost pressure creates a powerful inducement to lay off experienced hospital staff and hire younger, lower-wage workers for new outpatient clinics. Large wage differentials between workers across sites may also impede cooperation among hospitals, outpatient clinics, and home health agencies.

Banking

In the last chapter we introduced elements of the transformation of business organization in banking. In the 1970s each branch mimicked a vertically integrated firm. Since then, check processing and other back-office operations have been unbundled and reassigned to specialized processing operations, initially internal to each bank and increasingly contracted out to specialized firms (Figure 4). In the view of many bank

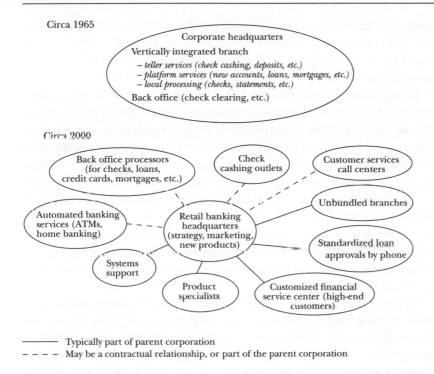

Figure 4. Network forms of business organization in retail banking

managers, back-office functions are "nonstrategic" operations and cost rather than profit centers.[11]

Today the customer contact functions of the traditional branch are rapidly being reorganized into separate self-service, routine customer service (delivered via call centers), and walk-in financial planning operations. So that they may offer more integrated packages of services, banks have begun seeking alliances with brokerage firms and even insurance companies. To differentiate their credit cards, many banks now offer affinity cards and tie-ins (e.g., with airlines) that give customers special deals on nonbank products.

Trucking

Outsourcing, just-in-time manufacturing, and the need for greater responsiveness throughout the economy are leading to new business relationships in the long-distance trucking industry.[12] After deregulation in the late 1970s, prices dropped and service options multiplied, as did the number of firms and owner-operators. At the same time, big firms grew still bigger; the market share of the four largest general freight carriers rose from 25 to 30 percent at the time of deregulation to recent levels around 50 percent.

Deregulation brought lower prices but uneven service. Many shippers found it difficult to work with scores of carriers and concluded that poor service offset the benefits of low prices. Many large shippers are reducing the number of trucking firms they hire to a more manageable group of "core carriers." On average, shippers used nearly fifty carriers in 1990; some analysts expect the number to be halved by 2000. "Common carriage," trucking services available to anyone at published rates (the norm before deregulation), may all but disappear. At the same time, many manufacturers that once owned their own trucks have outsourced the function. Long-term contracts between shippers and carriers are replacing in-house fleets as well as trucking services purchased on the spot market.

Shippers that seek closer relationships with their own customers negotiate arrangements with trucking companies to improve service. In addition to cost, trucking firms may compete on door-to-door delivery, damage rates, and responsiveness in settling claims. Because shippers also buy raw materials or intermediate goods, supply-chain integration may extend backward as well as forward. Just-in-time production makes trucking a critical link in the chain. Successful supply-chain integration can yield substantial cost savings where there are stable business relationships and complementary technologies.

With electronic data interchange, truckers can schedule equipment and drivers according to their customers' production schedules. Shippers will know where their goods are, and so will their customers. Global position satellite tracking and communications will put the trucking company (and, by extension, the shipper) in continuous contact with the driver. Less sophisticated firms are likely to find themselves at the margins of the industry, hauling for small producers, taking overflow and low-value goods.

Telecommunications

Before 1984 telecommunications in the United States functioned largely as a monopoly, subject to federal and state regulation.[13] The monopolist, AT&T, was the archetypal hierarchy. Standard operating procedures were handed down through functional divisions, with communication between divisions occurring only at middle or upper management levels.

The 1984 divestiture agreement reflected the belief that AT&T's "natural monopoly" in long-distance service had broken down. Decentralizing technologies such as microwave and satellite links, it was thought, meant that telecommunications services could become a competitive industry. Divestiture broke up the vertically integrated phone system in two ways. First, it deregulated long-distance, equipment manufacturing, and equipment installation markets. Second, AT&T lost its local Bell operating companies. In their place, seven regional companies provided local phone service. The AT&T divestiture, therefore, created a less vertically integrated industry in which competing equipment producers and equipment installers, monopoly local phone service providers, and competing long-distance providers operated in separate markets.

New services provided by new entrants have further fragmented the telecommunications market. Wireless services grew much faster than initially expected. Cable television companies and long distance companies may eventually sell local telephone services. Calls over the Internet provide a new kind of "bypass" of phone companies and phone charges. With continuing technological change and great uncertainty, waves of mergers, acquisitions, and alliances have swept through telecommunications and related industries, including home entertainment. (Some deals fall apart almost as soon as they are announced.) Unlike in health care, where networks have been a response to cost pressures, the ever-shifting alliances in telecommunications and related businesses represent a strategic response to uncertainty. Firms seek simultaneously to minimize risks and to position themselves in markets that sometimes grow at annual rates of 50 percent or more.

One of the consequences of restructuring will probably be continuing decline in the number of good jobs in the old, established telecommunications firms. Although these companies continue to pay relatively well, there is much less upward mobility than in the past. Before divestiture, management positions above the first level were filled exclusively from within.[14] Many of the old job ladders remain formally in place, but downsizing and restructuring mean that few people now climb them. Meanwhile new promotion policies allow external recruitment to fill "skill gaps."

Wages, benefits, and career paths will likely be under continuing pressure in the future, while new jobs of two types will be created in large numbers. There will be many and extraordinary opportunities for people who can help conceive, create, and market new products (e.g., Internet services). There will also be many low-wage, low-to-moderate-skill jobs to help implement these services. Examples of the latter include direct-selling, customer-service, and help-line work. (Telemarketers at new, nonunion firms earn $7 with no benefits.)[15]

Silicon Valley

Many people associate Silicon Valley, the high-technology region around San Jose, California, with computer hardware (Apple, Hewlett-Packard) and components (Intel). The area is also a center for computer-related services, home to Netscape, Intuit, and an ever-shifting population of small companies that develop specialized software and service products. The companies in the valley form highly fluid networks.[14] Some people work for a dozen employers in as many years. Venture capital firms and consultants help keep these networks vibrant.

Firms that specialize in software development, marketing, and finance cooperate with one another and with firms that specialize in hardware. Vertical integration is rare even among the larger companies. Sun Microsystems, for example, buys chips, disk drives, and other hardware components, taking advantage of the latest technologies. It focuses its own efforts on the design of work stations as high-performance system components. In recent years the company has moved heavily into operating systems and software tools, including the new Java programming language. Decentralized decision making, rather than hierarchy, has been common. During the 1980s Hewlett-Packard reorganized into semiautonomous divisions, each based on a particular product market segment. When a division grew too large, top management broke it up into smaller units. Since 1990 Sun has operated as five semiautonomous divisions that can compete with one another.

Silicon Valley companies battle fiercely. They compete for people, ideas, and funds as well as in product markets. At the same time, they cooperate in a variety of ways and at a variety of levels. Managers and engineers not only move among companies; they trade information in social settings (bars and restaurants, softball games, the supermarket). Engineers and computer specialists call their friends in competing firms when stumped by problems. (Engineers everywhere talk shop, but the free and easy environment of the valley encourages informal communication, in contrast with, say, the computer firms clustered around Boston.) Companies in Silicon Valley cross-license many patents, which helps keep entire industry segments on the technological frontier. Joint ventures and strategic alliances are common. Companies routinely share information with customers and suppliers. Information circulates through industry associations, trade shows, technical conferences, and, today, electronic mail. Many engineers' primary professional loyalties are to peers rather than employers. Some say that they "work for Silicon Valley," that their current employer is paying them for what they could and would be doing in any case. Companies try to hold on to employees by offering perks such as Friday beer blasts and on-site health clubs, not to mention lucrative stock options for the most valued workers, but people continue to circulate. Secrets are hard to keep, innovation flourishes, and some people get rich.[17] Engineers move into management. Venture capitalists (some of them former engineers) step in to help guide the fortunes of rapidly growing firms, sometimes putting their own people into managerial positions.

Three features of network structures in Silicon Valley stand out: firms simultaneously cooperate and compete; companies cannot expect to retain substantial numbers of long-term workers who might develop firm-specific skills; and the benefits of the system flow largely to high-skill autonomous workers. At least until they burn out or their knowledge becomes obsolete, managers and engineers can cope with job instability thanks to informal social networks. Indeed, they sometimes benefit; the failure or merger of an employer may be the impetus for founding a startup. Less skilled workers do not enjoy comparable opportunities.[18]

Implications for the Employment Relationship

In Chapter 2 we presented evidence that jobs and careers are tied to individual firms less frequently than in the past. The changes in business organization discussed in this chapter suggest that single-firm careers may become even more of a rarity in the future. Many workers now find themselves isolated in small, low-wage establishments such as check-processing operations, telephone call centers, the neighborhood Blockbuster video store, or a streamlined bank branch staffed by part-time workers. A growing number of those with better-paid positions find their prospects for internal advancement cut short by firm-level restructuring.

If a system of firm-specific jobs and internal labor markets has broken down, there may be no institutionalized way for displaced workers to find new jobs that use their skills. (Silicon Valley is unique; many efforts to replicate it in other settings have failed.) Even if they find a similar position in another firm, even within the same network, displaced workers lose accumulated job rights based on firm-specific seniority—rights to bid on opportunities for promotion, longer vacations, vesting of future pension contributions, and so on.

Networks create a continuing need for workers to move across firm boundaries, but in most cases no institutions exist to expedite mobility. For instance, a manager of a Minneapolis-St. Paul health care firm we interviewed noted that closer cooperation between hospitals and physicians' practices might entail "sharing" of nurses and other personnel, even if the two facilities functioned as separate firms. But she did not know whether or how this could be accomplished. Or consider the example of a community hospital in Watsonville, California, that operates its own home health care agency where nurses work part-time in the hospital and part-time in home health care. This arrangement benefits both the nurses and their patients. Nurses not only appreciate the variety; hospital work helps them keep abreast of new knowledge and practices. If the hospital and the home health agency were separate firms, even within a network, firm-specific jobs and internal labor markets might hamper this kind of mobility.[19]

Even where workers do not move across firm boundaries, cooperation may be desirable. Care might be improved, for example, if nurses employed in a hospital, a physicians' group practice, and a home health agency jointly planned treatment for patients. Such workers develop common expectations about compensation and working conditions, the more so if they work together over lengthy periods. Large differences in pay, benefits, and other job rights can harm cooperation, whereas comparable treatment could improve performance. Unless constrained by law, custom, or collective bargaining agreements covering multiple employers, the current system of firm-specific job rights provides no means for achieving comparability.

If firm-specific jobs and internal job ladders hinder interfirm mobility and cooperation, what could replace them as means of organizing work, pay and benefits, career mobility, and learning? Within business networks, if the relationships between firms are long-lived, jobs and career paths that are network-specific, rather than firm-specific, might be created. In other cases, network instability, widespread independent franchisees, and the isolation of many service workers in small establishments outside the boundary of any network mean that jobs and careers will have to be built within occupations, industries, and/or geographical areas. In the unionized construction industry, for example, training and job assignments are tied to particular occupations, such as carpentry, within a geographical region.

Implications for Economic Inequality

Although there is no consensus on the reasons for increasing wage inequality in the United States, changing business organization has played some role, in at least three different ways.[20] First, wage-based competition has contributed to outsourcing and network formation. In a less competitive environment, firms with sufficient market power can earn above-normal profits and share these profits with workers, including lower-wage workers. Collective bargaining is one means by which large firms in the past distributed some of their above-normal profits to lower-wage workers. Even in the absence of a union, internal rules and customs often constrained within-firm wage inequality. Increased product-market competition, particularly in recently deregulated industries such as telecommunications and airlines, has reduced these above-normal profits. To compensate, some firms have simply cut the wages of their workers.

Outsourcing and network formation also redistribute bargaining power from low-wage to high-wage workers—and from low-skill to high-skill workers. When both hold jobs in the same firm, the desire to limit within-firm inequality, motivate workers, and retain their cooperation may limit pay differences. High-wage workers may get less and low-wage workers more than if employed in separate firms. Networks and outsourcing segregate high- and low-wage workers, leading to greater inequality. A manager we interviewed at Core States Financial Corporation, a Philadelphia-based bank, noted that the bank's back-office check-processing employees did the same work as those in specialized processing companies but earned more because the culture of banks discouraged reductions in wages and benefits. Managers, he said, believed that "you need a nice office" and that "bank accoutrements" should be provided for all employees. But Core States, too, was succumbing to wage-based competition. The company has established a subsidiary for check-processing and other back-office work in a low-wage area of New Jersey. In the future, this manager predicted, Core States would directly employ only "highly professional" workers at the high wages and benefits that had earlier been customary.

Collective bargaining agreements have sometimes constrained wage inequality—but not always. The agreement between American Airlines and the Allied Pilots Association, for example, requires that association pilots fly all American's aircraft. American, however, has established four short-haul, regional airlines, the American Eagles. Under American Eagle contracts, pilots earn less, receive fewer benefits, and work more hours than the pilots who fly for American.[21]

Finally, networks can contribute to deunionization and thus to greater wage inequality.[22] U.S. labor law inhibits union organization and collective bargaining on any basis broader than the individual firm or establishment, so organizing the workers in a newly formed network may be difficult. In addition, because the per-worker cost of organizing is high in small establishments, union organizers tend to ignore them.[23] When a large firm restructures, workers who lose their jobs or move to a new subsidiary or affiliate may lose union representation or future opportunities to bargain collectively.

This pattern can be observed in several large service industries. In health care, where unionization has been most common in hospitals, union coverage is likely to decline, and intraindustry wage inequality increase, as workers migrate to other parts of networks. In telecommunications, AT&T and the regional operating companies, which have been downsizing, are more unionized than the newer long-distance providers, wireless firms, and other recent entrants. In 1996 the median hourly wage for cable TV and broadcasting workers (a mix including technical, sales, and clerical support staff) was $9, compared with $12.50 for workers in similar jobs in the old-line telephone industry (where 70 percent of workers belong to unions compared with 5 percent in cable TV and broadcasting).[24]

Implications for Economic Performance

Some recent changes in business organization promise to increase economic performance, others to decrease it. Larger firms and greater concentration may facilitate performance improvements through the engineering model, as illustrated by the tracking of package deliveries. In the design of new hotels, Interstate Properties, the chain mentioned in the preceding chapter, paid special attention to hard-to-clean areas such as room corners and baseboards (e.g., specifying rounded moldings). Standardization not only reduces design and construction costs; it facilitates engineering-based improvement in housekeeping, maintenance, and related services.

Business networks create potential for improved performance through collaboration across firm boundaries. In some cases, networks result in engineering improvements, as in the case of the standardization of ordering, billing, and payment procedures between a retailer and its major suppliers. In other cases, collaboration enhances the interpretive capabilities of one or both parties. With advice from a visiting nurse, for example, a home health worker may be able to tell whether a patient has suffered a relapse or is just having a bad day.

Networks sometimes lead to new products that combine complementary services into a single package. Health care networks integrate the services of insurers, physicians, hospitals, subacute and outpatient centers, home health care agencies, and nursing homes (or some subset of these) into a single "health care" service. In such cases, performance is enhanced if consumers find the new service package more valuable than the component services purchased separately.

Performance may decline if formerly integrated firms cut expenditures on training or research and development. With stable, long-term employment, firms could expect a return on investments in training and other forms of human resource development, whether the workers were clericals or R&D engineers and scientists. Oligopoly itself created incentives for R&D spending because, with limited competition, each firm knew it would reap much of the benefit of its investment.[25] Vertical disintegration and weaker ties between workers and firms reduce or eliminate one set of incentives to invest in people and technology, although they may create other incentives (e.g., entrepreneurial R&D strategies in place of the defensive approach of the old AT&T).

Outsourcing can give new life to the unrationalized labor-intensive work system, because it facilitates wage cutting to levels that make unrationalized labor-intensive jobs more attractive to employers than jobs in other work systems. Since the unrationalized system is characterized by poor quality and productivity, the result is often lower performance.

Business networks have the potential to improve productivity, increase service quality, and enhance flexibility. They make it easier for companies to adapt to changing technology and consumer preferences. But changes in business organization also contribute to greater economic inequality and, for many American workers, heightened job insecurity and reduced opportunities for advancement and career development. These negative effects, in turn, reduce incentives for workers to deliver high-quality service and therefore diminish the potential for improvement.

These drawbacks need not exist. They are the result of institutions rooted in the traditional view of employment within unitary firms. If the United States were to move away from a firm-based system of employment regulation and toward a system of employment rights and obligations based, as appropriate, in business networks, industries, occupations, or geographical areas, the nation could enjoy the benefits of networks at a lower social cost. In the next two chapters we show what such a system might look like and how it might be created.

7 Creating Multiemployer Institutions: Career Paths and Performance Improvement

Getting ahead wasn't supposed to be like this, was it? You thought you would start on the bottom rung of the old career ladder and climb. The implicit promise: Do what you're told, wait your turn, and with seniority, you will be tapped to rise. But millions of Americans who hoped to grasp the next rung—or even hold on to the one they've reached—have discovered that they are grabbing air.

Louis S. Richman, "How to Get Ahead in America," Fortune, *May 16, 1994*

For all their faults, hierarchical firms offered secure, predictable career paths for workers. They provided structures within which performance gains, of both the engineering and the interpretive type, could be realized. These gains laid the foundation for wage increases. In contrast, the developments in business strategy and organization described in the previous chapter have ambiguous implications for both performance and career paths. Vertical disintegration makes firms more nimble, but new forms of business organization do little to improve worker skill. Nor do they automatically foster cooperation or knowledge sharing among workers, within a firm or across firm boundaries. Outsourcing to low-wage firms, finally, discourages workers from acting in ways that would contribute to performance gains.

The story is similar for career paths. Economic restructuring creates new opportunities: Americans no longer need be "organization men" (and women) in order to climb career ladders. Yet business reorganization does not by itself create institutions that can help workers prepare for or find good jobs. Some workers, of course, can navigate the rapidly

changing employment scene on their own. But for others, the breakdown of the vertical firm means uncertainty and confusion.

The new patterns of business organization need to be supplemented
by institutions designed to promote worker cooperation and learning
across firm boundaries and to support careers that span multiple employers. Without such institutions, Americans will reap only a fraction of
the benefits potentially available from the economic dynamism of recent years. The United States has few such institutions today, in part because it had less need of them in the past. Even so, there are examples,
some current and some historical, that show the way. Although no
single case provides a model that can be copied everywhere in the
service economy, taken together they suggest the structures needed and
the policies that would foster those structures.

The Institutional Context

Multiemployer career paths top the list of needs. In the cases below in
which these career paths are well developed, associations of workers—
most commonly labor unions—administer systems of job mobility,
training, and skills standards. Sometimes employer associations share in
these responsibilities. But individual employers acting alone will not
make investments whose benefits they cannot capture. Only if firms can
be sure that others will reciprocate do they have reason to help workers
acquire anything other than firm-specific skills.

Some countries require firms to join employer associations, making it
easier for firms to reach agreements to share the costs of general training.
In the United States, where membership in trade and industry associations
is voluntary, "free-rider" problems are common. In construction, for instance, free-riding nonunion contractors hire workers trained through apprenticeship programs jointly supported by unions and associations of
unionized employers. The nonunion contractors avoid the costs of
training while gaining the benefits of access to skilled workers (see below).

American firms typically join business groups in order to influence
the groups' positions on lobbying issues. Associations rarely include all
major firms in an industry or locality, since firms do not all have interests in common. Even if they did, members might have trouble agreeing
on any except lowest-common-denominator actions. The construction
example below illustrates that nonunion training programs developed
by employers without worker representation may be too narrow to meet

the long-term needs of either employers or workers. Nor can government take the place of worker associations. Government agencies lack an insider's view of skill requirements, work practices, and the mobility patterns and career objectives of workers in an occupation, industry, or business network. (This is one reason government training and job-matching programs rarely function well, especially beyond entry-level positions.) Schools—whether public or private, "academic" or vocational—and employment agencies likewise lack inside knowledge.

Worker associations, then, are indispensable for creating institutions that can promote multiemployer careers and knowledge sharing. Of course, this does not mean that other actors are irrelevant. Government can encourage these activities and help fund them. Schools and employment agencies can provide essential services. Employer associations can represent the interests of firms. But it would be difficult to see how any of these groups could take the place of worker associations.

Multiemployer institutions address two basic types of problems. The first is mobility from "bad" jobs to good. This problem is most acute for workers in unrationalized labor-intensive and tightly constrained jobs. Even if wages at the bottom of the earnings distribution go up as a result of collective bargaining and direct policy intervention—as we advocate in Chapter 8—some jobs will still pay poorly. The people who hold these jobs need access to career paths that will help them move into better positions so that "bad" jobs can, for those workers who so desire, became the bottom steps on a staircase rather than dead ends. The second problem, employment insecurity, mainly affects those in the semiautonomous and high-skill autonomous work systems. Employers as well as employees stand to benefit from making it easier for workers to share know-how and change jobs within an occupation, industry, or business network.

Linking Bad Jobs to Good: Mobility between Work Systems

Most of the classic dead-end jobs can be found in the unrationalized labor-intensive and tightly constrained work systems. The people who hold these jobs cannot improve their lot much by holding onto them, and they may have trouble moving into substantially better positions.[1] Even when a worker demonstrates reliability and good interpersonal skills in a McDonald's, other potential employers may never know about it. Particularly in employment-starved areas, young workers often remain indefinitely in jobs paying close to the minimum wage. In the Wonder Years young, less-educated white males often found good jobs through friends, relatives, and community contacts.[2] Informal social networks less often give young workers access to better-paying positions today. There are fewer high-wage manufacturing jobs. Employment is stagnant or shrinking in big-city employers such as government, hospitals, and utilities, in which earlier generations of African Americans often found good jobs. Moreover, good service sector jobs now often require post–high school education.

From Fast-Food Jobs to Better Opportunities

McDonald's outlets in Harlem average fourteen applications for each opening and tend to hire workers who are already in their twenties.[3] Several foundations have explored the possibility of creating career pathways from fast-food jobs to better-paying employers. Such connections would benefit both workers and employers. If workers performed acceptably in a fast-food job, they would be able to move into a better position. Fast-food employers could expect to attract better applicants and avoid rapid turnover among uncommitted workers. Employers with good jobs available could hire workers who had demonstrated their reliability and willingness to learn. These firms would benefit from lower screening costs and turnover.

Stuart Ray, owner of forty Burger King restaurants in western Michigan, has linked his outlets with local manufacturing firms.[4] By holding out the promise of eventual movement into better jobs, Ray has sought to attract better workers and reduce turnover. Ray is unusual as a fast-food employer. Even before he began this job-linking program, his Burger Kings had annual labor turnover in the 90–100 percent range, less than half the levels common in the industry. This suggests human resources practices substantially superior to the norm. Ray is unusual, too, in not worrying about losing his best workers but instead perceiving a chance to reduce average turnover.

Community Career Ladders in Wisconsin

In Madison, Wisconsin, and surrounding Dane County a committee of leaders from business, labor, government, and nonprofit groups sponsored a feasibility study of "community career ladders" that would provide employers with better-qualified workers and offer workers training, support services, and a progression of job opportunities.[5] A local newspaper editor launched the initiative, proposing to hire workers with job experience in fast foods into shipping and receiving jobs at his paper.

After the feasibility study, union-employer consortia formed in three major area industries: health care, insurance, and manufacturing. In each of these industries, restructuring and technological change had raised skill requirements, and qualified workers were sometimes in short supply. The health care consortium is considering a training curriculum for entry-level occupations and an upward mobility program for low-wage workers. In order to address a shortage of computer specialists, the consortium in insurance plans a pilot information systems training program for both entry-level workers and experienced clerical employees wishing to upgrade.

Cape Cod Hospital Career Ladders

The specialized training and credentials needed for better jobs in hospitals limit upward mobility for housekeepers, food service workers, and many clericals. Since the 1980s Cape Cod Hospital (CCH), in Hyannis, Massachusetts, has provided education and training to help such workers qualify for vacant positions.[6] The CCH Career Ladders program includes on-the-job training, mini-apprenticeships called "traineeships," and both in-house and external coursework. So far, most of the internal promotions have been from entry level to clerical positions and lower-level technical positions such as electrocardiogram technician. Only recently have a few participants broken through to technical and nursing positions that require two years or more of specialized training.

A joint committee of three hospital managers and three officials of the local union runs Career Ladders. When a position opens, the committee first considers the most senior applicant. If that person is not qualified, the committee turns to the next most senior, and so on. Deliberately avoiding the creation of an expensive training bureaucracy, Career Ladders has focused on practical measures for minimizing the obstacles to advancement that lower-level employees face. Some workers, for example, could not afford to accept a part-time opening at a higher level because their take-home pay would go down until they could convert to a full-time position. To open up such opportunities, the CCH contract gives upgraders the right to work two part-time positions, for example, sixteen hours in a part-time phlebotomist opening and twenty-four hours as a housekeeper. Providing upgraders with up-front tuition for courses eliminated another obstacle. Even though fees were modest, up-front tuition led to a doubling of enrollment in courses. (Workers who fail to complete a course must pay for it.)

Related practices at CCH include:

- Training that is closely job-related and avoids classroom settings, based on the principle that it is easier to learn when you know how you will use the knowledge.
- Job shadowing, so that people can see if they really want a particular position.
- Trial periods that give workers an opportunity to demonstrate their qualifications. (Management retains the option of sending people back to their old jobs, but that rarely happens.)
- "Reasonable" entry requirements, with selection criteria relevant to on-the-job performance.

Defining job requirements has proved to be the most time-consuming aspect of the committee's work. Upper-level managers generally prefer modest qualifications to reduce the costs of upgrade training. Union officials usually concur, because this improves access for workers lower down the job ladder. Line supervisors, supported by their workers, often press for tough qualifications to safeguard status (and in some cases to ensure that incumbents can continue passing jobs on to relatives and friends).

Although the CCH program involves only one employer, it could be adapted to a multiemployer setting. Health care employers and unions in a locality would have to agree to make job definitions and skill requirements comparable across facilities. Seniority rules would have to accommodate workers who upgrade by changing employers. Employers and unions would have to agree to share training costs. The steering committee would have to include members from each participating employer or else provide for representation through an employer association. Such changes would not necessarily be easy, but these are the kinds of problems multiemployer union-management consultation arrangements and multiemployer collective bargaining are equipped to solve.

Building Career Paths

The examples above illustrate two different ways of coupling bad jobs to better ones. The Dane County and Cape Cod programs construct vertical ladders with contextually similar but progressively higher levels of skill. The fast-food experiments operate on the premise that it can be enough to demonstrate reliability and perhaps some generic competencies in an entry-level position. These two approaches are, in principle, capable of creating staircases to a large group of only loosely related job opportunities. The skill-commonality approach, which economizes on training costs but can link a bad job only to a limited set of good jobs, would constrain worker opportunities more, at least in some local or regional labor markets. The generic-competency approach entails higher training costs but is less dependent on local concentrations of employment in particular industries or occupations.

Both approaches can link unrationalized labor intensive or tightly constrained jobs with semiautonomous and, ultimately, some high-skill autonomous jobs. Check proofers, for example, might gain access to semiautonomous clerical jobs through the generic-competency approach. In this case, because the links would reach into jobs in many occupations and industries, the best form of worker association might be a local central labor council, a regional body that includes representatives of various local unions.[7]

Nurses' aide, licensed practical nurse, and registered nurse occupations might be linked through the skill-commonality approach since all work in similar patient-care settings. A multiemployer career path from aide to licensed practical nurse to registered nurse is a genuine possibility where unions or associations of workers exist (or can be organized). The career path could be developed by a labor-management council that included representatives of each worker association together with local health care employers. (British Columbia's Healthcare Labour Adjustment Agency, described below, illustrates the type of structure that could manage occupational upgrading.) The labor-management council could work with local educational institutions (e.g., community colleges) to develop curricula and seek financial support from state and local governments.

Child care workers and elementary schoolteachers likewise share overlapping skill sets. Child care workers who formed associations and worked with teachers' unions and associations of school boards, teachers' colleges, and state departments of education could develop career paths, perhaps to teacher's aide and then to teacher.

Multiemployer Institutions above the Entry Level

Like those seeking to move from low-paid jobs to better ones, workers above the entry level need institutions that provide multiemployer career paths. New institutions are also needed to promote economies of depth and coordination by making it easier for workers to share learning across firm boundaries.

Some observers believe career paths above entry levels are becoming individualized and unpatterned, characterized by frequent changes not only of employer but of occupation and industry. If this were the case, the prospects for creating multiemployer career paths and channels of worker communication would be poor. In fact, there is little evidence that careers are becoming highly disordered. When workers change employers, they often remain within the same occupation or industry. The share of workers who spent eight or more years in one occupation during the decade remained the same (68 percent) in the 1980s as in the 1970s. The share of workers who spent at least eight years in a given industry changed from 63 percent in the 1970s to 59 percent in the 1980s. In contrast, the share of workers who spent eight or more years with one firm declined from 67 percent to 52 percent.[8]

The continuing strength of worker attachments to occupation and industry throughout much of the services leaves us optimistic about prospects for expanding multiemployer career paths beyond the traditional professions and skilled crafts in which they have long existed. There are, to be sure, important differences between the latter jobs and many service jobs in which workers could benefit from multiemployer institutions. Professional and craft workers enjoy widely accepted occupational credentials. Their experience is recognized and portable. By contrast, employers may not accept or value the experience of workers (including many technicians) who lack formal credentials. And only the current employers of many semiautonomous workers are likely to acknowledge the worth of their experience-based know-how. Workers in unrationalized labor-intensive and tightly constrained service jobs are worst off; in the eyes of employers, there is little to distinguish them from someone who walks in off the street. Moreover, professional and craft workers have a strong occupational consciousness that smooths the way for communication and learning even among strangers. (Occupational consciousness is both cause and consequence of strong professional associations and craft unions.) In many other service jobs, worker identification with occupation, industry, or business network is weaker.[9] This makes it harder to create worker associations based on occupation, industry, or network. Union representation in the services is relatively high in bureaucratic services (education, transportation, communications, utilities, government, and hospitals) but under 11 percent elsewhere in the services (Table A-3). Nevertheless, several of the cases below illustrate multiemployer career paths and worker communication channels outside the traditional professions and skilled crafts.

Construction

Production processes in construction resemble those in the services more than those in much of manufacturing. Each construction project differs. The industry remains dominated by small firms that operate in highly competitive and unstable markets.[10] These firms need workers, including some with high-level skills, but they must also be able to lay them off when the project is finished. Specific skills attach to specific occupations (such as carpenter or electrician) and transfer easily from job to job. Because workers move around, firms have little motivation to train them.

Construction trade unions, organized by occupation, have helped solve the skill and labor allocation problems in this industry. Collective bargaining between a local occupational union and an association of employers creates institutions that train workers (contributing to economies of depth) and helps them pursue multiemployer career paths. Joint union-employer boards administer apprenticeships financed by contributions from the wage and benefit package negotiated with all unionized contractors in a locality.[11] Union-operated hiring halls refer workers to jobs. Employers agree to fill job vacancies from the hiring hall before looking elsewhere. Joint union-employer pension and health plans cover all union members who work in a locality; reciprocity across union locals moves pension contributions back to the primary location when a member works elsewhere temporarily. Portable benefit plans, along with hiring halls, facilitate mobility.

These multiemployer institutions have long existed for high-skill autonomous construction crafts. Of greater relevance as a model for lower-wage services, many of the same structures also serve construction laborers.[12] Moreover, the Laborers International Union of North America (LIUNA) and associations of unionized employers have recently begun to transform laboring work into a higher-skilled occupation. Employers and skilled construction workers traditionally perceived laboring as classic unrationalized labor-intensive work. Laborers were "hod carriers." They carried, pushed, dug, dragged, and cleaned up. In contrast to the established crafts, there were, until recently, no apprenticeship or certification programs. That began to change in the early 1980s, when LIUNA and the Associated General Contractors (AGC) developed a series of modular training courses.

Safety provided the initial impetus: laborers hired to remove as-
bestos from buildings had to know how to protect their own health and
that of the people who would be living and working in the buildings.
Local affiliates of LIUNA and AGC then began to offer related types of
training, including lead paint abatement, hazardous waste handling,
and OSHA rules. The menu later expanded to include operating fork-
lifts and other equipment, pouring concrete, and mason tending.
LIUNA was partly responding to technological changes that it perceived
as a threat to "hod carrying" work. Contractors supported training because they were having trouble finding capable workers during the
1980s construction boom. By the early 1990s apprenticeship programs
were initiated. These may serve to elevate further the status and skill of
journeyperson laborers as well as create stepping-stones for laborers
into the established crafts. By 1997, LIUNA delivered training to fifty
thousand of its half million members in construction, twice as many as
received training as recently as 1988.[13]

LIUNA operates "referral services" that allocate jobs in the order in
which members sign up. (A worker does not lose her place on the list if
she takes a job that lasts less than some minimum period.) Employers
can ask for laborers with training or experience in particular skills. Laborers, like members of other construction unions, typically need to
work only about one thousand hours to receive a year's pension credit.
Working forty to one hundred sixty hours in a quarter suffices to maintain family health care benefits. Workers can also bank credits toward
future health and pension benefits when they put in large numbers of
hours in good times.

In the construction industry as a whole, the decline of unionization
in the past two decades has brought back problems that apprenticeship
was designed to solve. Far fewer workers now get apprenticeship
training. Open-shop employers (those not covered by collective bargaining agreements) once were able to count on hiring workers with
good skills, but today they often cannot. A few large nonunion companies have been able to afford their own training, holding on to employees by offering superior wages and benefits. In some localities, AGC
chapters operate apprenticeship programs in which open-shop employers participate. (AGC includes both union and open-shop chapters.) These programs have rarely been as successful as their union
counterparts. Some nonunion employer-run programs concentrate on
meeting immediate needs through on-the-job training, sacrificing the

breadth of traditional apprenticeship with its mix of classroom instruction and on-the-job mentoring. And unions in the 1990s still accounted for 85 percent of graduations from apprenticeship, even though union coverage had shrunk to less than 25 percent.[14]

The inability of nonunion construction firms to develop sustainable training programs suggests the importance of worker organizations in creating successful multiemployer institutions. Productivity statistics for the construction industry also show the devastating impact of the decline of training coupled with wage and benefit declines that led experienced workers to leave the industry. From the late 1940s to the mid-1960s, productivity growth in construction actually exceeded that in manufacturing. But since 1965 productivity in construction has dropped back to the levels of the late 1940s.[15] In addition to the loss of economies of depth since the 1960s, fewer owners now come up through the ranks. The increasing social distance between workers and managers, architects, and engineers may have corroded economies of coordination, which are critical on major construction projects that may involve dozens of subcontractors and occupations. In sum, the self-regulation of the high-skill autonomous work system appears to have been partially supplanted by unrationalized labor-intensive work (with a few larger firms moving toward semiautonomous jobs).

Movies and Television

Since the decline of vertically integrated Hollywood studios in the 1950s, motion picture and television production has been characterized by shifting alliances of firms and workers (most of them high-skill autonomous workers) brought together on a temporary basis.[16] Actors, writers, camera operators, lighting technicians, and set designers rarely have long-term jobs with an employer. Many intersperse work in the entertainment industry with other jobs. Unions, organized by occupation or groups of related occupations, create the principal tie between workers and employers. The major unions include the Screen Actors' Guild, the Writers' Guild of America, the Directors' Guild of America, and the International Association of Theatrical and Stage Employees, which represents technical and craft workers.

These unions bargain with the Alliance of Motion Picture and Television Producers, an employer association that represents large studios and many independent producers. Union contracts include a roster system under which each union refers its members to jobs in order of seniority.

The unions also organize auditions, operate training programs for craft workers, and, jointly with employers, administer multiemployer health insurance and pension plans. Workers who move between occupations—playing a bit role in one movie and helping with props on another—may belong to more than one union. Union contracts provide workers with residuals (fees for the reuse of movies, television programs, and commercials on which they worked in the past). Residuals serve as a kind of supplementary unemployment benefit for those who cannot currently find a job in their specialty. They enable workers to take extended, lower-paid temporary employment in another industry (e.g., as a waiter or waitress) and then come back to entertainment when they get the opportunity.

Waitresses

Like the male-dominated laborer occupation, the historical example of female-dominated waitress unions offers lessons for a broad cross-section of unrationalized labor-intensive service occupations. Beginning in the early twentieth century waitresses established their own locals, separate from waiters, within the Hotel and Restaurant Employees Union.[17] These locals operated much like those in construction. They bargained collectively with local restaurant associations, established hiring halls, and required employers to hire only union members or to give preference to workers referred through the hiring hall. They also established health and welfare funds. Like their counterparts in construction, waitress unions generally did not seek to restrict layoffs. Instead of protecting the right to a particular job with a particular employer, they aimed to provide members with employment security within the occupation. Laid-off workers simply went to the hiring hall for another job. When business was bad, unions allocated the available work among all members.

Waitress unions also promoted economies of depth. Although they rarely operated formal apprenticeship programs, they provided training designed to define and diffuse occupational "best practices" (for example, keeping straight the orders for a large party). Experienced waitresses mentored newcomers, helping them learn to deal with rude customers or turn aside unwanted advances. Because the formal knowledge base is modest, the informal worker-to-worker transfer of contextual knowledge was probably the chief means by which waitresses achieved economies of depth.

Hotel Workers

The multiemployer San Francisco Hotels Partnership Project seeks performance improvement within unrationalized labor-intensive and semiautonomous occupations.[18] Started in 1993 and formalized in a collective bargaining agreement the next year, the Partnership includes twelve San Francisco hotels and union locals, affiliates of the Hotel and Restaurant Employees and the Service Employees. A joint union-management steering committee has charge of funds from employer contributions and state training agencies.

The Partnership is organized around problem-solving teams with members drawn two-thirds from labor and one-third from management, plus a neutral facilitator. Some teams are multiemployer, others single-employer. Multiemployer teams deal with common issues such as the design of training materials. Each hotel has one or more teams that address site-specific issues such as safety and work on common issues identified by the steering committee.

Some team activities have been directed mainly at engineering-type performance gains. (For example, a group of doormen at one hotel changed the way they handled baggage for large tour groups.) Using survey and focus group results, a multiemployer team rewrote guidelines for training curricula and suggested "best practice" training methods, including peer mentoring. The new training programs systematize the kind of person-to-person communication that the interpretive model requires. Even for housekeepers, the Partnership facilitator believes that workers' ability to interpret and respond to customer needs—for example, to direct a frantic businessman to a copying machine—can help attract conventions to San Francisco.

Wisconsin Regional Training Partnership

The Wisconsin Regional Training Partnership (WRTP) was founded in 1992. It includes more than forty mostly unionized manufacturing firms that employ about sixty thousand workers in the Milwaukee area, many in semiautonomous jobs and a smaller number in tightly constrained and high-skill autonomous ones.[19] The partnership also includes several industrial unions. Although WRTP does not have service sector members today, its experience is instructive because it is the largest new U.S. regional organization of its kind and because it plans to expand to service industries in the future. Governed by an executive council of business, labor, and government leaders, WRTP operates through worksite-specific labor-management committees and multiemployer labor-management working groups.

As in the San Francisco Hotels Partnership, a major focus is training and performance improvement. Member firms have sought to raise their investment in training production workers and to structure their hiring and promotion criteria around newly defined skill standards.

WRTP skill standards build on training modules in basic skills (e.g., reading, simple arithmetic), process or problem-solving skills (e.g., working in teams), and job-related technical skills (e.g., welding sheet metal). Basic and process skills (and credentials) are common to all member firms. Most of the technical skills are relevant to more than one firm.

WRTP provides employment-linked training for dislocated and disadvantaged workers enrolled at local technical schools. It offers youth apprenticeships for high school students. Because of its origins in manufacturing, some WRTP skill standards and training draw partly on the engineering model. But process and technical skills also have substantial interpretive components. Training takes place within firm-level and multiemployer skills centers, with heavy reliance on peer mentoring. The Partnership distills and diffuses the lessons of successful (and not so successful) experiences in the various skills centers.

The British Columbia Health Care Labor Adjustment System

In British Columbia as in the United States cost pressures have led to reductions in hospitalization and the elimination of some hospital jobs.[20] With restructuring beginning, British Columbia announced plans to insulate hospital workers from large wage cuts and the threat of unemployment. The provincial government brokered a "health accord" between the Health Employers' Association of British Columbia and three hospital unions representing nurses, technicians, and other nonmanagement workers. Under this agreement hospital workers whose jobs disappear can expect to be placed elsewhere in the public or publicly funded nonprofit sector, usually in health care. Before the accord, job rights for most workers were hospital-based, even though collective bargaining took place on a multiemployer basis. Contract provisions governed changes in duties, layoffs, and outsourcing. Pay increases, promotions, paid vacations, and layoffs depended on hospital-specific seniority.

The accord established a government-funded Healthcare Labour Adjustment Agency under a board of directors composed of union and management representatives and a neutral chair. Its major duties include:

- *Administering a "priority job placement program" for displaced hospital workers.* All health care facilities in the province must list their job openings with the agency. In the absence of internal candidates, displaced hospital workers receive priority over outsiders. Any hospital that plans to lay off a worker must retain that worker on its payroll for up to a year or until he or she can be placed. The worker must ordinarily accept any job assigned by the agency, with limits on pay cuts and commuting distance. An employer must accept an assigned worker unless it can convince the agency that the worker is unqualified. Displaced workers carry their previously accumulated seniority with them to a new job.

- *Administering a voluntary transfer and relocation program.* A hospital worker who wishes to transfer to another health care facility may register with the agency and receive a job referral through the agency's placement system.
- *Administering retraining for displaced workers.* The agency funds retraining proposals submitted by joint labor-management committees at each health care facility. (Workers who move into a new job in the same occupation may nonetheless need training—e.g., nurses leaving a hospital for home health care or general-duty nurses moving to a specialized ward.)

Although the British Columbia system was originally developed as a temporary means of helping displaced workers, it could easily become a vehicle for supporting multiemployer career paths for all workers, not just those laid off. Such a system not only has the potential to create lateral mobility within occupations but could make it possible for workers to move from unrationalized labor-intensive jobs (such as housekeeper) to semiautonomous or high-skill autonomous jobs (such as licensed practical nurse).

Prospects for New Multiemployer Institutions

The cases above describe multiemployer institutions now in operation. There are other jobs for which such institutions could be useful. We examine three at some length: high-skill autonomous technicians, semiautonomous clerical workers, and unrationalized labor-intensive nurses' aides. We also discuss several others in more abbreviated fashion.

Technicians

As in blue-collar crafts, occupational communities and worksite-based groups are critical repositories of know-how in a wide variety of specialized technical jobs, ranging from emergency medical technicians to air traffic controllers. Ethnographic studies show that technical workers often downplay the importance of formal training compared with experience.[21] In a few cases, such as radiological and other laboratory technicians, occupational communities are well developed. But often these communities are informal and localized, sometimes bound together by little more than weak social ties (e.g., among copier repair technicians). Word-of-mouth may help technicians find new jobs, but the process is haphazard.

Many technicians work in hierarchically structured organizations that offer few opportunities for advancement without leaving the occupation. Skills may be invisible to those outside the occupational community. Low status and modest pay hamper recruitment, training, and retention. Employers rarely address these problems unless poor performance or high turnover forces the issue. A single firm, moreover, might not be able to provide the diversity of competencies and contexts necessary for training well-rounded technicians. Even in a big company, managers may skimp on training for fear of losing technicians to another division.

Technical occupations, then, seem ripe for multiemployer career paths and worker communication channels rooted in occupational associations. Indeed, such associations have begun to form. The Society for Technical Communications, initially established in 1960, has more than twenty thousand members, most of them technical writers, editors, or illustrators. The society provides members with information on job openings and promotes economies of depth by publishing handbooks and manuals. (Typical publications bear titles such as *Guidelines for Beginning Technical Editors* and *Guide to Preparing Software User Documentation.*) The System Administrators' Guild, established in 1992, likewise provides a medium for computer specialists to share technical problems and solutions.[22] In another example, the long-established Society of Automotive Engineers has created an affiliate for mechanics called the Service Technicians Society (mentioned in Chapter 5). The impetus has come largely because new skills are needed to cope with the sophisticated electronics in new cars. These systems require a family of diagnostic techniques that are quite different from those for traditional vehicle systems and unfamiliar even to highly experienced mechanics.

Clerical and Administrative Support Workers

After growing by 21 percent from 1979 to 1989, clerical employment in the United States declined slightly from 1989 to 1996. Secretarial jobs grew by about 5 percent between 1979 and 1989 but fell by 20 percent from 1989 to 1996.[23] Clerical employees who once could count on single-firm careers and perhaps opportunities to advance through internal job ladders may now find themselves contingent workers.[24] At the same time, technological change and organizational restructuring have raised the status and sometimes the wages of office workers with demonstrated expertise in using computers and software, from basic word processing, spreadsheet, and database packages to more specialized desktop publishing, accounting, and financial planning programs. Moreover, "delayered" hierarchies open new opportunities for those with administrative skills.[25]

The clerical workers most hurt by automation and corporate restructuring include those whose know-how was specific to a firm, establishment, department, or work group. Much of the knowledge required to navigate computer systems, for example, remains nontransferable. A customer service representative we interviewed at Mount Rushmore Mutual (an insurance company discussed in earlier chapters) said it had taken her nearly two years to get up to speed on the eighty-three customized software packages used in the head office, although she already had worked with company products and software in field offices. Even when semiautonomous clerical workers have transferable knowledge, they may have no way of demonstrating it to a new employer.

The labor market for temporary clerical workers mirrors developments in office occupations as a whole. People with the competence and confidence to take initiative immediately (e.g., drafting letters, organizing meetings, making travel arrangements) may benefit from temporary employment. They can "screen the employer," as one put it. Temporary assignments may also allow workers to balance work and family life or pursue assignments that keep them technologically up-to-date. But many clerical temporaries scramble to get enough work and must keep up their computer skills on their own time.

Temporary help firms have computer-based learning programs that allow people to practice on new releases of word processing or spreadsheet packages.[26] But despite efforts by Manpower to change the public image of "staffing firms," John Milkint, president of Flexiforce, a temporary agency based in Milwaukee, says: "As an industry ... we are only a facilitator. Regardless of what anybody else tells you about training, we can let someone brush up on their keyboarding skills, we can give them a word processing package to practice, we can let them come into our office ... but to take someone with no skills and give them skills, no one in this industry does that no matter what they might say."[27]

Despite the rising importance of computer skills, our interviews suggest that many female office workers continue to place high value on variety in their jobs and think of their primary strengths as interpersonal. They may be less inclined than men to favor the creation of new and specialized suboccupations or to focus narrowly on their technical skills. For example, rather than monopolizing responsibility for local area network (LAN) operations to gain bargaining power, some women who oversee office computer networks regard this as simply a part of their long-standing mission to keep the office running smoothly. Assessing the interpersonal, interpretive skills of "office management"—as opposed to certifying that someone has taken a course in "teamwork" (or LAN management)—may be difficult. But the problem is hardly unique. Employers are already used to evaluating managers and professionals on hard-to-measure nontechnical skills, and many should welcome institutions that help raise skill levels for clerical and administrative workers.

Employer and office worker representatives, for example, could cooperate to plan training and certification programs with portable credentials and organized career paths.[28] As off-the-shelf software replaces customized programs and more firms replace proprietary networks with "intranets," computer skills will become more generic and thus transferable. Young people might earn entry-level credentials through "school-to-career" programs; community colleges could help upgrade the skills of experienced workers. New entrants to the occupation could shore up basic skills through short training modules before going on to more specialized courses as at the Wisconsin Regional Training Partnership. Some of this training can be delivered over the Internet, but worker and employer representatives could also establish community-based centers that would give clerical workers a place to meet face-to-face and learn from one another. Job-listing services might eventually evolve into hiring halls if multiemployer career paths became better ordered and if community-based centers contracted with employers to supply experienced and credentialed workers. Worker associations and employers could cooperate to create explicit linkages, based on training and skill certification, between routine clerical or administrative work and jobs requiring higher levels of competency and responsibility. Just as experience with graphics software prepares workers to move into desktop publishing or even graphic design, billing and bookkeeping clerks could, with training, move into accounting. Apprenticeships could also help clerical and administrative workers make the leap into higher-level occupations. These might, as in construction, be funded through a combination of lower wages during training and contributions set through labor-management negotiation.

Nurses' Aides

Many new jobs for nurses' aides in long-term care will open as the baby boom generation grows older. In the past, as we saw in Chapter 3, the work of aides in nursing homes, home health agencies, and other long-term care settings was organized either as low-wage, high-turnover, unrationalized labor-intensive work or as semiautonomous work characterized by stronger ties among employees, employers, and those they serve. At present, the unrationalized labor-intensive approach predominates. Workers and those they care for suffer the consequences.

Unions represent 13 percent of nursing home employees and a smaller fraction of those in long-term care overall.[29] Often, union formation represents a response to low-quality practices: low wages and benefits and unrealistic work standards generate collective anger that leads to support for a labor organization. As with old-style industrial unionism, adversarial labor-management relations may still leave workers excluded from efforts (should there be any) to improve quality in nursing homes. On the other hand, unions, once in place, tend to stabilize the workforce by raising wages and benefits. This improves quality by maintaining workers' relationships with residents.

Multiemployer, occupationwide associations of aides could help spread high-quality practices and discourage low-wage, high-turnover practices. (The same argument holds for associations of child care workers.) They could also contribute to training and mentoring programs, as at Cooperative Home Care Associates (Chapter 5). And they could expand upward mobility through career ladders that spanned worksites, so that experience as an aide could lead to other opportunities in health care (as at Cape Cod Hospital) or social service. Aides who did not see themselves as trapped might be better able to sustain the energy and patience necessary to deliver quality long-term care.

As care proliferates outside nursing homes (in assisted living settings and home health care), moreover, occupational associations that elevate the status, competency, and commitment of caregivers may be the only way to safeguard basic standards of care. In such dispersed settings, state regulations and inspections, never very effective even in nursing homes, will be even less able to enforce even minimum levels of decency.

Of course, employers who cannot imagine how to profit except by sweating workers in unrationalized labor-intensive jobs will resist the emergence of occupational associations. Administrators and directors of nursing who view unions as protectors of bad workers and unconcerned with quality will also be doubtful. Even workers at good homes will not automatically see occupational associations as in their interest if their own experience identifies unionism with poorly managed, lower-quality homes. Moreover, building an occupational association from the limited base in individual unionized homes would require cooperation across the smorgasbord of unions with bargaining rights today.[30] As in other service industries, labor organizations, supported by changes in public policy, will have to reinvent themselves to play a significant role in improving performance and job quality in long-term care.

Managers, Sales Associates, and Teachers

Like tributaries into a river, developments in other major occupations flow in the same direction as the three examples above. Public policy should seize on this similarity and push the shift toward multiemployer careers and interpretive model performance improvement throughout the services.

Managers. In the wake of extensive downsizing, Charles Heckscher interviewed middle managers—the archetypical company "men" (and occasionally women)—in nine large manufacturing firms. Despite widespread bitterness, some managers were beginning to embrace a "professional" orientation that redefines the reciprocal obligations of employee and employer.[31] These managers accepted, in principle, that the company's commitment to them depends on its marketplace success. In place of the "feudal community" of the old hierarchy, they shared a "community of purpose" with those with whom they worked. Their loyalty was increasingly to the particular project in which they were engaged rather than to the company.

To help managers cope in a world of more transient attachments, Heckscher advocates new supporting institutions: more investment by companies in keeping managers' portable skills current, job-matching institutions, occupational associations that can represent managers' interests with employers, tax changes to encourage saving for periods between "projects," and private income insurance. Even so, given their privileged position in the old bureaucracies, middle managers, for the most part, may well suffer a decline in wages and status.

Professional Sales Associates. As we saw in Chapter 4, the retail industry has, since the 1960s, relied less on the semiautonomous work system, with high turnover one result. Since 1993 the National Retail Federation (NRF), an industry association, has led an effort to develop new, portable credentials, or "skill standards," for the industry's customer-contact workers.[32] The president of NRF has expressed the hope that the new "Professional Sales Associate" credential could address the industry's reputation for "employee turnover, less than adequate customer service and low employee productivity."[33] The initial standards require associates to demonstrate understanding of "duties and tasks" specific to retail (e.g., monitoring inventory, providing personalized customer service), to improve "foundation skills" (e.g., reading comprehension and teamwork), and to develop their "personal qualities" (e.g., a positive demeanor and good ethics).[34] In King of Prussia, Pennsylvania, in June 1997, NRF opened a pilot training school to deliver training linked to the new standards using self-paced computerized instruction, workshops, mentored internships, and college certification. A dozen other pilot business-education-government partnerships across the country coordinate school-to-work, welfare-to-work, degree, and incumbent worker training programs geared to the new standards.

In much of retailing, skill standards alone will not reorient business strategies and lead to work reorganization. Indeed, almost as soon as the standards development effort began, voices within the industry argued that certification could fuel wage demands or spur union organizing that would erode thin profit margins. But without a stronger role for labor, which has been a bit player in the national development of standards and invisible in most local implementation efforts, it is not clear that the industry can overcome free-rider problems or its addiction to low labor costs. In principle, nonetheless, retail skill standards could be used to recreate across firms some of the types of mobility found in department stores in the 1950s.

Teachers. Teaching, though a recognized profession, has not typically been the site of significant collective reflection and interpretive performance improvement. Within bureaucratic school systems, teachers saw closing "their" classroom doors as the only way to preserve professional autonomy.[35] Labor relations took on many of the features of the adversarial industrial model of unionism, focusing on wages and benefits, detailed work rules, and employment security linked to individual schools (notwithstanding teachers' portable credentials and pensions). School boards and principals retained formal control over management, including curriculum, lesson planning, hiring, promotion, and discipline.

In the wake of concerns about the quality of public education, some schools have begun to open the classroom door, embracing an interpretive approach to student learning and the practice of teaching and seeking to make "learning to learn" more than a slogan.[36] In part, this is a matter of adapting to the cognitive styles of individual students. As in the Writing Project methods described in Chapter 5, teachers try to listen more carefully to students, "interpreting" what they hear. Team teaching helps, along with multischool networks of teachers who can share stories about their successes and failures. Although they have not yet done so, teachers' unions could encourage or initiate these innovations.

Some teachers' unions have sought greater classroom autonomy together with greater control over professional standards as a means of enhancing educational quality. In Cincinnati, curriculum councils of teachers seek to improve teaching methods in ten subject areas. Toledo and Cincinnati assign experienced teachers to observe and work with beginning teachers, helping them set and reach goals for improvement. The experienced teacher recommends to a joint union-management board whether or not the new teacher should be retained. The recommendations have almost always been heeded. In Cincinnati, when principals performed evaluations, more than 98 percent of beginning teachers were retained; with peer review, the rate is now around 95 percent. More important, assessments by experienced teachers have proven effective in improving classroom performance, whereas the pro-forma appraisals of principals had been nearly useless.[37]

Teachers' unions and school districts have also begun to construct multischool career paths. In Cincinnati, teachers and principals jointly screen applicants for openings; when qualifications are substantially equal, seniority in the district governs the choice. With teachers making more of the decisions, central administrative staff has fallen by 70 percent (including instructional supervisors). A districtwide career ladder allows teachers to progress from intern to resident to career teacher and finally to lead teacher. Those who change schools as they advance professionally contribute to the diffusion of expertise on which the interpretive model depends.[38]

Reconstructing Career Paths and Improving Performance

In the old employment system, there were sharp institutional boundaries between workers who had good jobs in large, stable firms and those on the "outside." Non-college-educated workers, if they were white and male, could often use informal social networks of family and friends to move from a "bad" job (typically unrationalized labor-intensive or low-wage tightly constrained) to a high-wage tightly constrained or semiautonomous job in a large firm. Once on the "inside," they could expect job security and, often, opportunities for advancement. Performance-improving communication between workers, if it took place, did so within the firm.

Based on the analysis in Chapters 1 to 6, Tables 12 and 13 summarize the structure of the economy and labor market in the 1960s and the mid-1990s. (Unlike in earlier tables, in Tables 12 and 13 we place the higher-wage work systems closer to the top.) Increasing inequality has manifested itself in the widening wage gap between high-skill autonomous workers and those in tightly constrained and unrationalized labor-intensive jobs. Insecurity in good jobs has stemmed especially

Table 12. Work systems, business organization, and career paths, circa mid-1960s.

Middle-class wages and security rooted in individual firms		
Work system	**Business organization**	**Career paths**
High-skill autonomous (professional, upper managerial)	Growing firms, many hierarchical, vertically integrated; some non-profit organizations Some professional partnerships	Some across employers Some within one organization
Semiautonomous (middle managerial, many administrative, clerical, sales employees)	Predominantly growing or stable firms, sometimes hierarchical	Most within one organization
Tightly constrained	Stable, often unionized firms	Many within one organization
Unrationalized labor-intensive	Predominantly small firms (including manufacturing)	No advancement within or across organizations; mobility across organizations

Table 13. Work systems, business organization, and career paths, circa mid-1990s.

More low-wage, dead-end jobs; fear of layoff from good jobs		
Work system	**Business organization**	**Career paths**
High-skill autonomous	Less stable firms, some growing rapidly, some slowly, sometimes linked in business networks; fewer vertical hierarchies Some professional partnerships	Some across employers Some within one organization
Semiautonomous	Less stable, less hierarchical firms, sometimes linked in business networks	Some one-firm careers; more attachments for a few years (with firm-specific skills little help to mobility)
Tightly constrained	Rising numbers in small service establishments (which may be part of a large firm); some outsourcing to new subsidiaries or independent firms (check processing, telephone call centers)	Few within one organization
Unrationalized labor-intensive	Small establishments and firms	No advancement within or across organizations; some horizontal mobility within occupation across employers (nursing homes, child care)

from the impact of changes in business organization on semiautonomous jobs.

As Table 14 shows, a new labor market system could emerge with the widespread embrace of interpretive approaches to performance improvement and the strengthening of multifirm career paths in the ways

Table 14. Work systems, business organization, and career paths, circa 2010.

Fewer low-wage jobs; more staircase careers		
Work system	**Business organization**	**Career paths**
High-skill autonomous	Business networks widespread, some decentralized "virtual" networks of professionals	Most across employers within occupation/profession
Semiautonomous (expansion of interpretive approach to performance improvement blurs boundary with high-skill autonomous and entry-level jobs)	Business networks widespread; some stable regional networks with dominant lead firms (health care, large firm retail, telecommunications); other networks more fluid, resembling construction (managerial and administrative services; small-firm retail)	Intraindustry and interindustry staircase careers—extended attachments at several firms or networks; significant opportunity to move into high-skill autonomous jobs
Entry-level (tightly constrained or unrationalized labor-intensive)	Small or large establishments with employment linkages to larger firms or business networks	Advancement to semiautonomous jobs through firm-based, community-based, occupational, and industry-specific career pathways

outlined in this chapter. This table is necessarily speculative; it is particularly hard to say how business organization might change should multiemployer institutions grow stronger. As in construction and in Hollywood, we expect that the spread of multiemployer career ladders would reinforce the tendency of technological change and competitive pressures to break down old-style integrated firms. In the new system, institutional boundaries would blur; distinctions in pay, status, and career opportunities between workers in different firms and between long-term and contingent workers would decline. People who began their work lives in "bad" jobs would have access, through more formalized institutions, to good jobs with the same or a different employer.

Workers whose informal social networks did not put them in contact with good jobs would find it easier to escape low-wage, dead-end jobs. Once in a good semiautonomous or high-skill autonomous job, a worker could advance economically and develop skills within an occupation, industry, or business network along established multiemployer career paths. The distinction between single- and multiemployer careers would blur, and a worker could combine both kinds of advancement over the course of a working life. A nurse, for example, might start out in a home health agency, move to a nursing home and then to general-duty nursing in a hospital, and finally advance within the hospital to more specialized nursing or supervisory work.

Because multiemployer institutions would channel displaced workers into roughly comparable jobs with other firms, losing a job would not be the calamitous event it often is today. Employers would find it easier to adjust their labor needs to changing product market conditions without resistance or resentment from workers. Of course, the downsizing of an entire occupation or industry would still create displacement that multiemployer institutions alone could not solve. But where, as in banking today, some firms shrink while others expand, the new institutions would help workers manage the transition. And by promoting both voluntary mobility and interfirm communication among workers, they would help improve economic performance.

8

A New Deal for a New Economy

The brain of modern man is short of a sort of fish-glue; that is why his mind does not settle, and is thick with sediment—new theories, old practice, new practice, old theories.

—*Alexander Herzen*, My Past and Thoughts (Letter to Turgenev), 1862

In this book we have described three roots of economic anxiety. The first is our collective failure to imagine ways of improving the economic performance of much of the service sector. Because of this failure, the United States has been unable to generate the kind of broadly based improvements in living standards that prevailed in the manufacturing-led Wonder Years. Second, many workers are stuck in low-wage, dead-end jobs, most of them in the unrationalized labor-intensive work system. Finally, fragmented and fluid patterns of business organization chip away at security and career prospects, especially for workers in semiautonomous jobs.

We cannot improve service sector performance by using the methods that worked in mass manufacturing. In too much of the service sector there is too little scope for standardizing and rationalizing production. Even if this were possible, how many of us would want to work in cookie-cutter jobs or consume homogenized service products? Likewise, it would be hard to recreate stable firms in much of today's economy, because of fast-paced technological change, shifting consumer demand patterns, and a highly competitive business environment. Nor would this be desirable, because innovation bubbles up from the same turbulence that buffets Americans as workers. Even if we could restore the one-company careers of the past, how many of us would prefer the conformity and deference to organizational whims that was the price of inclusion in the old hierarchies?

Rather than go back to the past, we must relieve economic anxiety by attacking its contemporary roots. We begin with the one root that can be drastically stunted, although not uprooted entirely: the unrationalized labor-intensive work system. We propose using the minimum wage and other wage-setting policies to reduce the number of unrationalized jobs. Such policies would have two effects. First, employers would find it cheaper to use automation rather than people for mindless, boring tasks. Second, when jobs cannot be automated, employers would have incentives to redesign work, jointly with their employees, to take advantage of a workforce that turns over less quickly and has more experience and commitment to the job. The policies we urge would also limit the encroachment of wage-based competition in the other work systems.

We next turn to service sector performance improvement, in particular to public policies that would foster performance gains through economies of depth and coordination. Although government cannot raise performance directly, it can support research and other activities that make workers and employers more likely to. Better economic performance would lay a foundation for wage growth.

We also propose incentives for workers and employers to construct the kinds of multiemployer institutions described in the preceding chapter. These could begin to ease fears of job loss by marking out staircase career paths among multiple employers, providing opportunities for training and learning, and enhancing career security (if not necessarily security in a particular job). These institutions would also contribute to performance improvement by creating venues for work-related communication, shared learning, and definition of best practices.

Finally, our fourth set of policy proposals would foster the growth of worker associations on a multiemployer basis. These associations would play two roles. As unions have long done, they would bargain collectively over wages and working conditions, thereby raising wages and preventing jobs from sliding in the direction of low-wage, unrationalized labor-intensive work. Just as important, they would be an essential element in establishing multiemployer career paths and promoting economies of depth.

Taken together, the policies we propose would reduce economic inequality and improve economic performance. They would restore real wage growth, especially for lower-income service workers. They would narrow the differences (in status and skill as well as in pay) between jobs in the four work systems, between those employed by different firms and in different industries, and between permanent and contingent workers. They would enable Americans to change jobs more easily, to seek opportunities and build careers. In sum, they would rebuild for a service-dominated economy some of the best features of the Wonder Years. The policies we recommend would not attempt to resurrect or reimpose the institutional system of the past. Instead, building on the distinctive features of today's potentially dynamic service economy, they would make markets work better in both economic and social terms.

America Still Needs a Raise

Meaningful improvement in unrationalized and tightly constrained jobs requires measures that will directly raise wages and benefits. Proposals for strengthening the minimum wage and other direct wage-setting policies can be counted on to divide employers and employees, Democrats and Republicans. Opponents, including many economists, argue that using public policy to set wages directly or to encourage collective bargaining will increase unemployment and hurt those whom such policies are intended to help. But as we see below, empirical studies cast doubt on the presumption that modest increases in the minimum wage raise unemployment. And job-creating policies could offset any unemployment that might result from more substantial hikes in the minimum wage.

Increasing the Minimum Wage

The minimum wage is the most powerful instrument for raising earnings at the bottom of the labor market. It not only has direct effects on pay for workers who earn the minimum but also tends to raise wages and reduce turnover for those earning within a few dollars of the minimum.

Minimum wage earners are concentrated in the service sector, especially retail trade.[1] These workers are not, by and large, teenagers with part-time jobs. More than 70 percent of those whose pay went up because of the 1990 increases in the federal minimum wage were age twenty or older. Thirty percent were the sole wage earners in their families. On average, minimum wage earners account for half their family's total earnings. Minimum wage workers are three times more likely than others to live in poverty; a minimum wage worker employed full-time, full-year, earns $10,712, about two-thirds the poverty level for a family of four. An estimated one-third of the pay increases resulting from the 1990 and 1991 hikes in the federal minimum wage went to families in the lowest decile of the earnings distribution. These same increases rolled back roughly 30 percent of the 1979–89 increase in economywide wage dispersion.

Even after the 1997 increase the real value of the minimum hourly wage ($5.15 in 1997) remained only about 75 percent of its peak real value, reached in 1968, and just over 80 percent of its 1979 level. As of 1998, restoring the minimum to the inflation-adjusted level of 1968 would require an increase to almost $7.00 an hour. Moreover, the minimum wage during the Wonder Years did not simply maintain its real value but rose with national labor productivity (Figure 5), allowing low-wage workers to share in the expansion of the national economic pie. The value of the federal minimum wage would have to rise to more than $10.50 (as of mid-1998) to reach its level relative to productivity in 1968.

The higher the minimum wage, the more plausible the oft-expressed concerns that low-wage and entry-level jobs would be lost. Prices for Big Macs and other low-cost service products might also rise. But these concerns have often been overstated. After state minimum wages were hiked 8 and 11 percent in Texas and New Jersey, respectively, teenage employment in fast-food restaurants actually rose.[2] After a 1988 increase in the minimum wage, teenage employment in California climbed relative to that in other states. After increases in the federal minimum wage in 1991, low-wage employment increased or remained stable in the states most affected, that is, those that had not already set the state minimum above the federal level. The early returns indicate that the 1996 hike in the minimum wage from $4.25 to $4.75 had little impact on employment.[3]

Why have increases in the minimum wage not caused employment declines? One explanation is that minimum wage hikes can reduce turnover and hence the number of unfilled jobs.[4] For example, the great majority of fast-food restaurants have jobs open at any point in time (more than 80 percent even in the 1980s, when unemployment was much higher than in the late 1990s). Before the 1988 federal minimum wage increase, surveys indicated some two hundred thousand vacancies in the eating and drinking industry. Employers required to pay higher wages would discover compensating benefits in lower recruit-

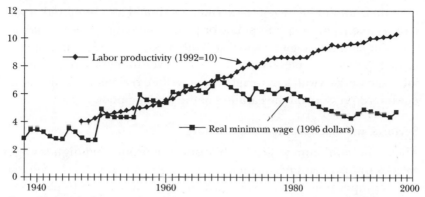

Source: Productivity figures are from U.S. Department of Labor, Bureau of Labor Statistics, output per hour of all persons in the non-farm business sector. Minimum wage deflated using the CPI-U-X1.

Figure 5. The minimum wage and labor productivity

ment and turnover costs. (Recall the estimate in Chapter 3 of the costs of turnover in nursing homes: four thousand dollars per job.)

Unlike recent modest increases, big hikes in the minimum wage might cause job losses, especially in the unrationalized labor-intensive and tightly constrained work systems. But this is desirable. It would improve service quality in work previously performed in the unrationalized system. It would raise conventional productivity measures through automation and elimination of tightly constrained jobs.

During the Wonder Years Congress boosted the minimum wage periodically, but the expanding market for mass-produced goods, supported by collective bargaining, kept employment expanding. If higher minimum wages and an expansion of collective bargaining did not sufficiently stimulate demand today, we could deploy the kind of work-spreading and job-creating policies that are outlined later in this chapter.

Despite the recent increases, the minimum wage should be raised much more. One way to accomplish this is to increase the minimum wage $1 per year until it reaches 90 percent of its 1968 level relative to productivity. (This would have been about $9.25 per hour in 1997.) Thereafter, the minimum should be indexed to the average wage. While waiting for the federal government to act, local governments should enact "living-wage ordinances" that set minimum wages for municipal government contractors and employers that receive public subsidies. States should raise their minimum wages.[5] Governments should also require that welfare recipients moving into public or private sector jobs receive at least the minimum or living wages to which others are entitled. In the absence of such policies, employers will have incentives to replace their current low-wage workers with lower-paid former welfare recipients, putting more downward pressure on the earnings of the working poor.

Sectoral and Occupational Wage Setting

Above the minimum wage, mechanisms for promoting higher wages vary by industry and occupation. Prevailing wage laws discourage low-wage competition by requiring government contractors to pay an industry- or occupation-specific minimum well above the overall minimum wage. They apply in construction under the federal Davis-Bacon Act and state equivalents. The federal Service Contract and Walsh-Healey acts apply to services and manufacturing, respectively.

In construction, the prevailing wage often meant the union wage when union coverage was high. Federally and in some states, it is now roughly equal to the somewhat lower average wage. In states that repealed prevailing wage laws in construction, wages have declined and apprenticeship programs have atrophied.[6] As we saw in Chapter 7, construction productivity has also declined substantially. This natural experiment in deregulation of the construction industry is an unqualified failure.

Industry dynamics in construction indicate that stronger occupational wage standards would lead to a better trained workforce and substantially higher quality and productivity. Similar dynamics are at work in a number of services. Where federal, state, and local governments have the leverage and the knowledge, they should establish occupational wage standards that would boost performance. The public sector foots much of the bill for labor-intensive social services. Distribution of funds for such services could be conditioned on providers meeting an occupational wage and benefit minimum.

Since 1991, for example, a national campaign has advocated a "Worthy Wage" for child care workers, originally aimed at raising average wages to $10 per hour.[7] Research cited in Chapter 3 suggests that children suffer developmentally from high turnover and unskilled caregiving. A Worthy Wage would lower turnover and improve quality. Government could require that child care providers receiving public subsidies abide by a Worthy Wage standard. An occupational wage standard would similarly improve quality in long-term care and community-based mental health-mental retardation services.[8] When government accounts for only a small share of the market—for example, temporary office work—paying an above-market wage for contracted services might serve to demonstrate the potential for performance improvement.

Equivalent Compensation for "Nonstandard" Employment

Roughly 20 percent of the service sector workforce consists of part-timers. Ten percent is made up of temporary and contract employees and others with nonstandard employment arrangements (see Chapter 2). Many Americans prefer part-time or temporary positions, which may make it easier to balance work and family or work and education. But low pay and meager benefits compared with those of full-time and permanent workers who perform the same tasks encourage low-wage, high-turnover work systems. Therefore, states and the federal government should take steps to equalize hourly equivalent compensation for part-time, temporary, and full-time employees in jobs requiring substantially equivalent skill, effort, and responsibility. Federal law should pro-rate employee benefits for nonstandard employees.[9] The federal Equal Pay Act, which requires employers to pay equal wages to men and women who do equal work, provides a model. The same rule, as well as other federal and state labor and employment laws, should apply to "dependent contractors" (i.e., nominally independent contractors who work mostly or exclusively for a single client).[10]

Promoting Performance Improvement in the Services

In the scientific management tradition, managers and the technical experts who reported to them were responsible for performance. Firms relied on cost accounting and engineering measures to track efficiency. The discussion of performance improvement in Chapter 5 suggests a different view of performance and how it can be improved, especially in the services. Performance improvement in the interpretive model, and even in recent engineering-model reforms, depends on the participation of workers. This participation must be actively engaged rather than passive, committed rather than coerced. The "soft" technologies of interpretation, teamwork, and communication become as important as machines in generating performance gains based on economies of depth and coordination.

Governments cannot and should not try to micromanage performance, but they can and do influence the framework and knowledge base on which private sector performance improvement builds. The U.S. government spends about $70 billion annually on research and development. But here as elsewhere, policy remains stuck in the past. The broad directions of U.S. technology and science policies were set in the early years of the cold war and have changed relatively little since. At least a dozen federal agencies spend money on R&D and implement technology and science policies ranging from support for university research to exploration of space to finding cures for disease. By and large, these agencies ignore the human dimensions of technology and science. Moreover, because most federal R&D spending is linked with missions such as defense, in which agencies contract to purchase equipment, not services, the manufacturing-oriented perspective linked with scientific management and the engineering model remains dominant.

The end of the cold war has brought little overall change. Agencies jealously guard their prerogatives and their budgets. A bewildering array of federal laboratory facilities—some six hundred—go about their business, all but invisible to policymakers. Responsibility for R&D spending and related policies is spread among many congressional committees and executive agencies. Because there is no overall federal R&D budget, determining public spending on, say, "human factors engineering" would require a special budgetary cross-tabulation. It is difficult even to estimate federal spending on well-defined scientific fields such as chemistry.[11] Accordingly, a first step toward reorienting technology policy is for federal statistical agencies to collect more accurate data on technology spending as it relates to the services and on what that money is buying.[12] The federal government should then fund R&D on the human-centered dimensions of performance much more liberally. It should do so for the same reasons that government funds other areas of (nonmission) R&D, namely, that individual firms cannot in general expect to benefit economically from R&D results that are available to all.

There are other steps government can take that would be easy and inexpensive. The Commerce Department's Malcolm Baldrige Award, given to companies that exemplify quality practices, has helped influence what leading-edge companies regard as best practices. Although service firms are eligible, the award continues to go mostly to manufacturing firms. More important, award criteria reflect the engineering model. They pay little attention to the interpretive dimension. And because only firms can enter, the awards do not recognize or assess multi-employer institutions for their contributions to performance. (Much the same is true of private sector quality programs, such as ISO 9000.)

To remedy these deficiencies, Baldrige criteria (and those of state and local awards) should be revised for evaluating service industry performance. The federal and state governments should award small seed-money grants to local multiemployer institutions (unions and occupational and industry associations as well as labor-management consortia). Such grants could document the extent to which their recipients help improve performance among their members. After accumulating case knowledge of what distinguishes performance-enhancing multiemployer institutions, the federal and state governments should develop awards specifically to recognize their contribution. As with the current Baldrige program, winners should be required to share information with other similar institutions.

Federal, state, and local governments could also begin to mark out a path for the rest of the service economy. All Americans deal with the courts and police, tax authorities and other public sector agencies (including motor vehicle departments). These bureaucracies could improve their day-to-day performance by developing better interpretive capacities and achieving economies of depth and coordination. (The cynical response this suggestion may elicit simply demonstrates how much it is needed.) Such improvements might begin to change the attitudes of Americans toward their government.

Currently, public policy neither encourages nor discourages communication, consultation, and shared learning among workers, especially across firm boundaries, which we argued in Chapter 5 is a necessary ingredient in improving performance. To help workers share their knowledge and contribute to innovation and performance improvement, state or federal agencies with responsibilities for performance-related matters (e.g., the Commerce Department) or labor-management cooperation (e.g., the Federal Mediation and Conciliation Service) could convene short local conferences. In addition to workers, these conferences should include technical experts (who may view production methods and practices differently than workers) and managers (whose own interpretive skills are especially important and who may need to be persuaded that workers can contribute to performance improvement). With the help of, and at the request of, locally based multiemployer institutions, such meetings should be planned around the concerns of particular occupations, industries, or business networks (or groups of these). State or federal law should give employees the right to a limited amount of time off from work to attend such conferences, for example, two or three days per year.

Employers who fear that proprietary know-how might leak out during such meetings should be reassured by examples of industrial districts such as Silicon Valley (Chapter 6), where firms compete fiercely and successfully even as workers move among firms and managers and professionals routinely talk shop with one another. Higher levels of cross-firm communication among lower-level workers would likewise contribute to the pace of innovation.

Launching Multiemployer Institutions

Chapter 7 emphasized the importance of strengthening multiemployer institutions that take responsibility for training and career ladders, and promoting work-related communication. Government policy should encourage and facilitate such institutions, without dictating their structure, governance, and activities. Public officials cannot know in advance whether the multiemployer institutions that will best serve particular groups of workers and employers should be organized by occupation, industry, business network, geographical region, or some combination of these. And within the broad set of activities that multiemployer institutions can usefully undertake, policymakers cannot know which activities will be most appropriate for which institutions. Public policy must, therefore, be flexible, allowing institutional structures to emerge organically.

Likewise, policy should not try to dictate governance procedures. Some sort of worker representation is essential, as we argued in Chapter 7. Beyond this, policy should be neutral on participation and apportionment of responsibility among employers, governments, and representatives of consumers or other stakeholders. Policy should also be neutral as to whether the institutions are established and operate through collective bargaining, consortia, or other means.

Government can help multiemployer institutions get started through planning grants and other forms of seed funding (to groups of workers or workers jointly with other stakeholders). Very modest grants helped launch the San Francisco Hotels Partnership, Cape Cod Career Ladders, and Wisconsin Regional Training Partnership described in Chapter 7.

Some resources for such seed funding can come from "workforce development reform," consolidation of scores of existing, separate employment and training programs into one or several block grants to the states. Many of the existing programs are, in a sense, Band-Aids for the bleeding of the Wonder Years economy. As that economy began to break down and the wages of less educated workers plummeted, special programs proliferated for disadvantaged workers and those displaced by federal action (e.g., trade liberalization and the Clean Air Act).

The mediocre record of existing employment programs has given government-supported training a bad name in some quarters. These critiques fail to recognize the context within which today's programs operate. Many of them channel people into dead-end jobs; partly because trainers lack deep links to employers or worker associations, even longer-term training directs people into positions for which demand is unpredictable and career ladders have broken down.

The current government employment and training system is not, in sum, a system at all. Still, misguided attempts at reform would make a bad situation worse. A shift to block grants to states might be taken by Congress as an opportunity to slash funds or to eliminate the equity emphasis of current programs for displaced and disadvantaged youth and adults. Regional redistribution of funds could reduce support for poor workers in communities where unemployment and underemployment are highest in favor of affluent suburban areas.

To ensure that workforce development reform helps relieve rather than worsen economic anxiety, Congress, states, and substate regions need to set guidelines and allocate money based on an understanding of what an effective new system would look like. They should give high priority to workforce development projects that

- train workers drawn from groups of at least three firms;
- include significant participation by worker representatives;
- have strong connections to groups of employers that pay a living wage and offer opportunities for career advancement;
- train and mentor workers consistent with productive, high-quality forms of work organization;
- develop, implement, or deliver portable credentials (such as skill standards);
- create structured opportunities for workers to advance above the entry level;
- create new forms of employment and income security above the level of the individual firm;

- demonstrate the potential to increase employer and worker investment in learning (e.g., by spreading apprenticeship-type approaches to training and mentoring);
- have developed criteria for evaluating their success in promoting workforce development and agree to share their assessments with others.

The federal program that comes closest to pointing in the right direction is skill standards development. Since 1992 voluntary partnerships in twenty-two industries have developed (and, in some cases, implemented) skill standards. (The effort led by the National Retail Federation, discussed in Chapter 7, began as a skill standards voluntary partnership.) The National Skill Standards Board, created in 1994, supports the development of "occupational cluster" skill standards in broadly defined sectors such as manufacturing, sales jobs in retail and wholesale trade, and, it is anticipated, business and administrative services (in essence, clerical and administrative jobs). Cluster standards give workers greater opportunity and mobility.

Canada has deployed a related approach by supporting more than twenty sectoral human resource councils over the past dozen years.[13] The electrical and electronics industry sectoral council now requires member companies to spend a portion of payroll on general training. Worksite committees that include worker representatives oversee the expenditure, even in nonunion facilities. Canadian sectoral councils have also focused on issues such as the organization of work and development of skill standards. Canadian sectoral councils exist in service industries such as tourism, trucking, software development, and auto repair, as well as in manufacturing.

Multiemployer Careers in Deregulating and Restructuring Industries

In 1996, after AT&T announced it would lay off forty thousand workers, Labor Secretary Robert Reich initiated a national debate about corporate responsibility. Reich put forward a Wonder Years conception of corporate responsibility, advocating incentives and mandates to induce firms not to downsize.[14] In our view, trying to turn back the clock to an age when individual firms could be the prime locus of security for breadwinners is a losing proposition. But that does not mean firms have no responsibility for providing employment security or creating the skills on which they depend.

In particular, firms that are downsizing or otherwise restructuring should accept part of the task of building a new employment system. For example, policymakers might have insisted on a quid pro quo for deregulation of telecommunications: multiemployer cooperation in managing the new and less stable market for outside craft workers, technicians, and even customer service representatives. Further deregulation should be so conditioned. In banking, sectoral councils that draw on the experience of the British Columbia Health Accord could help displaced back-office and platform workers, tellers, and loan officers find jobs that draw on their experience. Mergers—of hospitals, banks, or telecommunications companies—should also be analyzed from the standpoint of workers and the industry training system as well as consumer interests. Just as companies sometimes sell off pieces of an acquisition to satisfy regulators that competition will be maintained in particular market segments, they could be required to participate in or fund sectoral institutions to help manage the postmerger multifirm labor market.

Corporate Responsibility Contributions

The unwillingness of firms to finance training at a multiemployer level has been a long-standing obstacle to multiemployer careers. One way around this problem is to require firms to pay corporate responsibility contributions, equal to a small percentage of payroll, to multifirm institutions that satisfy criteria such as those described above for receiving workforce development seed funding. A number of countries require firms to spend a small percentage of payroll on training.[15] Government could subsidize collective training by allowing a tax credit for some part of the contribution to multi-employer funds.

Portable Benefits

The federal government currently subsidizes single- and multiemployer health insurance and pensions through the tax code. (Both employer and employee contributions to health insurance premiums are tax exempt; employer and employee contributions to retirement plans are taxed only when the worker receives pension income, not at the time of contribution.) A simple, desirable alteration in the tax code would remove the subsidy for single-employer plans (while grandfathering existing plans).[16]

New Unions for a New Economy

The National Labor Relations Act (NLRA), passed in 1935, establishes the right of workers to join unions. It helped spread industrial unionism, following an era in which craft unionism predominated.

Today U.S. labor law reforms must be equally bold, ushering in another change in the dominant mode of worker representation.

After six decades of statutory amendments and judicial interpretations, the NLRA has become a straitjacket. It offers most workers only a single choice: they may join, by majority vote, a worker association modeled on the traditional industrial union, or else do without collective representation altogether. The main features of the industrial union model include collective bargaining at the level of the worksite or firm, a sharp division between the rights and duties of labor and those of management, wages and contractual job rights linked to particular positions within the firm, and a grievance procedure through which unions can challenge managerial violations of workers' job rights. This form of unionism met the needs of workers in much of the economy of the Wonder Years.

Today many Americans take this industrial model to be synonymous with union representation (just as they did the craft model in the 1920s). With the relative decline of old-style mass manufacturing, moreover, many American workers have come to view unions as irrelevant to their needs. But as we have seen, alternative forms of collective representation and collective bargaining exist.

Our labor law reform proposals aim at the same goals as other policies in this chapter: to improve wages and other employment outcomes directly, to enhance economic performance through skill-intensive work systems, and to foster multiemployer institutions that would support both career aspirations and performance improvement. Worker associations, including unions and professional associations, are crucial to the achievement of these goals.

Multiemployer Collective Bargaining

Because firms and establishments are smaller on average in the services than in manufacturing, organizing and bargaining collectively at the level of the establishment or firm is unlikely to be effective in raising wages or providing satisfactory levels of employment security and career advancement. To protect workers and influence business strategy and work systems, unions must be able to bargain jointly with multiple employers on behalf of workers in an occupation, industry, or business network, often within a small geographical area. This does not mean that all terms and conditions of employment must be uniform across employers. Multiemployer bargaining in the United States and elsewhere allows for separate, more detailed subagreements with smaller employer groups and individual employers.

Federal labor law does not prohibit multiemployer collective bargaining, which exists in a few industries, such as construction and motion pictures. But the law discourages new multiemployer bargaining relationships and provides little support for maintaining existing ones. For example, the National Labor Relations Board (NLRB), which is charged with determining the appropriate bargaining unit, has favored narrow units, typically within a single firm or establishment, on the assumption that workers in such units form a "community of interest." Unions have also favored narrow units because they perceive them as easier to organize. Not even the NLRB, moreover, can require units to combine for bargaining purposes. For several bargaining units to negotiate together, all the relevant unions and employers must voluntarily agree to joint bargaining. (Any union or employer may withdraw from a joint bargaining arrangement before a new round of bargaining begins.)

An alternative rule would permit units to bargain jointly if a majority of the workers in each unit voted to do so. This rule would support multiemployer bargaining but still allow majority decisions within each firm- or establishment-specific unit. Individual units could withdraw only if their workers so voted in an election. Employers would not be allowed unilaterally to withdraw from joint bargaining arrangements. New units could join an existing multiemployer bargaining arrangement if a majority of their workers voted to do so.[17]

A more substantial departure from current practice would permit workers within a geographical area to seek representation and collective bargaining on a multiworksite basis (without first organizing into worksite-specific units). To permit this, the NLRB should be given the authority to certify broad occupational, sectoral, or network-based bargaining units. All the employers in such a unit would be required to bargain jointly with the union selected by a majority of workers. (The NLRB should be allowed to certify a broad unit of this type only if the workers seeking union representation request it; employers should not be allowed to frustrate collective bargaining by forcing a broad unit against workers' wishes.)

"Prehire" agreements could also be used to foster multiemployer bargaining where workers are highly mobile. Under such agreements, an employer and union agree that the union will represent workers that are subsequently hired (e.g., musicians hired for a Broadway production). If employees subsequently hired desire to, they may vote to decertify the union.

Prehire agreements are currently permitted only in construction (in recognition of the transient nature of worker-employer relationships there). Rather than exempt particular occupations or industries from the ban on prehire agreements, the law should allow these agreements throughout the economy. Because it is impossible to predict the spread of short-term employment relationships, it is appropriate to allow prehire agreements generally.[18]

There is another obstacle to multiemployer bargaining, especially within business networks. With few exceptions, the law prohibits a union from using economic pressure on, or an agreement with, one firm to achieve recognition or economic gains from another firm. The ban on these "secondary pressures" is often justified by the argument that an "innocent" third party should not be inserted into a dispute between a union and an employer. But in business networks, as well as in traditional subcontracting arrangements, the only way for a union to achieve recognition by one employer (a janitorial service contractor, say, or a home health care provider) may be to use economic pressure on another firm (such as a building owner or HMO). Absent such secondary pressures, successful unionization of one firm's workforce may simply lead other firms to sever their ties with that firm. Congress, recognizing this principle in the network-dominated garment and construction industries, exempted those industries from the ban on secondary pressures; otherwise collective bargaining would probably never have taken hold in either. With the spread of business networks and increasingly fragmented industries, it is time to end the ban on secondary pressures, at least where the purpose is union recognition.[19]

Expanding Collective Rights for High-Skill Autonomous and Semiautonomous Workers

Many high-skill autonomous and some semiautonomous workers are not guaranteed associational rights under the NLRA because they perform "managerial" or "supervisory" duties (such as hiring and directing the work of others). Companies are allowed to fire or otherwise discriminate against such workers if they join a union or association. The theory behind these legal provisions is that workers who make decisions "in the interest of" an employer would have a conflict of interest if they were allowed to bargain with that employer. The implicit assumption is that the interests of employers and workers are so antithetical that no one can serve both simultaneously.

There are examples, however, of unions that have successfully carried out "managerial" duties. Some teachers' unions take responsibility for hiring and performance evaluation (as we saw in Chapter 7). Indeed, outside the tightly constrained work system (and, some would say, in it), nearly all employees, in effect, manage themselves. It is thus not very realistic to assume that workers and employers, particularly in the service sector, must be viewed as two armed camps designated "labor" and "management." In addition, if firms are not going to take responsibility for training and promoting economics of depth in a more dynamic economy, worker associations (including occupational unions) should be allowed to take up the slack.

The NLRA should, therefore, be amended to grant associational rights to currently excluded high-skill autonomous and semiautonomous workers. One step in this direction would be to limit the supervisory and managerial exclusions to those who have substantial discretion to set company policy or whose primary job is to carry out an employer's labor relations policy, as recommended by the presidentially appointed Commission on the Future of Worker-Management Relations.[20]

Employer-Worker Consultation

Some proposals for reforming labor law suggest that employees be given new forums for expression, such as works councils or employee participation committees, at individual worksites or firms.[21] Such reforms could promote work reorganization in some nursing homes, insurance companies, and schools. But where turnover is high, worksite- or firm-level labor-management consultation is of little use. In such situations, public policy should facilitate consultation on a multiemployer as well as a single-employer basis. The San Francisco Hotels Partnership and the Wisconsin Regional Training Partnership make extensive use of both single- and multiemployer consultation, which prove useful on different issues.

Multiemployer labor-management consultation is often necessary to the ongoing operation of multiemployer institutions, such as training programs and job-matching systems, that can improve employment security and economic performance. Multiemployer collective bargaining may not always be the right vehicle for establishing multiemployer institutions or consultative relationships. Some workers (e.g., in professional and technical occupations) may want those outcomes but not want collective bargaining. Some nonunion workers and employers may want to participate in multiemployer institutions established by unionized employers. (The WRTP includes some nonunion firms.) Sometimes the units that make sense for collective bargaining, whether single- or multiemployer, differ from the units that make sense for other labor-management activities such as training or job matching. Think of bad-job-to-good-job linkages that rely on general competencies rather than skill commonalities, as for fast-food workers. It is unlikely that fast-food workers would want to bargain jointly with, say, office clerical workers, about pay and working conditions. But both fast-food and clerical workers may be interested in talking to employers about ways to create career paths that link the two sets of jobs. In such instances, multiemployer consultation without collective bargaining may be desirable.

To encourage these possibilities, we propose that elected single- or multiemployer worker committees, established on a voluntary basis, be given rights to consult with employers in an industry, occupation, or business network. These committees would not have the right to bargain collectively or to make binding decisions about any aspect of the employment relationship but would simply meet with employers. For this reason, a showing of 15 or 20 percent support among the relevant group of workers should be sufficient to establish a committee, whose members would then be elected by those workers. The NLRB could be given the power to certify committees and election results and to make rules regarding the scope of representation.[22]

Completing the Circle: The End of Unemployment

In his book *The End of Work,* Jeremy Rifkin makes one of the more recent in a long line of apocalyptic predictions that automation and information technologies will create an ever-expanding army of the unemployed.[23] Our analysis provides no support for such dire prophecies. Nonetheless, some observers may expect policies like those we propose, especially for raising wages, to create unemployment, in part by encouraging automation and self-service. Some would also say that higher wages at the bottom of the wage scale are self-defeating, leading to growth of the informal low-wage economy. Other critics might compare labor markets in Europe and the United States and conclude that there is a trade-off between the quantity and quality of jobs. A country can have low unemployment or it can maintain the relative earnings of workers at the bottom of the income distribution, but, these observers would suggest, it cannot do both.[24]

Without trivializing the technical and political challenges of avoiding unemployment while raising wages, we believe the existing situations in Europe and the United States hardly span all possible ways of organizing a postindustrial economy. Rethinking policy requires recognizing, once again, how preconceptions based on the era of mass manufacturing limit the imagination. During the Wonder Years factory workers rarely took other jobs when demand dropped. Unemployment compensation simply maintained their buying power. Underlying this policy was the assumption that the slump would be temporary and that renewed expansion would put people back on their old jobs.

Indeed, the idea of unemployment as it is understood today emerged in the United States only with the rise of mass production.[25] In earlier years, when the nation was largely rural, people produced many goods and services locally or at home, from raising livestock and crops to making furniture and clothes to taking care of children.

To deal with variable labor demand and the possible shortfall in available jobs, public policy needs to ease movement in and out of the labor force, as happened more or less spontaneously in earlier times. The nation cannot return to the self-sufficiency of the nineteenth century, but people should be able to leave the labor force and take on other meaningful roles without the stigma or economic waste associated with "unemployment."

More fluid entry and exit have already begun. With more women in the labor force, and more men again taking an active role in raising children, responsibility for primary caregiving in better-off dual-earner families now shifts more easily in response to the employment opportunities of each partner. And if lifelong learning—for personal enrichment as well as to improve job opportunities—is to be more than a slogan, education will have to become more accessible for people of all ages, whether in or out of the labor force. (We will have to understand that the Internet will not make learning easy and automatic, any more than television did.) National or community service offers a third alternative. Work requirements for welfare recipients could be folded into community service programs involving people with many levels of skill and education, avoiding the stigma of old-style jobs programs (and today's welfare reforms).

Money is the key to many of these shifts. Will people with decent jobs be willing to help stabilize the incomes of others? That will require Americans to see their contributions as providing security and a richer life for themselves as well as for others. People will also need to perceive government programs as effective. With these points in mind, we offer some concrete suggestions. Sketchier and more speculative than those earlier in the chapter, these proposals suggest simply that aggregate employment problems can be solved.

Flexible Contributory Funds

Unemployment insurance, individual retirement accounts, and pensions could be transformed into flexible contributory funds that people could tap in a wider range of circumstances: to supplement earnings during national or community service, while caring for children or elderly relatives, during training and education. With safeguards so that people do not end up old and destitute or depending unfairly on the generosity of others, accounts might even be drawn down for extended sabbaticals during middle age. Such changes should help dissolve the anachronistic and artificially sharp distinction between working life and retirement.

Shorter Work Time

Many people in the United States already put in a "substandard" work week in the form of involuntary part-time employment. More people might voluntarily choose part-time work if they received hourly compensation comparable to that of full-time workers (as proposed above). Raising wages for people in the bottom half of the earnings distribution could also reduce the number of families with children in which both parents feel they must always work full-time. Lowering the threshold above which workers must be paid overtime, finally, might shorten the average work week.[26]

Subsidized Community-Based Employment

New public works programs are generally considered inconceivable in the United States. People commonly assume they would be too expensive. Opponents also argue that this kind of program stigmatizes recipients and would be inefficiently run. On the other hand, if cost pressure and employment instability climb the education and wage ladder, new public employment programs could lose some of their association with welfare. If people with proven competencies are idle, it may be easier to revive the depression-era conviction that unemployment is a waste: surely these talents could be put to use.

A decentralized process for planning and administering publicly supported employment could help alleviate concerns about waste. Worker associations and multiemployer partnerships could help manage the flow of workers between private sector jobs and community service. Construction unions could provide labor for building affordable housing. The actors', musicians', and writers' guilds could staff cultural activities. Associations of physicians and nurses could provide health care in underserved urban or rural areas. Worker associations and community groups could submit proposals to a local board, which would select projects for funding. Because such work would generate a greater sense of security even for their members who currently have good jobs, worker associations might subsidize the wages of those employed in community projects, for example, through income insurance funds.[27]

Keeping Score in Postindustrial America

As noted in Chapter 2, gross domestic product—the value of all goods and services produced in the domestic economy—is a problematic measure of material well-being in a service-dominated economy. Nonetheless, many Americans take for granted that this is the best (or only) way to measure national economic welfare. They might be surprised to find that this measure has existed only since the rise of national income accounting in the 1930s and 1940s.[28] Of course, GDP never was a comprehensive measure of national welfare. (Among other things, it does not include nonmarket production or estimates of environmental damage. It does not include the value of leisure time. It does include spending on the military and prisons.) GDP was acceptable as a proxy for material well-being in the mass production era when growth was driven by the increasing output of a slowly changing basket of standardized products. As services have come to dominate the economy, GDP has become increasingly dubious as a measure of national well-being.

The genuine progress indicator (GPI), one of the recent attempts to develop a better measure of national welfare, shows improvement from the late 1940s to around 1970 but steady deterioration since then.[29] Much of the deterioration stems from the inclusion of measures of environmental harm, depletion of nonrenewable resources, rising income inequality, and crime. The GPI also accounts for the artificial inflation of GDP as more household services (such as child care, elder care, meals, and cleaning) have been provided in the market rather than outside it. Critics complain that indicators such as the GPI simply measure what their constructors value. That is equally true of GDP, of course. Any good index of national welfare *should* measure our progress in terms of the outcomes we value as a society.

The increasingly obvious inadequacy of GDP as a proxy for national welfare gives the United States an opportunity to reinvent the way we evaluate the performance of the economy. To help guide the nation in this process, the federal government could create a high-level commission charged with defining a set of alternative indicators. Such a "National Progress Commission" might be asked to formulate measures that compensate for some of the most glaring deficiencies of the GDP and that more directly measure whether gains in economic performance are broadly distributed and benefit society as a whole. To be useful, such an exercise would have to go much further than consideration of "adjustments" to the Consumer Price Index. Measures that might be considered include inequality in income and wealth, levels of poverty, life expectancy, education investment and outcomes, and environmental quality.

The Wonder Years emerged in stages, not overnight. A long series of technological innovations, many of them incremental and not very visible, prepared the way for large-scale production of standardized goods. The "invention" of the industrial corporation and the growth of large-scale oligopolies stabilized markets for high-volume goods, from steel rails to cigarettes to automobiles. Industrial unions won shopfloor protections suited to factory work and negotiated an end to the industrial unrest of the 1930s. The combination of the federal minimum wage, unemployment insurance, social security, industrial unions, and industry-wide pattern bargaining helped generate the mass consumption that drove economic expansion until the 1970s.

We believe the country should emulate the kind of system building that helped generate the Wonder Years. This should be done not by trying to shore up obsolete institutions but by building an economic system that will generate broad-based prosperity in our new, postindustrial society.

In outlining the basic features of a new U.S. economic system, we have said little about manufacturing and less about international trade and investment. It has, of course, become fashionable to bemoan (or celebrate) the paralysis of domestic economic policy that supposedly results from international competition and highly mobile capital. The size of the U.S. economy and a modest ratio of imports to domestic consumption, however, give the nation room to maneuver. Labor market transformation can begin in the large number of jobs within nonmobile services insulated from international competition. The creation of "new unions" in substantial numbers of these jobs could change American politics enough to put in place complementary reforms in manufacturing and in international economic institutions (over which the United States still has disproportionate influence). The experience of the Wonder Years suggests that we can implement the international pieces of a new system last. The global trade and financial institutions that helped spread prosperity in the Wonder Years did not begin to emerge until the late 1940s, long after the New Deal in the United States.

Some may see our recipes as interventionist and technocratic, as little more than a rehash of traditional New Deal liberalism. We suggest that they look again and digest more fully the extent of our reliance on geographically decentralized self-governance by business, labor, and local community organizations. Our New Deal for the New Economy shares some features with its Rooseveltian namesake: a concern for combining equity with economic growth and a belief that active government policy can help to solve economic problems. But our view of the appropriate role of government differs from that of traditional American liberalism. We do not believe that government officials or their advisers could ever have enough knowledge to create or implement public programs that would solve the problems of the service economy. We agree with conservatives who argue that the most important knowledge about economic processes cannot be centralized and, indeed, cannot even be made explicit. (Recall the emphasis in Chapter 5 on the importance of "knowing how" as opposed to "knowing that.") For this reason, we do not propose any new "big government" programs. We rely on government only to make and enforce a few basic rules (such as minimum wages) and to set broad, general goals (such as improved economic performance in the service sector). Government should not try to decide in detail how to achieve these goals. Those decisions should be left to geographically decentralized, self-governing groups that have the local knowledge necessary to craft workable policies.

Conservatives often glorify the decision-making ability of individual entrepreneurs. Our proposals also depend on entrepreneurship for innovation and practical solutions to economic problems. But we do not believe that atomized businesses are the only source of entrepreneurial ability. Associations of businesses, associations of workers, and local community organizations can also be entrepreneurs. Our proposals aim to encourage these associations to use their creative abilities to solve important public problems. A reader of Tocqueville might interpret our proposals, with their focus on associations, as reinforcing what is special about American democracy and culture. They are also a way of making American capitalism safe again for the middle and working classes, a prerequisite to the revival of both economic prosperity and vibrant political democracy.

The idea of explicitly regulating the basis of competition may sound to some like a threat to free enterprise. In fact, such regulation accentuates the difference between capitalism and feudalism.[30] Feudal lords knew well enough how to sweat peasants. Competition over the distribution of output and, indirectly, the intensity of labor was all they did know. (As absentee landlords of unrationalized labor-intensive work processes, they neither organized the production process nor sought to improve its efficiency.) Today, ruling out low-wage strategies is simply a way of making our postindustrial economy less feudal, reorienting it to stimulate and harness human creativity.

Whether the United States can renew itself in the ways we have outlined without a deeper crisis remains unclear. If waves of corporate downsizing build to another high crest, they could generate political support among upper-income groups and professionals for policies that would also benefit those in the lower-paying work systems. But before wishing too hard for a "heightening of the contradictions," we should remember that systemic crises can veer off in perverse directions as well as generate constructive change.

Our hope is that, before the United States loses its way, enough people will rally around progressive reform. We have written this book on the assumption that meaningful reform comes about not only in reaction to economic pain but also because it is seen as possible. The fate of America and its workers is not determined by technology or by markets or by globalization. It is subject to our collective control. Once that fact is grasped, once problems are recognized as soluble, they become amenable to resolution through politics. We acknowledge that there are many issues we have not addressed, many questions yet unanswered. But as any machinist knows, a "blueprint," even if generated by a computer, does not tell you precisely what to do. It is a guide, subject to interpretation. We know enough to get started. We know roughly as much as Roosevelt did in 1935. The time has come to create a New Deal for a New Economy.

Appendix A

Services Compared with
Manufacturing: Jobs and Productivity

Table A-1. Annual average employment in manufacturing and services, by race/ethnicity (in millions of workers and percent)

	1979		1989		1996	
	millions	%	millions	%	millions	%
Manufacturing						
White	18.0	82	16.2	78	14.7	75
Black	2.2	10	2.1	10	2.1	10
Hispanic	1.4	6	1.8	9	2.0	10
Other	0.4	2	0.7	3	0.9	5
Services						
White	48.1	83	58.5	78	62.8	75
Black	6.1	11	8.6	11	10.0	12
Hispanic	2.7	5	5.1	7	7.5	9
Other	1.4	2	2.4	3	3.4	4

Source: See Table 3.

Notes: Percentages in each column may not add to 100 because of rounding. All those of Hispanic origin are classified only as Hispanic.

Table A-2. Annual average employment in manufacturing and services, by level of education (in millions of workers and percent)

	1979		1989		1996	
	millions	%	millions	%	millions	%
Manufacturing						
Less than high school	6.4	29	4.1	20	3.0	15
High school diploma	9.8	45	9.5	46	7.9	40
Some college	3.3	15	3.7	18	5.0	25
Four-year college degree	1.7	8	2.4	11	2.8	14
Postgraduate education	0.8	4	1.1	5	0.9	5
Services						
Less than high school	11.5	20	10.3	14	9.5	11
High school diploma	22.6	39	27.7	37	24.9	30
Some college	11.7	20	17.3	23	25.7	31
Four-year college degree	7.1	12	11.1	15	15.8	19
Postgraduate education	5.4	9	8.2	11	7.8	9

Source: See Table 3.

Table A-3. Union coverage in manufacturing and service industries

	% of employees covered by a collective bargaining agreement	
	1986	**1996**
All workers	19.9	16.2
All private workers	15.2	11.0
Manufacturing	25.8	18.3
All services	18.1	15.7
Transportation	46.7	38.6
Communications	43.9	25.8
Utilities	37.8	33.9
Wholesale trade	8.2	6.7
Retail trade	7.8	6.2
Finance, insurance, and real estate	4.2	4.0
Private households	0.5	1.2
Business and repair	6.7	3.8
Personal services	10.0	8.7
Entertainment and recreation	13.9	10.3
Hospitals	18.5	16.2
Medical except hospitals	9.5	8.7
Education	41.0	40.8
Social services	13.1	9.2
Other professional	4.3	2.9
Public administration	36.2	37.2

Source: Barry T. Hirsch and David Macpherson, *Union Membership and Earnings Data Book: Compilations from the Current Population Survey,* 1997 edition (Washington, D.C.: Bureau of National Affairs, 1997), Tables 1A, 1B, 7A, 7C, and calculations based on Tables 7A and 7C.

Table A-4. Median hourly wages in manufacturing and services, by sex (in 1996 dollars)

	Manufacturing				Services			
	1979	1989	1996	% change, 1979–96	1979	1989	1996	% change, 1979–96
Men	$14.84	$13.92	$12.55	−15	$13.19	$12.26	$11.23	−15
Women	9.01	9.49	9.15	2	8.48	9.03	9.00	6
Wages for women as % of those for men	61	68	73			64	74	80

Source: See Table 4.

Table A-5. Median hourly wages in manufacturing and services, by race/ethnicity (in 1996 dollars)

	Manufacturing				Services			
	1979	1989	1996	% change, 1979–96	1979	1989	1996	% change, 1979–96
White	$13.21	$12.65	$12.40	−6	$10.60	$10.54	$10.38	−2
Black	10.60	9.49	9.00	−15	8.91	8.86	8.30	−7
Hispanic	9.54	8.86	8.00	−16	9.01	8.22	7.75	−14
Other	11.03	10.76	10.00	−9	10.60	10.76	10.00	−6
Wages for blacks as % of those for whites	80	75	73		84	84	80	
Wages for Hispanics as % of those for whites	72	70	65		85	78	75	

Source: See Table 4. All those of Hispanic origin are classified only as Hispanic.

Table A-6. Median hourly wages in manufacturing and services, by level of education (in 1996 dollars)

	Manufacturing				Services			
	1979	1989	1996	% change, 1979–96	1979	1989	1996	% change, 1979–96
Less than high school	$10.54	$8.86	$8.00	−24	$6.89	$6.33	$5.60	−19
High school diploma	12.62	11.39	10.25	−19	9.54	8.86	8.50	−11
Some college	14.46	13.92	12.35	−15	10.60	10.35	9.69	−9
Four-year college degree	18.55	18.98	18.46	−1	13.46	14.68	14.42	7
Postgraduate education	23.13	24.34	25.18	9	16.73	18.83	19.62	17
Less than high school as a % of high school	84	78	78		72	71	66	
High School as a % of four-year college	68	60	56		71	60	59	

Source: See Table 4.

Table A-7. Alternative work arrangements in manufacturing
and major service industries, 1995 (in thousands
of workers and percent of industry employment)

	Independent contractors		On-call and day laborers		Temporary help agency workers		Workers provided by contract firms	
	Thousands	%	Thousands	%	Thousands	%	Thousands	%
Manufacturing	416	2	123	1	395	2	115	1
All services	5710	6	1530	2	745	1	504	1
Transportation and public utilities	415	5	181	2	90	1	87	1
Wholesale and retail trade	1070	4	287	1	96	0.4	79	0.2
Finance, insurance, and real estate	798	10	37	0.4	89	1	45	1
Other services[a]	3370	8	956	2	457	1	211	0.4
Public administration	25	0.4	69	1	14	0.2	82	1

Sources: February 1995 data from the Current Population Survey and our calculations based thereon, as reported in *Contingent and Alternative Employment Arrangements,* Bureau of Labor Statistics Report 900 (Washington, D.C.: Bureau of Labor Statistics, August 1995); and *Employment and Earnings,* March 1995, p. 29.

[a]Includes business and repair services, personal services, entertainment and recreation services, and professional services.

Table A-8. Part-time workers in manufacturing
and major service industries, 1979–1996 (in percent)

	1979	1989	1996
Manufacturing	4	4	5
All services	23	23	23
Transportation, communications, and utilities	9	9	10
Wholesale trade	7	8	8
Retail trade	38	38	37
Finance, insurance, and real estate	13	12	12
Business and repair services	20	19	16
Personal services	46	38	34
Entertainment and recreation services	40	36	37
Professional services	23	25	24
Public administration	7	7	6

Source: See Table 3.

Note: Part-time work is defined as less than 35 hours/week.

Table A-9. Output per labor-hour in major U.S. sectors
(average annual percent change)

	Manufacturing	All nonfarm business
1960–96	2.8	1.7
1960–73	3.3	3.0
1973–79	2.1	1.1
1979–96	2.8	1.0
1979–90	2.6	1.0
1990–93	2.7	1.3
1993–96	3.4	0.5

Source: Bureau of Labor Statistics based on estimates of real output from the Bureau of Economic Analysis (in the Department of Commerce) and BLS estimates of hours worked.

Table A-10. Labor productivity growth in manufacturing
and in service industries before and after 1977
(average annual percent change)

Industry (SIC code)	Initial year	Before 1977	1977–95
Manufacturing	1949	2.5	2.5
Railroad transportation (4011)	1947	4.1	7.0[a]
Trucking, except local (4213)	1954	2.5	3.6[b]
U.S. Postal Service (43)	1967	1.0	0.9
Air transportation (parts of 4512,4513,4522)	1947	7.3	3.0
Petroleum pipelines (4612,4613)	1958	7.3	1.2
Telephone communications (481)	1951	6.2	5.3
Gas and electric utilities (491,492,493)	1947	5.7	0.8
Hardware stores (525)	1972	0.0	1.3
Department stores (531)	1967	2.5	2.3
Variety stores (533)	1967	−1.4	1.5
Food stores (54)	1958	1.8	−0.9
Grocery stores (541)	1972	−1.0	−0.9
New and used car dealers (551)	1958	2.5	1.1
Auto and home supply stores (553)	1972	2.6	1.8
Gasoline service stations (554)	1958	3.9	3.1
Men's and boys' clothing stores (561)	1967	2.1	2.7
Eating and drinking places (58)	1958	0.8	−0.3
Drug stores (591)	1958	4.2	0.3
Liquor stores (592)	1972	−1.5	0.9
Commercial banks (602)	1967	1.8	2.2
Hotels and motels (701)	1958	2.5	0.1
Laundry, cleaning, and garment services (721)	1958	1.7	−0.6
Beauty and barber shops (723,724)	1972	−0.5	1.4
Automotive repair (753)	1972	−0.8	0.6

Source: Computed from Bureau of Labor Statistics annual output-per-hour data by Standard Industrial Classification (SIC) code.

[a]Series ends in 1993.

[b]Series ends in 1989.

Table A-11. Labor productivity growth in manufacturing
and selected service industries, 1977–1994
(average annual percent change)

Manufacturing	2.45
Transportation and utilities	1.51
Transportation	0.58
Communications	4.53
Public utilities	0.65
Trade	2.06
Wholesale trade	3.30
Retail trade	1.29
Finance, insurance, real estate	0.16
Other services	−0.56
Hotels and lodging	−1.53
Personal services	0.87
Business and other services	−0.42
Automotive repair	−1.26
Miscellaneous services	−0.20
Motion pictures	1.65
Amusement services	0.98
Health services	−1.84
Legal services	−2.77
Education services	0.01
Membership organizations and social services	−0.18
Private households	2.18

Source: L. Slifman and C. Corrado, "Decomposition of Productivity and Unit Costs," unpublished paper, Board of Governors of the Federal Reserve System, November 18, 1996.

Note: Based on Bureau of Economic Analysis output data by 2-digit SIC code and on hours of labor input. Hours of labor input include estimates for nonprofit institutions and private households. Calculations assume self-employed workers work the same number of hours as full-time wage and salary employees in each industry.

Appendix B
Employment Estimates
by Work System

In order to calculate the employment figures for each of our four work systems (Tables 7 and 8), it was necessary to assign each three-digit occupation (as tabulated in the Current Population Survey [CPS]) to one of the four systems. In some cases we assigned all workers in a given occupation to one work system. In other cases we split the occupation between two or more work systems based on our knowledge of the characteristics of the jobs performed by those in that occupation and on case studies. This procedure was necessary because no existing surveys collect information that is directly related to the distinguishing features of the four work systems. The classifications for 1996 are shown in Table B-1.

Table B-1. Classification of occupations

Work system	3-digit CPS occupations and occupation codes
Tightly constrained	Lowest-wage 75 percent of sales counter clerks and cashiers (codes 275–276); all telephone operators (code 348); all bank tellers (code 383); all data entry keyers (code 385); 50 percent of assemblers (code 785) randomly chosen from the highest-wage 75 percent of assemblers; second-lowest wage quartile of machine operators in codes 703–733; second-lowest wage quartile of machine operators in codes 738–779; second-highest wage quartile of production inspectors, testers, samplers, and weighers (codes 796–799).

Table B-1. (Continued)

Unrationalized labor-intensive	All street and door-to-door sales workers (code 277); all news vendors (code 278); lowest-wage 50 percent of sales-related occupations (codes 283–285); lowest-wage 25 percent of administrative support occupations (codes 303–389) except adjusters and investigators in codes 375–376, computer equipment operators (codes 308–309), telephone operators (code 348), bank tellers (code 383), and data entry keyers (code 385); all private household occupations (codes 403–407); all guards and correctional institution officers (codes 424–432); all service occupations except protective and household (codes 433–469) except dental assistants (code 445) and barbers, hairdressers, and cosmetologists (codes 457–458); lowest-wage 25 percent of barbers, hairdressers, and cosmetologists (codes 457–458); lowest-wage 75 percent of farming, forestry, and fishing occupations (codes 473–499) except farm operators and managers (codes 473–476) and captains and other officers of fishing vessels (code 497); all carpet installers (code 566); all drywall installers (code 573); lowest-wage 50 percent of painters (code 579); lowest-wage 25 percent of assemblers (code 785); lowest-wage 25 percent of machine operators in codes 703–733; lowest-wage 25 percent of machine operators in codes 738–779; lowest-wage 50 percent of fabricators and hand-working occupations (codes 783–784 and 786–795); lowest-wage 50 percent of motor vehicle operators (codes 803–814); all handlers, equipment cleaners, helpers, and laborers (codes 864–889).
Semiautonomous	Lowest-wage 75 percent of executive, administrative, and managerial occupations and selected supervisors, except accountants and auditors, underwriters, and management analysts (codes 4–37 except 23, 24, and 26; supervisors in codes 303–307, 413–415, 433, 448, 456, 503, 553–558, 613, 628, 803, 828, 843, and 864); lowest-wage 25 percent of technicians and related support occupations (codes 203–235); lowest-wage 75 percent of retail and personal services sales workers in codes 263–274; highest-wage 25 percent of sales counter clerks and cashiers (codes 275–276); highest-wage 50 percent of sales-related

Table B-1. (Continued)

Semiautonomous *(continued)*	occupations (codes 283–285); highest-wage 75 percent of administrative support occupations (codes 303–389) except adjusters and investigators in codes 375–376, computer equipment operators (codes 308–309), telephone operators (code 348), bank tellers (code 383), and data entry keyers (code 385); lowest-wage 50 percent of computer equipment operators (codes 308–309); all dental assistants (code 445); middle-wage 50 percent of barbers, hairdressers, and cosmetologists (codes 457–458); highest-wage 25 percent of farming, forestry, and fishing occupations (codes 473–499) except farm operators and managers (codes 473–476) and captains and other officers of fishing vessels (code 497); 25 percent of assemblers (code 785) randomly chosen from the highest-wage 75 percent of assemblers; highest-wage 50 percent of machine operators in codes 703–733; highest-wage 50 percent of machine operators in codes 738–779; highest-wage 50 percent of fabricators and hand-working occupations (codes 783–784 and 786–795); lowest-wage 50 percent of production inspectors, testers, samplers, and weighers (codes 796–799); highest-wage 50 percent of motor vehicle operators (codes 803–814); lowest-wage 50 percent of rail transportation occupations (codes 823–826); lowest-wage 75 percent of water transportation occupations (codes 828–834); lowest-wage 50 percent of material-moving equipment operators (codes 843–859).
High-skill autonomous	Highest-wage 25 percent of executive, administrative, and managerial occupations and selected supervisors, except accountants and auditors, underwriters, and management analysts (codes 4–37 except 23, 24, and 26; supervisors in codes 303–307, 413–415, 433, 448, 456, 503, 553–558, 613, 628, 803, 828, 843, and 864); all accountants and auditors (code 23), underwriters (code 24), and management analysts (code 26); all professional specialty occupations (codes 43–199); highest-wage 75 percent of technicians and related support occupations (codes 203–235); all sales supervisors and proprietors (code 243); all sales representatives for finance and business services (codes 253–257); all sales representatives for

Table B-1. (Continued)

High-skill autonomous (*continued*)	commodities except retail (codes 258–259); highest-wage 25 percent of retail and personal services sales workers in codes 263–274; all adjusters and investigators in codes 375–376; highest-wage 50 percent of computer equipment operators (codes 308–309); all protective service occupations except guards and correctional institution officers (codes 413–423); highest-wage 25 percent of barbers, hairdressers, and cosmetologists (codes 457–458); all farm operators and managers (codes 473–476); all captains and other officers of fishing vessels (code 497); all precision production, craft, and repair occupations except carpet installers, drywall installers, and the lowest-wage 50 percent of painters (codes 503–699 except 566, 573, and the lowest-wage 50 percent of 579); all printing machine operators (codes 734–737); highest-wage 25 percent of production inspectors, testers, samplers, and weighers (codes 796–799); highest-wage 50 percent of rail transportation occupations (codes 823–826); highest-wage 25 percent of water transportation occupations (codes 828–834); highest-wage 50 percent of material-moving equipment operators (codes 843–859).

The 1979 CPS occupation codes differ somewhat from those for 1996. To generate the figures reported later in Tables 10 and 11 (at the end of Chapter 4), we converted the 1979 occupation codes to their approximate 1996 equivalents using the matching scheme in Gloria Peterson Green, Khoan Tan Dinh, John A. Priebe, and Ronald R. Tucker, "Revisions in the Current Population Survey Beginning in January 1983," *Employment and Earnings* (February 1983), 7–14. Then we derived and compared results for two ways of allocating occupations among the four work systems. One allocation scheme used was identical to that in Table B-1. The second differed from it in three ways as suggested by the analysis of changes in work systems over time described in Chapter 4. Under this second approach, we

- assigned all motor vehicle operators to the semiautonomous category (instead of splitting them 50–50 between semiautonomous and unrationalized labor-intensive);
- assigned the highest wage 75 percent of sales-related occupations to the semiautonomous category (instead of splitting them 50–50 between semiautonomous and unrationalized labor-intensive); and
- assigned all administrative support occupations (except adjusters and investigators, computer equipment operators, telephone operators, bank tellers, and data entry keyers) to the semiautonomous category.

Notes

Chapter 1. Recreating the Prosperity of the Past in the Economy of the Future

1. Smith was dismissive of services, in part because the personal and household servants employed by the upper classes in England seemed to him unproductive: "The labour of the menial servant, on the contrary [the comparison is with "the labour of the manufacturer"], does not fix or realize itself in any particular subject or vendible commodity. His services generally perish in the very instant of their performance, and seldom leave any trace or value behind them." He goes on to state that the same can be said of the services provided by army and navy, king or queen, as well as "churchmen, lawyers, physicians, men of letters of all kinds; players, buffoons, musicians, opera-singers, opera-dancers, &c." See Adam Smith, *An Inquiry into the Nature and Causes of the Wealth of Nations*, vol. 1 (London, 1887 [reprint of 6th ed.]), pp. 335–336.

2. We use the framework (but not all the terminology) for characterizing the U.S. mass production economy found in Michael J. Piore and Charles F. Sabel, *The Second Industrial Divide: Possibilities for Prosperity* (New York: Basic, 1984).

3. Angus Madison, *Dynamic Forces in Capitalist Development: A Long-Run Comparative View* (Oxford: Oxford University Press, 1991), table C.11, p. 275.

4. Frederick Taylor's studies of efficiency in machine shops and steel mills laid the foundations for scientific management, sometimes also known as Taylorism. Taylor believed that it was possible to find the one best way to perform each manufacturing operation through "scientific" techniques such as time-and-motion study; and that, once these methods had been determined, all workers should be forced to follow them. Frederick W. Taylor, *The Principles of Scientific Management* (New York: Harper & Brothers, 1911).

5. Alfred D. Chandler, Jr., *Scale and Scope: The Dynamics of Industrial Capitalism* (Cambridge: Belknap Press/Harvard University Press, 1990).

6. Piore and Sabel, *Second Industrial Divide*, pp. 79–82.

7. This figure compared with 31 percent in 1938 and 33 percent in 1973. See Paul Bairoch, "International Industrialization Levels from 1750 to 1980," *Journal of European Economic History* 11 (1982), table 2, p. 275.

8. *U.S. Industrial Competitiveness: A Comparison of Steel, Electronics, and Automobiles* (Washington, D.C.: Office of Technology Assessment, 1981).

9. Advisory Council on Unemployment Compensation, *Report and Recommendations* (Washington, D.C.: Advisory Council on Unemployment Compensation, 1994), pp. 34–41.

10. We estimated an upper bound on the number of service jobs directly exposed to international competition by adding together all employment in communications, finance, insurance, and computer and data processing; one-quarter of all employment in engineering and management services; and 10 percent of all employment in hotels and lodging, motion pictures, amusement and recreation services, health services, legal services, and educational services. This adds up to a total 11 percent of employment in services. The data used for these calculations are from the U.S. Department of Labor, Bureau of Labor Statistics, Current Employment Statistics survey for 1997.

Chapter 2. The Service Economy and the Service Worker

1. The statistics on Wal-Mart and General Electric come from *Fortune*, May 15, 1995.

2. Thomas A. Stewart, "A New 500 for a New Economy," *Fortune*, May 15, 1995, pp. 166–178.

3. Government classifications illustrate the ambiguity of the distinction between services and goods. Computer software, for instance, has been counted as a service industry, even though much software is reproduced and distributed in a fashion similar to manufactured products. The value of the software stems almost entirely from its design (conception), generation (programming, debugging), documentation (instructions for use), and maintenance (including updates). In contrast to a pair of blue jeans or a TV set, physical reproduction is incidental. The same is true for audio (and video) recordings, where nearly all the value added is in the conception and execution of the recorded performance; nonetheless, in the national income and product accounts, recordings have always appeared under goods. The reasons for these differences are at least in part historical. In the early years of computing, consulting firms developed many software programs. In contrast, the manufacture of early phonograph records was technologically challenging and the costs high, so it looked like a goods-producing industry to statistical agencies. Because software, like recordings, can be shipped and stored, some types of software are being reclassified as part of manufacturing under the 1997 North American Industry Classification System.

4. Although the calculation of productivity allows for nonstandard products and changes in product attributes (too often referred to simply as "quality" improvements), measurement of productivity remains easiest in industries that produce standardized goods that do not change much over time. This is one reason we often use the looser term "economic performance" rather than productivity, with its connotations of measuring the output of homogeneous products.

5. Government, which we treat alongside private services in this book, employed about 19 million Americans in 1996. More than 16 million of those worked in state and local government, counting those in public schools, included under "professional services" in Table 3.

6. In 1979 women filled 52 percent of service jobs, men 69 percent of manufacturing jobs. Throughout this chapter we compare services solely with manufacturing because manufacturing has been the focus of so much popular and policy attention. Together, manufacturing and services account for about 93 percent of all U.S. employment. The remaining 7 percent consists of agriculture, forestry, fishing, mining, and construction (which, along with manufacturing, make up the goods-producing sector). All employment data cited in this chapter are based on our calculations from the combined outgoing rotation groups of the Bureau of Labor Statistics' 1979, 1989, and 1996 Current Population Surveys.

7. The shares of workers receiving health and pension benefits also declined in the 1980s, although the share receiving pension benefits recovered slightly in the 1990s. Service workers are less likely than manufacturing workers to receive pension and health insurance benefits, except in government and communication/utilities. For pension data, see *Employment-Based Retirement Income Benefits*, Special Report and Issue Brief no. 153 (Washington, D.C.: Employee Benefit Research Institute, September 1994). For health insurance data, see *Employment-Based Health Benefits: Analysis of the April 1993 Current Population Survey*, Special Report and Issue Brief no. 152 (Washington, D.C.: Employee Benefit Research Institute, August 1994); and *Sources of Health Insurance and Characteristics of the Uninsured*, Issue Brief no. 179 (Washington, D.C.: Employee Benefit Research Institute, November 1996). There are no comprehensive sources of data on employee benefits other than pensions and health care.

8. Frank Levy and Richard J. Murnane, "U.S. Earnings Levels and Earnings Inequality: A Review of Recent Trends and Proposed Explanations," *Journal of Economic Literature* 30 (September 1992), 1333–1381. See also Lawrence Mishel, Jared Bernstein, and John Schmitt, *The State of Working America, 1996–1997* (New York: M. E. Sharpe, 1996), and Peter Gottschalk, "Inequality, Income Growth, and Mobility: The Basic Facts," *Journal of Economic Perspectives* 11 (Spring 1997), 21–40.

9. Robert H. Frank and Philip J. Cook, *The Winner-Take-All Society* (New York: Free Press, 1995), provides an economic interpretation and numerous illustrations of this sort of status competition.

10. See, for example, Dave E. Marcotte, "Skills, Wages, and Careers: Essays on the Emerging Economy and Its Implications for Education and Training Policies," Ph.D. dissertation, School of Public Affairs, University of Maryland, 1994; Stephen R. Rose, *Declining Job Security and the Professionalization of Opportunity*, Research Report no. 95-04 (Washington, D.C.: National Commission for Employment Policy, 1995); Peter Gottschalk and Robert Moffitt, "The Growth of Earnings Instability in the U.S. Labor Market," *Brookings Papers on Economic Activity 1994* 2, 217–254; and Daniel Polsky, "Changes in the Consequences of Job Separations in the U.S. Economy," manuscript, University of Pennsylvania, 1996. All these studies are based on the Panel Study of Income Dynamics (PSID), which tracks individuals over time. They show small declines in job stability for men between the 1970s and 1980s. (The PSID does not contain enough data on women to permit similar calculations.) Studies based on the Current Population Survey (CPS) show little or no overall decline in job stability during the 1980s, but because the CPS contains information on different workers at different points in time, rather than following the same people over time, we consider the PSID studies more reliable. Studies based on the CPS include Kenneth Swinnerton and Howard Wial, "Is Job Stability Declining in the U.S. Economy?" *Industrial and Labor Relations Review* 48 (January 1995), 293–304; Francis X. Diebold, David Neumark, and Daniel Polsky, *Job Stability in the United States*, Working Paper no. 4859, National Bureau of Economic Research, Cambridge, Mass., September 1994; and Kenneth Swinnerton and Howard Wial, "Is Job Stability Declining in the U.S. Economy? Reply to Diebold, Neumark, and Polsky," *Industrial and Labor Relations Review* 49 (January 1996), 352–355.

11. The figures cited in this paragraph are from Henry S. Farber, *The Changing Face of Job Loss in the United States, 1981–1995*, Working Paper no. 382, Industrial Relations Section, Princeton University, May 1997, pp. 64, 67, and 68.

12. Kenneth Swinnerton and Howard Wial, unpublished data; Polsky, "Consequences of Job Separations."

13. Robert Valletta, "Has Job Security in the U.S. Declined?" *FRBSF Weekly Letter*, no. 96-07, Federal Reserve Bank of San Francisco, February 16, 1996, uses CPS data

to show that permanent dismissals trended upward from 1968 to 1993 and that the share of unemployment accounted for by permanent dismissals became more sensitive to economic fluctuations after 1980.

14. Marcotte, "Skills, Wages, and Careers."

15. These findings are based on analysis of involuntary job losers in the late 1980s compared with the late 1970s; they refer specifically to wage declines of 10 percent or more. See Polsky, "Consequences of Job Separations."

16. U.S. Department of Labor, Bureau of Labor Statistics, *Employment and Earnings,* January 1997, p. 159.

17. There is no generally accepted meaning for contingent work. Some analysts define it as anything other than a full-time, long-term job (and include, for example, part-time work). Others prefer narrower definitions.

18. On the limitations of BLS data, see Edwin R. Dean and Kent Kunze, "Bureau of Labor Statistics Productivity Measures for Service Industries," in *The Service Productivity and Quality Challenge,* ed. Patrick T. Harker (Dordrecht: Kluwer, 1995), pp. 11–42.

19. Michael F. Mohr, "Recent and Planned Improvements in the Measurement and Deflation of Services Outputs and Inputs in BEA's Gross Product Originating Estimates," in *Output Measurement in the Service Sectors,* ed. Zvi Griliches (Chicago: University of Chicago Press, 1992), pp. 25–71. In three roughly overlapping industries, BLS and BEA generate productivity growth estimates that can be compared. For communications, BEA reports recent growth at 4.5 percent annually and BLS at 5.3 percent. In utilities, the BEA figure is 0.65 percent per year and the BLS figure 0.8 percent. In retail trade, the BEA figure is 1.3 percent and BLS figures range from −0.9 percent to 3.1 percent for twelve subindustries, with the unweighted arithmetic average of the BLS retail subindustries at 1.4 percent annually.

20. Because computer systems are used throughout the economy, the techniques for assigning "imputed" values to improvements in performance affect not only the productivity series estimated for the computer manufacturing industry but the productivities of all industries that purchase computers (because these purchases are inputs to the production process), including banking, insurance, retailing, and other information-intensive service industries.

21. Stephen V. Burks, *Final Report: OTA Project on Trucking Industry Productivity,* report prepared for the Office of Technology Assessment, March 1, 1995.

22. Jean Gadrey, Thierry Noyelle, and Thomas M. Stanback, Jr., *An Evaluation of Productivity Gains in Life and Property-Casualty Insurance in the United States,* Working Paper no. 92-01, Eisenhower Center for the Conservation of Human Resources, Columbia University, April 1992.

23. See Dean Baker, "Does the CPI Overstate Inflation? An Analysis of the Boskin Commission Report," in Dean Baker, ed., *Getting Prices Right: The Debate Over the Consumer Price Index,* Economic Policy Institute Series (Armonk, N.Y.: M.E. Sharpe, 1997), pp. 101–103.

Chapter 3. Work Systems

1. This vignette, including quotations, is drawn from T. Horowitz, "Mr. Eden Profits from Watching His Workers' Every Move," *Wall Street Journal,* December 1, 1994, p. A9.

2. This example is based on Susan C. Eaton, *Pennsylvania's Nursing Homes: Promoting Quality Care and Quality Jobs* (Harrisburg: Keystone Research Center, April 1997), pp. 24–25.

3. This section draws on interviews at the insurance company.

4. This example is based on the experience of Tom Peters, as drawn from his book *Liberation Management: Necessary Disorganization for the Nanosecond Nineties* (New York: Knopf, 1992), pp. 133–143.

5. Michael J. Piore, "Labor Standards and Business Strategies," in *Labor Standards and Development in the Global Economy*, ed. Stephen Herzenberg and Jorge F. Perez-Lopez (Washington, D.C.: U.S. Department of Labor, Bureau of International Labor Affairs, 1990), pp. 35–49.

6. Suzanne W. Helburn et al., *Cost, Quality, and Child Outcomes in Child Care Centers: Executive Summary*, Economics Department, University of Colorado at Denver, January 1995.

7. Calculations made from 1996 Current Population Survey.

8. Ellen Galinsky, Carollee Howes, Susan Kontos, and Marybeth Shinn, *The Study of Children in Family Child Care and Relative Care* (New York: Families and Work Institute, 1994).

9. Researchers observed 225 children in three metropolitan areas for an average of three hours each. To measure quality of care, the researchers noted whether a family child care provider would comfort children, let them cry, or scold them and whether providers tended to answer children in monosyllables or engaged them in conversation. Researchers also evaluated whether children appeared to trust the provider (e.g., did children resist being picked up?), and whether children ignored the provider.

10. Helburn et al., *Child Care Centers*, p.1, conclude: "Most child care is mediocre in quality, sufficiently poor to interfere with children's emotional and intellectual development.... Consumers ... show little differential effective demand for higher quality, in part because they have difficulty observing the quality of care the children actually receive. This means that there are few economic incentives to improve quality."

11. As Appendix B makes clear, the share of jobs in each work system depends on choices we have made about the assignment of different occupations. For example, we put 75 percent of technicians and all craft workers into the high-skill autonomous category.

12. The discussion that follows is based on Eaton, *Pennsylvania's Nursing Homes*. See also Larry W. Hunter, "Building Employment Relationships: The Case of the Massachusetts Nursing Home Industry," Ph.D. dissertation, Sloan School of Management, Massachusetts Institute of Technology, 1994.

13. Eaton, *Pennsylvania's Nursing Homes*, p. 28.

14. Both quotations are from Tom Daykin, "Wisconsin Nursing Homes Ask State to Cure Staff Woes," *Milwaukee Sentinel*, October 31, 1994.

15. Gooloo S. Wunderlich, Frank. A. Sloan, and Carolyne A. Davis, eds., *Nursing Staff in Hospitals and Nursing Homes: Is It Adequate?* (Washington, D.C.: National Academy Press, 1996).

16. Eaton, *Pennsylvania's Nursing Homes*, p. 41.

17. Hunter, "Building Employment Relationships," found that, in 20 percent of the 156 homes he surveyed in Massachusetts, more than half the aides had been at the home at least three years. At another 20 percent, fewer than 20 percent of aides had been there three years. Cited in Eaton, *Pennsylvania's Nursing Homes*, p. 20.

Chapter 4. The Dynamics of Change in Work Systems

1. This section is based on interviews. See also Thomas D. Steiner and Diogo B. Teixeira, *Technology in Banking: Creating Value and Destroying Profits* (Homewood, Ill.:

Dow Jones-Irwin, 1990); and *Choosing the Right Path to Virtual Banking: The 1994 Ernst & Young and American Banker Special Report on Technology in Banking* (New York: Ernst & Young, 1994).

2. Payments account for the great majority (over 90 percent) of retail banking transactions. Bank of America, for example, processes a daily average of more than 12 million checks, a million pieces of mail, and a comparable number of credit/debit card transactions. Daily deposits approach 1 million, with businesses accounting for about a third of the volume. ATM transactions and statements average more than half a million per day. Bank of America customer service representatives answer nearly one hundred thousand calls each day.

3. Jane S. Pollard, "Industry Change and Labor Segmentation: The Banking Industry in Los Angeles, 1970–1990," Ph.D. dissertation, University of California at Los Angeles, 1995. At one of the banks Pollard studied, proofers who could not process fourteen hundred checks an hour were dismissed. In a "proof-off" competition at another bank, the winner reached thirty two hundred checks an hour.

4. Programming a computer-based system to recognize handwritten numerals is a difficult task. Whereas the totals on credit card statements are machine printed in a known location with a standard font, handwritten checks contain ambiguities that must be interpreted. For instance, a 2 can look like a 7, a 3 like an 8—and lack of context limits the value of the error-detection and correction routines that help computers make sense of words and sentences. At the company we visited, the OCR system successfully reads the handwritten amounts on about half the checks received. If this amount is the same as the minimum payment due or the monthly statement total—which the OCR system can read without any trouble—the check is automatically passed along to be deposited. If not, the check is routed to an operator. Since 40 percent of customers pay the full amount or the minimum, 20 percent of all payments go forward without operator intervention.

5. John W. Verity with Robert D. Hof, "The Internet: How It Will Change the Way You Do Business," *Business Week,* November 14, 1994, p. 84.

6. Labor productivity for telephone operators has increased at 12 percent per year since 1950, according to calculations based on data in George Kohl, *Information Technology and Labor: A Case Study of Telephone Operators,* report prepared for the Communications Workers of America, Washington, D.C., n.d. Of course, it is not clear how much productivity would have risen if the labor inputs of customers were included in the calculations or if qualitative changes in service could be accounted for.

7. Calmetta Coleman, "Fliers Call Electronic Ticketing a Drag," *Wall Street Journal,* January 17, 1997, pp. B1, B8.

8. Connie Guglielmo, "Here Come the Super-ATMs," *Fortune,* October 14, 1996, pp. 232–234; "Technology in Finance," *The Economist,* October 26, 1996, survey section.

9. *CyberAtlas,* various dates, www.cyberatlas.com.

10. "Finance's Info-Tech Revolution," *Business Week,* October 28, 1996, pp. 129–150.

11. *Making Government Work: Electronic Delivery of Federal Services* (Washington, D.C.: Office of Technology Assessment, September 1993), pp. 41–42.

12. David Cay Johnston, "I.R.S. Admits Lag in Modernization, Urges Contract Plan," *New York Times,* January 31, 1997, pp. A1, A18.

13. This discussion is based on Michael H. Belzer, *The Trucking Industry: Structure, Work Organization, Productivity, and Labor Market,* report prepared for the Office of Technology Assessment, February 1995.

14. This case study is a composite based on field research at several companies. It is based in part on Françoise Carré, *Work Reorganization in the Insurance Industry*, report prepared for the Office of Technology Assessment, revised, June 3, 1997.

15. This section is based on Rosemary Batt, "Performance and Welfare Effects of Work Restructuring: Evidence from Telecommunications Services," Ph.D. dissertation, Sloan School of Management, Massachusetts Institute of Technology, July 1995.

16. *Virtual Banking.*

17. The discussion of banks in the Los Angeles area draws on Pollard, "Industry Change and Labor Segmentation," especially chaps. 6–7.

18. Of 33 senior managers Pollard interviewed in the early 1990s, 11 had started as tellers and 5 as mail handlers, secretaries, or platform workers. The other 17 were mostly younger and had entered in jobs that included human resources and data processing. Pollard, "Industry Change and Labor Segmentation," p. 244. Before 1970 men benefited disproportionately from upward mobility. Fifty-six percent of male bank employees, and a higher proportion of white males, were managers or professionals. Eighty-five percent of women worked as clericals.

19. This discussion draws from Michael H. Belzer, "Collective Bargaining after Deregulation: Do the Teamsters Still Count?" *Industrial and Labor Relations Review* 48 (July 1995), 636–655, and from Belzer, *Trucking Industry*.

20. According to one survey, 73 percent of drivers acknowledge violating federal or state regulations; fully two-thirds admit to driving more hours than the weekly maximum. Belzer, "Collective Bargaining after Deregulation." Participant-observation research conducted before the full impact of deregulation took hold revealed that "drivers often worked seventy to ninety hours a week and sometimes more." Lawrence J. Ouellet, *Pedal to the Metal: The Work Lives of Truckers* (Philadelphia: Temple University Press, 1994), p. 28.

21. This discussion is based on work by Ken Freeman, who conducted the interviews noted below during the spring of 1995.

22. "Contractor Purchasing," *Cleaning Management* (December 1994), 4. This survey also found large janitorial firms seven times more likely than small firms to provide health care benefits for their employees.

23. This account is drawn from Thierry J. Noyelle, *Beyond Industrial Dualism: Market and Job Segmentation in the New Economy* (Boulder, Colo.: Westview, 1987), pp. 19–49. Noyelle notes that, in addition to their lower payroll costs, the discounters turned over their inventories at twice the rate of the older department stores (six or seven times a year versus three or four).

24. Quotation from Noyelle, *Beyond Industrial Dualism*, p. 47.

25. The 1960 figure comes from Noyelle, *Beyond Industrial Dualism*, p. 47, and the 1996 figure from calculations based on the CPS.

26. Leonard A. Schlesinger and James L. Heskett, "Breaking the Cycle of Failure in Retail Trade," *Sloan Management Review* 32, no. 3 (1991), 17–28.

27. Louis Uchitelle, "'Good' Jobs in Hard Times," *New York Times*, October 3, 1993, p. D1. Benefits at Wal-Mart include health care, for which employees copay at about 30 percent, and profit sharing, which averages about 6 percent of annual pay.

28. Wage trends in semiautonomous jobs (but not the other three types) differ markedly depending on which of the two methods reported in Table 10 is used. In method 1 the lowest-wage clerical and retail workers are classified within the unrationalized labor-intensive work system in 1979 as well as 1996. In method 2 the lowest-wage clerical and retail workers are considered part of the semiautonomous work system in 1979 but placed in the unrationalized system by 1996.

29. The inflation-adjusted median wage for physicians declined 3.7 percent from 1995 to 1996. The mean physician wage fell much more dramatically. Calculations based on the CPS.

30. For an earlier version of this argument, see Lester Thurow, *Generating Inequality* (New York: Basic, 1975).

Chapter 5. Reorganizing Work

1. Eileen Appelbaum and Rosemary Batt, *The New American Workplace: Transforming Work Systems in the United States* (Ithaca: ILR Press, 1994), p. 102. On recent work reforms in services, see pp. 104–120.

2. Simultaneous engineering, a recent set of managerial reforms in manufacturing, aims for closer integration of product and process design to reduce time-to-market and ensure that product attributes (including cost and quality) are not compromised by manufacturing problems that appear after production begins. Some simultaneous engineering teams include production workers who, because of their shopfloor experience, can help identify process steps that might be awkward or difficult to perform.

3. See John A. Alic, "Who Designs Work? Organizing Production in an Age of High Technology," *Technology in Society* 12 (1990), 301–317.

4. Michael Piore, Richard K. Lester, Fred M. Kofman, and Kamal M. Malek, "The Organization of Product Development," *Industrial and Corporate Change* 3 (1994), 405–434, draw a similar distinction between two approaches to the design of manufactured goods.

5. A major problem in interpretive service work, and in the design of goods, is determining whether what the customer thinks she wants is what she actually needs or will ultimately find satisfying. In the engineering model, product design begins with the exploration and interpretation of customer desires, a process that may continue in iterative fashion as prototypes are tested and customer reaction gauged. However, this is separate from production (which may not begin until months or years later).

6. For an elaboration in the context of professional occupations, see Donald Schön, *The Reflective Practitioner* (New York: Basic, 1983).

7. The concepts of depth and coordination economies are related to Janice Klein's three dimensions: depth of knowledge, number of managerial/administrative activities, and job breadth. See Janice Klein, "Teams," in *The American Edge*, ed. Janice Klein and Jeffrey Miller (New York: McGraw-Hill, 1993), pp. 70–88. Our concept of coordination is narrower than Klein's managerial/administrative dimension: it does not encompass all the activities managers and administrators commonly perform, only those involved in coordinating work. Nor, for the reasons noted, do we use the category of job breadth (number of functional tasks in each job).

8. See John A. Alic, "Knowledge, Skill, and Education in the New Global Economy," *Futures* 29 (1997), 5–16.

9. After emigrating to the United States, the physicist Hans Bethe wrote to Arnold Sommerfeld, his former teacher in Germany: "What is most characteristic of physics in America is team work. Working together in large institutes, in each of which everything that exists in physics is being done, the experimentalist constantly discusses his problems with the theorist, the nuclear physicist with the spectroscopist.... More team work: The frequent conferences.... One discusses what one is just then interested in." Quoted in Michael Eckert, "Theoretical Physicists at War: Sommerfeld Students in Germany and as Emigrants," in *National Military Establishments and the Ad-*

vancement of Science and Technology: Studies in 20th-Century History, ed. Paul Forman and José M. Sánchez-Ron (Dordrecht: Kluwer, 1996), pp. 72–73.

10. Jody Hoffer Gittell, *Coordination, Control, and Performance of Interdependent Work Processes,* Harvard Business School Working Paper, September 1996.

11. Gittell, *Coordination, Control, and Performance.*

12. Jody Hoffer Gittell, *Obstacles to Crossfunctional Coordination: Lessons from the Airline Departure Process,* Harvard Business School Working Paper, April 1996.

13. This case is drawn from Sondra Perl and Nancy Wilson, *Through Teachers' Eyes* (Portsmouth, N.H.: Heinemann, 1986), pp. 3–17, 119–148, and 203–243.

14. The Xerox example comes from Julian Orr, *Talking about Machines* (Ithaca: ILR Press, 1996), pp. 125–143.

15. Such complaints can be registered against engineering documentation of all types, particularly when technical changes are frequent (and the documentation never catches up). Like the computer programs discussed later, manuals typically start out full of errors, but for manuals, unlike computer programs, there is little incentive to find and correct them.

16. The material on EMTs is drawn from Bonalyn Nelson, "Work as a Moral Act: How Emergency Medical Technicians Understand Their Work," in *Between Craft and Science,* ed. Stephen R. Barley and Julian E. Orr (Ithaca: ILR Press, 1997), pp. 154–184.

17. This discussion of software support workers is drawn from Brian T. Pentland, "Bleeding Edge Epistemology: Practical Problem-Solving in Software Support Hot Lines," and Stacia E. Zabusky, "Computers, Clients, and Expertise: Negotiating Technical Identities in a Nontechnical World," both in *Between Craft and Science,* ed. Barley and Orr, pp. 113–128 and 129–153.

18. In 1997 the Service Technicians Society (STS), an organization of automotive service technicians (i.e., auto mechanics), established an "STS Service Bay Bulletin Board" for just this purpose. STS is affiliated with the Society of Automotive Engineers (SAE), and the bulletin board can be reached from SAE's web site or directly at www.sts.sae.org:80.

19. This discussion is based on training documents used by the Philadelphia-based Cooperative Home Care Associates (CHCA), many of them prepared by Zara Joffe. It also draws on an interview with Scott Gordon, executive director in Philadelphia, and on Peggy Clark and Steven L. Dawson, *Jobs and the Urban Poor: Privately Initiated Sectoral Strategies* (Washington, D.C.: Aspen Institute, November 1995). Many of the practices at CHCA are also followed at other branches of the Home Care Associates Network (in the Bronx, Boston, Chicago, and Detroit).

20. This paragraph is based on interviews.

21. This discussion is based on interviews with MRM managers. See also Françoise Carré, *Work Reorganization in the Insurance Industry,* report prepared for the Office of Technology Assessment, revised, June 3, 1997.

22. The information on Southwest Airlines is drawn from Jody Hoffer Gittell, *Crossfunctional Coordination and Work Reorganization in the Service Sector,* report prepared for the Office of Technology Assessment, April 23, 1995.

23. This case draws on Thomas Bailey, Annette Bernhardt, David Jacobson, John Quigley, and Deborah Ziegler, *Job Quality and Productivity in Retail Trade,* draft report prepared for the Office of Technology Assessment, August 1994.

24. The discussion of UPS is based on interviews and on a ride-around with a UPS package delivery driver.

25. Bailey et al., *Job Quality.*

26. *Taco Bell 1994,* Harvard Business School Case Study no. 9-694-076, revised July 13, 1995.

Chapter 6. Business Organization

1. Calculated from U.S. Department of Commerce, Bureau of the Census, *Statistical Abstract of the United States 1996* (Washington, D.C.: U.S. Government Printing Office, 1996).

2. Gerald R. Moody, *Information Technology and the Economic Performance of the Grocery Store Industry,* Economics and Statistics Administration, U.S. Department of Commerce, Working Papers on Industrial and Economic Performance ESA/OPD 97-1, April 1997, pp. 6–7.

3. Allen N. Berger and Loretta J. Mester, "Efficiency and Productivity Trends in the U.S. Commercial Banking Industry: A Comparison of the 1980s and 1990s," paper presented at the Centre for the Study of Living Standards Conference on Service Centre Productivity and the Productivity Paradox, Ottawa, Ontario, April 11–12, 1997.

4. Eileen Glanton, "Ernst & Young, KPMG to Form Top Firm in Field," *Philadelphia Inquirer,* October 21, 1997, p. C–1.

5. Bennett Harrison, *Lean and Mean: The Changing Landscape of Corporate Power in the Age of Flexibility* (New York: Basic, 1994), pp. 8–12, likewise argues that economic concentration is occurring today without the centralization of production that accompanied it in the past.

6. Jean Gadrey, Thierry Noyelle, and Thomas M. Stanback, Jr., *A Critique of Eating-Drinking Places in the United States and a Comparison with France,* Working Paper no. 91–05, Université de Lille and Eisenhower Center for the Conservation of Human Resources, Columbia University, August 1991, table 3.

7. Marriott International, Inc., *Annual Report,* 1993, p. 2. The remainder of this discussion of hotels draws on Nathan Newman, *The Restructuring of the Hotel Industry,* report prepared for the Office of Technology Assessment, August 1994.

8. Larry Hirschhorn and Bob Guttman, *The Future of Law Firms,* report prepared for the Office of Technology Assessment, August 1994.

9. A great deal has been written about business networks, from many perspectives. For useful reviews, see Max H. Boisot, "Markets and Hierarchies in a Cultural Perspective," *Organization Studies* 7 (1986), 135–158, and Walter W. Powell, "Neither Market nor Hierarchy: Network Forms of Organization," *Research in Organizational Behavior* 12 (1990), 295–336.

10. This case is based on interviews with managers of hospitals, principally in Minneapolis–St. Paul, and with health care industry consultants.

11. Larry W. Hunter, University of Pennsylvania, personal communication, 1994.

12. This section is based on Michael H. Belzer, *Paying the Toll: Economic Deregulation of the Trucking Industry* (Washington, D.C.: Economic Policy Institute, 1994), p. 27; Belzer, *The Trucking Industry: Structure, Work Organization, Productivity, and Labor Market,* report prepared for the Office of Technology Assessment, July 31, 1995.

13. This section is based on Rosemary Batt, "Performance and Welfare Effects of Work Restructuring: Evidence from Telecommunications Services," Ph.D. dissertation, Sloan School of Management, Massachusetts Institute of Technology, July 1995; on personal communications with Jeffrey Keefe, Rutgers University; and on John A. Alic, *Employment Impacts of the National Information Infrastructure,* technical report (Washington, D.C.: Economic Policy Institute, March 1997).

14. Rosemary Batt, "From Bureaucracy to Enterprise? The Changing Jobs and Careers of Managers in Telecommunications Services," in *Broken Ladders,* ed. Paul Osterman (New York: Oxford University Press, 1996), pp. 55–80.

15. Rosemary Batt, personal communication, May 1997.

16. This section is based on AnnaLee Saxenian, *Regional Advantage* (Cambridge: Harvard University Press, 1994), pp. 29–57 and 133–159.

17. The movement of workers transfers ideas from firm to firm, creating benefits for all firms that exceed the total benefits that all firms could reap by holding onto their workers. Alan Hyde, "Real Human Capital: The Economics and Law of Shared Knowledge," unpublished manuscript, Rutgers University School of Law, Newark, 1997.

18. For a similar assessment, see Harrison, *Lean and Mean*, pp. 114–117.

19. Susan Eaton, personal communication, 1994.

20. Harrison, *Lean and Mean*, pp. 195–211, maintains that business networks have contributed to the growth of wage inequality. His arguments are complementary to those presented here.

21. Jody Hoffer Gittell, personal communication, 1995.

22. Richard Freeman and James Medoff, *What Do Unions Do?* (New York: Basic, 1084), pp. 90–93, show that unions reduce wage inequality not only among union members but in the entire U.S. economy.

23. Howard Wial, "The Emerging Organizational Structure of Unionism in Low-Wage Services," *Rutgers Law Review* 45 (Spring 1993), 671–738.

24. Calculations made from outgoing rotation groups of the 1996 Current Population Survey.

25. Industrial research arose in part through the efforts of large firms to defend their market positions. Leonard S. Reich, *The Making of American Industrial Research: Science and Business at GE and Bell, 1876–1926* (Cambridge: Cambridge University Press, 1985).

Chapter 7. Creating Multiemployer Institutions

1. Annette Bernhardt, of Columbia University's Institute on Education and the Economy, has studied two cohorts of the National Longitudinal Survey, which tracks young workers over time. She finds that in recent years such workers are more likely to circulate among low-wage positions, whereas in the 1970s young workers were more likely to advance by changing employers. Personal communication, May 1997.

2. See, e.g., Howard Wial, "Getting a Good Job: Mobility in a Segmented Labor Market," *Industrial Relations* 30 (Fall 1991), 386–416.

3. Katherine S. Newman, "Working Poor: Low-Wage Employment in the Lives of Harlem Youth," in *Transitions through Adolescence: Interpersonal Domains and Context,* ed. Julia A. Graber, Jeanne Brooks-Gunn, and Anne C. Petersen (Mahwah, N.J.: Lawrence Erlbaum, 1996), pp. 323–343.

4. Stuart Ray, personal communication, March 1997.

5. This section is based on an unpublished memo from the Jobs with a Future Work Group, Madison, Wis., January 24, 1995; on an interview with Terry Schnapp, Wisconsin Division of Industrial and Labor Relations, March 27, 1995; and on Laura Dresser and Joel Rogers, "Rebuilding Job Access and Career Advancement Systems in the New Economy," unpublished paper, Center on Wisconsin Strategy, Madison, undated.

6. This section is based on interviews with the hospital workers' union local president and the hospital's personnel director; on Cape Cod Hospital and Hospital Workers' Union Local 767, *Career Ladders Program,* revised 1990; and on *Opportunity Is the Rule, Not the Exception: A Qualitative Assessment of the Cape Cod Hospital Career Ladders Program,* Ford Foundation Project Report (Boston: University of Massachusetts-Boston, September 1993).

7. Some central labor councils, including those in Cincinnati and in Ithaca, New York, already provide employment and training services to nonunion as well as union workers. See Fernando Gapasin and Howard Wial, "The Role of Central Labor Councils in Union Organizing in the 1990s," in *Organizing to Win,* ed. Kate Bronfrenbrenner et al. (Ithaca: ILR Press, 1998), pp. 54–67.

8. These results come from Stephen Rose, *Declining Job Security and the Professionalization of Opportunity* (Washington, D.C.: National Commission for Employment Policy, 1995), p. 10, and personal communications with Rose. They are based on the University of Michigan's Panel Study of Income Dynamics. Rose finds that careers in bureaucratic service industries—public administration, transportation, communications, and elementary and secondary education—tend to be firm-specific. In all these industries, median occupational tenure was typically no higher than firm tenure. In other service industries, workers switch employers more frequently but stay in the same occupation. Examples include legal services, beauty shops, laundries, and hotels and motels. The ratio of occupational to employer tenure in these services falls between that in manufacturing (where median occupational tenure is 1.2 times employer tenure) and in construction (where occupational tenure is 2.3 times employer tenure). Stephen R. Maguire, "Employer and Occupational Tenure: 1991 Update," *Monthly Labor Review* 116 (June 1993), p. 53, Table 3.

9. For an illustration among clerical workers, see Stephen A. Herzenberg, "Worker Identity, Union Structure, and the Clerical Occupation," paper presented at the AFL-CIO/Cornell University Conference on Organizing, Washington, D.C., April 1, 1996.

10. This discussion is based on interviews with construction union and industry association officials. See also Clinton Bourdon and Raymond Levitt, *Union and Open-Shop Construction* (Lexington, Mass.: Heath, 1980).

11. For tax purposes, these are considered employer contributions. After union and employer representatives reach agreement in collective bargaining on total compensation per hour, the union allocates compensation among wages, joint health and welfare funds (e.g., health care and pension), and training funds. Irwin Aronson, personal communication, March 1998.

12. This discussion draws on Irwin Aronson and Stephen Herzenberg, "Careers in Laboring," paper prepared for the Russell Sage Foundation, Keystone Research Center, Harrisburg, 1998.

13. Telephone interview with William Duke, Laborers International Union of North America, February 1998.

14. The 85 percent figure is based on data from the Labor Department's Bureau of Apprenticeship and Training provided by Cihan Bilginsoy, University of Utah. Union coverage in construction comes from Barry T. Hirsch and David A. Macpherson, *Union Membership and Earnings Data Book: Compilations from the Current Population Survey,* 1997 ed.(Washington, D.C.: Bureau of National Affairs, 1997), pp. 82, 90.

15. Labor productivity estimates in construction for 1948–1994 are based on combining data on real value-added with data on hours of labor input of all persons. For data on real value-added (or "gross product originating") by industry, see the monthly *Survey of Current Business,* various issues. The Bureau of Labor Statistics provides data on hours of labor input by industry.

16. This section is based on Alan Paul and Archie Kleingartner, "Flexible Production and the Transformation of Industrial Relations in the Motion Picture and Tele-

vision Industry," *Industrial and Labor Relations Review* 47 (July 1994), 663–678; Archie Kleingartner and Alan Paul, "Bases of Member Attachment to Unions in Arts and Entertainment," in *Proceedings of the 44th Annual Meeting, Industrial Relations Research Association* (Madison, Wis.: Industrial Relations Research Association, 1992), pp. 18–31; and Susan Christopherson and Michael Storper, "The Effects of Flexible Specialization on Industrial Politics and the Labor Market: The Motion Picture Industry," *Industrial and Labor Relations Review* 42 (July 1989), 331–347. See also Michael J. Enright, "Organization and Coordination in Geographically Concentrated Industries," in *Coordination and Information: Historical Perspectives on the Organization of Enterprise,* ed. Naomi R. Lamoreaux and Daniel M. G. Raff (Chicago: University of Chicago Press, 1995), pp. 103–146.

17. This section is based on Dorothy Sue Cobble, "Organizing the Postindustrial Work Force: Lessons from the History of Waitress Unionism," *Industrial and Labor Relations Review* 44 (April 1991), 419–436.

18. This section draws on Deborah Moy, "An Overview of Work Areas of the San Francisco Hotels Partnership Project," unpublished manuscript, November 1996; and Dresser and Rogers, "Rebuilding Job Access."

19. This section is based on Phil Neuenfeldt and Eric Parker, "Wisconsin Regional Training Partnership: Building the Infrastructure for Workplace Change and Skill Development," AFL-CIO Human Resources Development Institute, Briefing Paper no. 96-01, January 1996; and Dresser and Rogers, "Rebuilding Job Access."

20. This section is based on interviews with representatives of British Columbia hospital employers and unions, the provincial Ministry of Health, and the Healthcare Labour Adjustment Agency.

21. This discussion draws on Stacia Zabusky and Stephen R. Barley, "Redefining Success: Ethnographic Observations on the Careers of Technicians," in *Broken Ladders,* ed. Paul Osterman (New York: Oxford University Press, 1996), pp. 185–214.

22. The descriptions of these two associations are based on Chris Benner, *Shock Absorbers in the Flexible Economy: The Rise of Contingent Employment in Silicon Valley* (San Jose, Calif.: Working Partnerships USA, May 1996).

23. Calculations based on the Current Population Survey.

24. 9.3 percent of clerical and sales workers lost their jobs in 1993–95, compared with 6.9 percent in 1987–89. Henry S. Farber, *The Changing Face of Job Loss in the United States, 1981–1995,* Working Paper no. 382, Industrial Relations Section Princeton University, May 1997, p. 69. See also Alice de Wolff, *Job Loss and Entry Level Information Workers: Training and Adjustment Strategies for Clerical Workers in Metropolitan Toronto,* report prepared for the Metropolitan Toronto Clerical Workers Labour Adjustment Committee, July 1995.

25. In a 1994 survey 71 percent of 174 members of Professional Secretaries International (PSI) reported that, since 1990, they had taken on duties previously performed by managers. New responsibilities included purchasing, hiring, training, and overseeing quality management programs. *The Impact of Restructuring on the Secretarial Profession: A Survey of Office Professionals* (Holland, Mich.: Administrative Development Institute, 1994). Fifty-five percent of those surveyed said restructuring had had a positive impact on their jobs; only 22 percent viewed it as negative. Anticipating more demand for broadly skilled office workers, one of the PSI members we interviewed predicted that her occupation would experience an increase in wages and status like that enjoyed in the 1980s by nurses—another occupation combining technical and interpersonal skills.

26. Among temporary help firms, Manpower has a reputation as a leader in the development of computer skills. According to Doris Seavey and Richard Kazis, *Skills As*

sessment, Job Placement, and Training: What Can Be Learned from the Temporary Help/Staffing Industry? (Boston: Jobs for the Future, 1994), the company spends about 2 percent of payroll on training (including equipment expenditures). Manpower's self-paced "Skillware" modules cover some one hundred fifty software packages. Under its arrangements with software developers, Manpower also pretests new office products and develops computer-assisted training programs.

27. Quoted in Katherine Sciacchitano, *Scrambling to Survive: Temporary Clerical Workers in a Midwestern City,* report prepared for the Office of Technology Assessment, 1995.

28. This paragraph draws on Alice de Wolff, "Careers in Office Occupations," draft paper prepared for the Russell Sage Foundation, Keystone Research Center, Harrisburg, April 1997, and on de Wolff, *Job Loss and Entry Level Information Workers,* pp. 88–89.

29. Hirsch and Macpherson, *Union Membership and Earnings,* p. 104.

30. The Service Employees International Union represents two-thirds of unionized nursing home workers, and industrial unions that happen to be locally powerful represent most of the others. Susan C. Eaton, *Pennsylvania's Nursing Homes: Promoting Quality Care and Quality Jobs* (Harrisburg: Keystone Research Center, April 1997).

31. Charles Heckscher, *White Collar Blues* (New York: Basic, 1995).

32. This section draws on research conducted with the assistance of Margaret Hilton, including interviews with Kathy Mannes and Rob Hall of the National Retail Federation in 1995. Information on retail skill standards can also be found at the web site of the National Retail Institute: www.nrf.com/nri.

33. Tracy Mullin, "Just Think of the Possibilities," *Stores: The Magazine for Retail Management* (February 1995), p. 8.

34. *Raising Retail Standards* (Washington, D.C.: National Retail Federation, 1994).

35. We owe this observation to David Bensman, Rutgers University.

36. Examples include New York's Central Park East Schools and Theodore Sizer's Coalition of Essential Schools. See Charles Taylor Kerchner, Julia E. Koppich, and Joseph G. Weeres, *United Mind Workers: Unions and Teaching in the Knowledge Society* (San Francisco: Jossey-Bass, 1997), pp. 53–69. On Central Park East, see Deborah Meier, *The Power of Their Ideas: Lessons for America from a Small School in Harlem* (Boston: Beacon Press, 1994).

37. Kerchner, Koppich, and Weeres, *United Mind Workers,* pp. 87–99. On Cincinnati, see Cincinnati Federation of Teachers, "Raising Professional Standards in Teaching," 1994.

38. Cincinnati Federation of Teachers, "The Career in Teaching Program," no date.

Chapter 8. A New Deal for a New Economy

1. This section is based mainly on David Card and Alan B. Krueger, *Myth and Measurement: The New Economics of the Minimum Wage* (Princeton: Princeton University Press, 1995). Similar findings for the most recent increases in the minimum wage (in 1996 and 1997) can be found in Jared Bernstein, *America's Well-Targeted Raise: Data Show Benefits of Minimum Wage Increase Going to Workers Who Need It Most* (Washington, D.C.: Economic Policy Institute, September 1997).

2. For the most recent evidence that fast-food employment rose slightly faster in New Jersey than in neighboring Pennsylvania after a 1992 New Jersey minimum wage increase, see David Card and Alan B. Krueger, "A Reanalysis of the Effect of the New Jersey Minimum Wage Increase on the Fast-Food Industry with Representative Pay-

roll Data," Working Paper no. 393, Industrial Relations Section, Princeton University, January 1998.

3. Jared Bernstein and John Schmitt, *The Sky Hasn't Fallen: An Evaluation of the Minimum-Wage Increase* (Washington, D.C.: Economic Policy Institute, September 1997).

4 For a formal model, see Card and Krueger, *Myth and Measurement,* pp. 369–383. See also William M. Boal and Michael R. Ransom, "Monopsony in the Labor Market," *Journal of Economic Literature* 35 (March 1997), 86–112.

5. Massachusetts, California, and Oregon have recently increased their minimums. As of 1997 ten cities had enacted living-wage ordinances.

6. Peter Philips, Garth Mangum, Norm Waitzman, and Anne Yeagle, "Losing Ground: Lessons from the Repeal of Nine 'Little Davis-Bacon' Acts," Working Paper, Department of Economics, University of Utah, February 1995.

7. For more on the Worthy Wage campaign, see National Center for the Early Childhood Work Force (NCECW), "The Worthy Wage Campaign," Washington, D.C., no date.

8. For a proposal along these lines for nursing home and home care aides, see Susan C. Eaton, *Pennsylvania's Nursing Homes: Promoting Quality Care and Quality Jobs* (Harrisburg: Keystone Research Center, 1997), pp. 48–50.

9. Because the federal Employee Retirement Income Security Act (ERISA) preempts state regulation of benefits, states could mandate only wage parity unless Congress amended ERISA.

10. Swedish and German law provide possible models for the United States. Swedish law provides a legal definition of "dependent contractors" and requires that they be covered by labor and employment laws. German law classifies these workers as "employee-like persons" and has a similar requirement. See Marc Linder, *The Employment Relationship in Anglo-American Law* (New York: Greenwood, 1989), pp. 246–247.

11. Agencies that fund research in chemistry include the scientific offices of all three military services, other defense agencies, the National Science Foundation, the National Institutes of Health, the National Aeronautics and Space Administration, the Departments of Energy and Agriculture, and the Environmental Protection Agency, plus still others having responsibilities that call for studies of the oceans and atmosphere.

12. Improvements in the government's estimates of R&D spending by nonmanufacturing firms have led to an order-of-magnitude increase in reported levels of R&D compared with the manufacturing sector of the economy (from 3–4 percent to more than 25 percent) since the early 1980s. Nonetheless, the statistics probably still undercount services-related R&D. See John A. Alic, "Technology in the Service Industries," *International Journal of Technology Management* 9 (1994), 1–14. Available data offer little insight into the content of services-related R&D or the work performed by the engineers and scientists employed in the service sector (more than half the total number of engineers and scientists in the labor force).

13. This paragraph is based on interviews with representatives of several Canadian sectoral councils, Canada's federal government, and the Canadian Labour Market Productivity Center, and on Andrew Sharpe, "Report to the Human Resources Development–Canada Interdepartmental Seminar on Sector Councils," unpublished paper, Centre for the Study of Living Standards, Ottawa, Ontario, November 26, 1996.

14. Robert B. Reich, *Locked in the Cabinet* (New York: Knopf, 1997), pp. 296–297.

15. *Worker Training: Competing in the New International Economy* (Washington, D.C.: Office of Technology Assessment, September 1990), p. 94.

16. In addition, employee representatives should have some say in governance of portable, multiemployer plans. Under current law, multiemployer benefit plans established by unions must be jointly administered by worker and employer representatives if they receive contributions from employers. Participants in TIAA–CREF (Teachers Insurance and Annuity Association–College Retirement Equities Fund, a multiemployer retirement plan that covers many workers in nonprofit higher education and research organizations) elect the plan's board of directors.

17. A British Columbia labor law reform commission made this proposal in 1992. See John Baigent, Vince Ready, and Tom Roper, *Recommendations for Labour Law Reform,* report to the British Columbia Ministry of Labour, September 1992. On legal issues and an alternative proposal that would give the NLRB the power to combine bargaining units, see Howard Wial, "The Emerging Organizational Structure of Unionism in Low-Wage Services," *Rutgers Law Review* 45 (Spring 1993), 671–738.

18. This recommendation was also made by Commission on the Future of Worker-Management Relations, *Report and Recommendations* (Washington, D.C.: U.S. Department of Labor and U.S. Department of Commerce, 1994), pp. 11–12; and Samuel Estreicher, "Labor Law Reform in a World of Competitive Product Markets," in *The Legal Future of Employee Representation,* ed. Matthew W. Finkin (Ithaca: ILR Press, 1994), pp. 13–56.

19. Secondary pressure need not rely on worksite pickets; the law could permit a collective bargaining agreement to specify that the employer will not do business with any other firm whose workers are not represented by a union or that does not agree to remain neutral during a union representation campaign. For additional arguments in favor of relaxing the ban on secondary pressures, see Howard Wial, "New Bargaining Structures for New Forms of Business Organization," in *Restoring the Promise of American Labor Law,* ed. Sheldon Friedman, Richard W. Hurd, Rudolph A. Oswald, and Ronald L. Seeber (Ithaca: ILR Press 1994), pp. 303–313. See also Dorothy Sue Cobble, "Making Postindustrial Unionism Possible," in *Restoring the Promise,* pp. 285–302.

20. Commission on the Future of Worker-Management Relations, *Report and Recommendations,* pp. 9–11.

21. See, e.g., Paul Weiler, *Governing the Workplace* (Cambridge: Harvard University Press, 1990), pp. 283–295; Janice R. Bellace, "Mandating Employee Information and Consultation Rights," in *Proceedings of the 43rd Annual Meeting, Industrial Relations Research Association* (Madison, Wis.: Industrial Relations Research Association, 1991), pp. 137–151.

22. Wial, "Unionism in Low-Wage Services"; Bellace, "Mandating Employee Information."

23. Jeremy Rifkin, *The End of Work: The Decline of the Global Labor Force and the Dawn of the Post-Market Era* (New York: Putnam's, 1995). For a more responsible treatment of similar issues, see Chris Freeman and Luc Soete, *Work for All or Mass Unemployment? Computerized Technical Change Into the Twenty-First Century* (London: Pinter, 1994).

24. For a range of perspectives on such questions, see Rebecca Blank, ed., *Social Protection Versus Economic Flexibility: Is There a Trade-off?* (Chicago: University of Chicago Press, 1994).

25. See Alexander Keyssar, *Out of Work: The First Century of Unemployment in Massachusetts* (Cambridge: Cambridge University Press, 1986); and the review of Keyssar's book by Michael J. Piore, "Historical Perspectives and the Interpretation of Unemployment," *Journal of Economic Literature* 25 (December 1987), 1834–1850.

26. On shorter work time, see Juliet B. Schor, *The Overworked American: The Unexpected Decline of Leisure* (New York: Basic, 1991), pp. 142–162.

27. One precedent for occupational solidarity: with nonunion firms expanding, construction unions sometimes agree to accept lower rates to win new work. By increasing dues, the unions are then able to subsidize the pay of workers on contracts bid at substandard rates. Personal communication with Irwin Aronson, March 1997. Of course, if union contractors seek to cut rates all the time, it can put the entire wage structure at risk. Thus, if community-based work were to expand, it would be necessary to prevent "regular" jobs from arbitrarily and routinely migrating into the lower-paid, "community-based" category.

28. This section draws on Fred Block, *Postindustrial Possibilities: A Critique of Economic Discourse* (Berkeley: University of California Press, 1990), pp. 155–188.

29. Clifford Cobb, Ted Halstead, and Jonathon Rowe, "If the GDP Is Up, Why Is America Down?" *Atlantic Monthly*, October 1995, pp. 59–78.

30. The argument in this paragraph is based on Robert Brenner's interpretation of the transition from feudalism to capitalism. See Brenner, "Agrarian Class Structure and Economic Development in Pre-Industrial Europe," *Past and Present* 70 (February 1976), 30–75.

Index

Airlines, 102, 119; car rentals and, 110; credit cards and, 113; electronic tickets of, 61; equipment use in, 62; flight departure processes of, 93, 94

Alliance of Motion Picture and Television Producers, 133

Allied Pilots Association, 120

American Airlines, 102, 120

Apprenticeship programs, 136, 160; construction work, 124, 131, 132, 133, 154; office work, 140–141; waitressing, 134

Associated General Contractors (AGC), 131, 132

AT&T, 8, 11, 108; defensive approach of, 121; divestiture of, 66–68, 114–115; internal changes of, 14; layoffs by, 160; stocks of, 22; telemarketers of, 116; unionization of, 120

Automation: in banking, 68–69; clerical workers and, 139; in financial services, 23; in manufacturing, 1, 5, 57–58; minimum wage hikes and, 150, 153; tightly constrained jobs and, 10, 58, 59, 78, 105; unemployment and, 166

Baldrige Award, 156–157

Banking: career paths in, 4, 69–70, 197n. 18; comparative wages in, 75; computer purchases in, 194n. 19; concentration in, 108; from home, 61–62; restructuring in, 59, 68–71, 112–113; sectoral councils and, 161; skill requirements for, 80; teller demand in, 47; transactions in, 196n. 2

Benefits, 192–193n. 7; in banking, 119; in construction, 132, 133; ERISA and, 205n. 9; for home health aides, 99; multiemployer, 206n. 16; for Wal-Mart employees, 75, 197n. 27

British Columbia Healthcare Labour Adjustment Agency, 129, 136–137

Burger King restaurants, 126

Business mergers: in banking, 69; career ladders and, 4; concentration and, 108; job loss and, 30; multiemployer institutions and, 161; in telecommunications, 115

Business networks, 108, 109–110, 118–119; economic inequality and, 119–120, 201n. 17; labor mobility and, 118; in mid-1990s, 146; multiemployer bargaining and, 164; potential of, 121–122; in Silicon Valley, 116–117

Business organization, 8–9, 107–122; ambiguous implications of, 123–124; antitrust laws and, 10; economic inequality and, 122; interpretive-model reforms and, 106; productivity prerequisites and, 18; public policy and, 16; work systems and, 52, 71–75, 145–146, 147

Call centers, 45, 69, 104, 107, 113

Cape Cod Hospital, 127–128, 141, 158

Capital: flexible, 108; inflexible, 109